D0992079

THE NEW
AMERICAN
RIGHT

THE NEW AMERICAN RIGHT

Edited by
Daniel Bell

CRITERION BOOKS   NEW YORK

To SAMUEL M. LEVITAS — executive
editor and guiding spirit of *The New
Leader,* who for the past twenty-five years
has steered that worthy publication to
the right of the left, and to the left of the
right, seeking always the road of freedom
and intellectual decency—this book is personally dedicated.

D. B.

Acknowledgments

SEVERAL OF the essays, as noted in
the first chapter, appeared earlier in different places. "The
Pseudo-Conservative Revolt," by Richard Hofstadter, was
based on a lecture delivered at Barnard College in spring
1954 in its series on "The Search for New Standards in
Modern America," and printed in *The American Scholar*,
Winter 1954-55. We are indebted to Dr. Basil Rauch,
chairman of the program in American Civilization at
Barnard, for releasing the essay prior to the publication
of the Barnard series in book form. "The Intellectuals
and the Discontented Classes," by David Riesman and
Nathan Glazer, appeared in *Partisan Review*, Winter
1955. "The Revolt Against the Elite," by Peter Viereck,"
was given originally before the American Historical Association in December 1954; sections of it have appeared
in *The Reporter*, December 30, 1954, and *The New
Leader*, January 24, January 31, 1955. "Social Strains in
America," by Talcott Parsons, appeared in the *Yale Review*, Winter 1955. "The Polls on Communism and Conformity," by Nathan Glazer and Seymour Martin Lipset,
was prepared for this volume but includes sections of a

review-article by Mr. Glazer in *Commentary*, August, 1955. "The Sources of the 'Radical Right,'" by Seymour Martin Lipset was prepared originally as a study by the Bureau of Applied Social Research for the Fund for the Republic, and it was published, in a somewhat different form from that which appears in this volume, in the *British Journal of Sociology*, June 1955.

The editor and publisher gratefully acknowledge the kindness of the authors and editors of periodicals in granting permission to reprint these essays.

My thanks to Nathan Glazer and Seymour Martin Lipset for the many discussions, out of which grew the suggestion for this volume, to William Phillips for encouraging the idea of publication and to Miss Kathleen Jett who typed considerable portions of the manuscript.

D. B.

The Contributors

DANIEL BELL is a former managing editor of *The New
Leader* and instructor in social science at the
University of Chicago. He is at present a lecturer
in sociology at Columbia University and labor
editor of *Fortune* magazine. His essays on work,
the sociology of leadership, and the intellectuals
have appeared in several books. A monograph on
the history of American Marxist parties, which appeared in the compendium *Socialism and American Life* (Princeton, 1952), is being revised and
expanded for publication by Doubleday-Anchor
books. Mr. Bell, with the assistance of William
Goldsmith, is at work on a volume on Communism
and the American Labor Movement, under a grant
from the Fund for the Republic.

RICHARD HOFSTADTER, professor of history at Columbia
University, and one of the leading young historians in the United States, is the author of *Social
Darwinism in American Thought* and *The American Political Tradition*. Both will appear in reprint,

the former by Beacon, the latter by Knopf-Vintage books. A recent work, *The Age of Reform,* an analysis of the populist and progressive movements, given as the Walgreen lectures at the University of Chicago, was published by Knopf. A volume by Professor Hofstadter and Walter Metzger on the history of academic freedom in America will be published by the Columbia University Press.

DAVID RIESMAN is best known for his book *The Lonely Crowd,* which, within five years of its publication, has been accepted as a contemporary classic. A former lawyer, Mr. Riesman is professor of social science at the University of Chicago and sometime visiting professor at Harvard, Yale and Johns Hopkins. He is the author, among other works, of *Faces in the Crowd,* a companion volume of case studies to *The Lonely Crowd;* a biography, *Thorstein Veblen,* and *Individualism Reconsidered,* a collection of essays.

NATHAN GLAZER, linguist and sociologist, was a collaborator of David Riesman on *The Lonely Crowd* and *Faces in the Crowd.* An associate editor of *Commentary* magazine for nine years, Mr. Glazer conducted its monthly department, "The Study of Man," and contributed more than a dozen highly regarded essays on ethnic groups, prejudice and social theory. Mr. Glazer, now an editor of Anchor Books, gave the Walgreen lectures at the University of Chicago in the spring of 1955 on Judaism in America. These will be published by the University of Chicago Press next year.

PETER VIERECK, historian and Pulitzer prize winning poet,

is a stormy petrel of the "new conservatism" in America. Professor of modern history at Mount Holyoke College, he is the author of *Metapolitics: From the Romantics to Hitler, Conservatism Revisited* and the *Shame and Glory of the Intellectuals*, as well as several books of poetry. Mr. Viereck, who lectured in Italy in 1955, is completing a new book of essays, in which *The Unadjusted Man* will appear, to be published by Beacon Press.

TALCOTT PARSONS, professor of sociology and chairman of the department at Harvard University, is one of the leaders of the dominant structure-function school in American sociology. His first book, *The Structure of Social Action*, was a synthesis of the work of Durkheim, Pareto and Weber. Together with several collaborators he has been seeking to create a general theory of social behavior. These attempts have resulted in a number of major works including *The Social System, Towards a General Theory of Action* (with Edward Shils), and *Working Papers in the Theory of Action* (with Robert F. Bales). His most recent book, with Robert F. Bales, is *Socialization and the Family*.

SEYMOUR MARTIN LIPSET, associate professor of sociology at Columbia University, is the author of *Agrarian Socialism*, a study of the Cooperative Commonwealth Federation in Canada; an editor, with Reinhard Bendix, of a reader in *Class, Status and Power*; and a co-author of a monograph on "The Psychology of Voting," which is included in the *Handbook of Social Psychology*, edited by Gardner Lindzey. His most recent book, *Union Democracy*, a study of the political process in the typo-

graphical union, will be published by the Free
Press in 1956. Together with his Columbia colleagues Richard Hofstadter, Herbert Hyman and
William Kornhauser (now at Berkeley), Professor
Lipset is completing an inventory of writings in
political sociology, under a Ford behavioral studies
grant.

Contents

1 Interpretations of American Politics   3
    DANIEL BELL

2 The Pseudo-Conservative Revolt   33
    RICHARD HOFSTADTER

3 The Intellectuals and the Discontented Classes   56
    DAVID RIESMAN AND NATHAN GLAZER

4 The Revolt Against the Elite   91
    PETER VIERECK

5 Social Strains in America   117
    TALCOTT PARSONS

6 The Polls on Communism and Conformity   141
    NATHAN GLAZER AND
    SEYMOUR MARTIN LIPSET

7 The Sources of the "Radical Right"   166
    SEYMOUR MARTIN LIPSET

Index   235

THE NEW
AMERICAN
RIGHT

1

Interpretations of
American Politics

DANIEL BELL

THIS BOOK presents a series of novel
essays on some recent political history, notably an examination of the "new American right" which had concentrated for a time around the leadership of Senator
McCarthy, and which continues today in large, if inchoate,
form. This is not, however, a book about Senator Mc-
Carthy, although two of the essays, by Talcott Parsons
and S. M. Lipset, offer some fresh insights into the flash-
fire spread of McCarthyism. McCarthyism, or McCarthy-
wasm, as one wit put it, may be a passing phenomenon.
This book is concerned not with these transiencies, but
with the deeper-running social currents of a turbulent
mid-century America.

This is a turbulence born not of depression, but of prosperity. Contrary to the somewhat simple notion that prosperity dissolves all social problems, we see that prosperity brings in its wake new social groups, new social strains and new social anxieties. Conventional political analysis, drawn largely from eighteenth and nineteenth century American experience, cannot fathom these new social anxieties nor explain their political consequences.

This book, by establishing a new framework, attempts to provide an understanding of these new social problems. This framework is derived from an analysis of the exhaustion of liberal and left-wing political ideology, and by an examination of the new, prosperity-created "status-groups" which, in their drive for recognition and respectability, have sought to impose older conformities on the American body politic. This framework, drawn from some of the more recent thought in sociology and social psychology, represents a new and original contribution which, we feel, extends the range of conventional political analysis. To an extent, this is a "thesis book." It does not present a "total" view of politics nor does it supplant the older categories of political analysis, but it does add a new and necessary dimension to the analysis of American society today. Equally important, and of more immediate relevance perhaps, the application of these concepts may allow us not only to understand some puzzling aspects of the last decade, but also to illuminate the sub-rosa political forces of 1956 and beyond.

Politics in the United States has been looked at, roughly, from three standpoints: the role of the electoral structure, of democratic tradition, and of interest groups, sectional or class.

Perhaps the most decisive fact about politics in the United States is the two-party system. Each party is like some huge bazaar, with hundreds of hucksters clamoring

for attention. But while life within the bazaars flows freely
and licenses are easy to obtain, all trading has to be conducted within the tents; the ones who hawk their wares
outside are doomed to few sales. This fact gains meaning
when we consider one of the striking facts about American
life: America has thrown up countless social movements,
but few political parties; in contradiction to European
political life, few of the social movements have been able
to transform themselves into political parties. Here is one
source of flux yet stability in American life.

"It is natural for the ordinary American," wrote Gunnar
Myrdal, "when he sees something that is wrong to feel
not only that there should be a law against it, but also that
an organization should be formed to combat it,"—and,
we might add, to change it. American reform groups have
ranged from Esperantists to vegetarians, from silver money
advocates to conservationists, from trust-busters to socialists of fifty-seven varieties. These groups, intense and
ideologically single-minded, have formed numerous third
parties—the Greenback Party, Anti-Monopoly Party, Equal
Rights Party, Prohibition Party, Socialist Labor Party,
Union Labor Party, Farmer-Labor Party, Socialist Party.
Yet none succeeded.

The wheat farmers of the north central plains have a
homogeneity of cultural outlook and a common set of
economic problems which national boundary lines cannot
bisect. Yet in Canada, the wheat farmers formed a Social
Credit Party in Alberta and a Cooperative Commonwealth Federation in Saskatchewan, while their brothers
in North Dakota could only, at best, form a Non-Partisan
League within the Republican Party in order to press
their interests.[1]

These factors of rigid electoral structure have set
definite limits on the role of protest movements, left and
right, in American life. ("Let me make the deals, and I
care not who makes the ideals," an American politician

has said.) They account in significant measure for the failure of the Lemke-Coughlin movement in 1936, and the Wallace-Progressive Party in 1948. They account for the new basic alliance between the unions and the Democratic Party. Whatever lingering hopes some trade unionists may have held for a labor party in the United States were dispelled by Walter Reuther at the C.I.O. convention in November 1954 when, in answering transport leaders such as Mike Quill, he pointed out that a third party was impossible within the nature of the United States electoral system. This is a lesson that every social movement has learned. And any social movement which hopes to effect or resist social change in the United States is forced now to operate within one or the other of the two parties. This factor alone will place an enormous strain on these parties in the next ten years.

The democratic tradition, the second of the interpretive categories, has played an important role in shaping American political forms. The distinctive aspect of the political tradition in the United States is that politics is the arena of the *hoi polloi*. Here the "common man" becomes the source of ultimate appeal if not authority. This was not so at the beginning. The "founding fathers," with the Roman republic, let alone the state of affairs under the Articles of Confederation, in mind, feared the "democratic excesses" which the poor and propertyless classes could wreak against those with property. Whatever the subsequent inadequacies of the economic interpretation of history in a complex society, it is clear that in 1787 self-consciousness of property, and a desire to limit the electoral role of the people, were uppermost in the minds of the "four groups of personalty interests which had been adversely affected under the Articles of Confederation: money, public securities, manufactures, and trade and shipping."[2] This was reflected in the precautions written into the Constitution: a non-popular Senate, selected by the States; an appointive judiciary holding office for life, and a President elected through the indirect and cumbersome means of an electoral college.

But these barriers soon broke down. The victory of the Jeffersonians was the first step in the establishment of a "populist" character for the American democracy. The Federalists, seeing the success of the Jeffersonian methods, realized the necessity of imitating those "popular, convivial and charitable techniques." As early as 1802, Hamilton, in a letter to Bayard, outlined a plan for a "Christian Constitutional Society," which would appeal to the masses "through a development of a 'cult' of Washington and benevolent activities."³ A Washington Benevolent Society was formed in 1808, but it was too late, the Federalists had already lost. Thirty years later their spiritual descendants, the Whigs, beat the Democrats at their own game. Casting aside Henry Clay, whose "Hamiltonian" views were too well-established, the Whigs nominated General William Henry Harrison, the hero of the battle of Tippecanoe, against Andrew Jackson's successor, Martin Van Buren.

"If General Harrison is taken up as a candidate," said Nicholas Biddle, the former head of the National Bank, in some direction to party managers (which might not have echoed so strangely in 1952), "it will be on account of the past. . . . Let him say not one single word about his principles, or his creed—let him say nothing—promise nothing. Let no Committee, no convention—no town meeting ever extract from him a single word about what he thinks or will do hereafter. Let the use of pen and ink be wholly forbidden."⁴

The "cider election" of 1840 was a turning-point in American political life. Harrison traveled from place to place in a large wagon with a log cabin on top, and a barrel of hard cider on tap for the crowds. Daniel Webster, with the fustian of the demagogue, expressed deep regret that he had not been born in a log cabin, although his elder siblings had begun their lives in a humble abode. Whig orators berated Van Buren for living in a lordly manner, accusing him of putting cologne on his whiskers, eating from gold plate, and of being "laced up in corsets such as women in town wear and if possible tighter than the best of them."

The lesson was clear. Politics as a skill in manipulating masses became the established feature of political life, and the politician, sometimes a front-man for the moneyed interests, but sometimes the manipulator in his own right, came to the fore. Increasingly, the upper classes withdrew from direct participation in politics. The lawyer, the journalist, the drifter, finding politics an open ladder of social mobility, came bounding up from the lower middle classes. The tradition of equality had been established. The politician had to speak to "the people" and in democratic terms.

If the politician spoke to the people, he acted for "interests." The awareness of the interest-group basis of politics, the third of the categories, goes far back to the early days of the republic. Madison, in the oft-quoted Number Ten of the Federalist Papers, had written, "the most common and durable source of factions has been the various and unequal distribution of property. Those who hold and those who are without property have ever formed distinct interests in society." James Harrington's maxim that "power always follows property," "I believe to be as infallible a maxim in politics, as that action and reaction are equal in mechanics," said John Adams, the outstanding conservative of the time.[5] The threat to property on the part of the small farmer and the landless formed the basis of the first disquiet in American politics. The Shaysites in Massachusetts and other insurgents, General Henry Knox complained to George Washington, "believe that the property of the United States has been protected from the confiscations of Britain by the joint exertions of all." Madison, looking to the future, anticipated that "a great majority of the people will not only be without land, but any other sort of property." When this has occurred, he predicted, the propertyless masses will "either combine under the influence of their common situation; in which case the rights of property and the public liberty will not be secure in their hands; or what is more probable," he continued, with the lessons of the Roman demagogues in mind, "they will become tools of opulence and ambition, in which case, there will be equal danger on the other side."[6]

The early factional struggles in American political life, rustic in form because of the agrarian weight of the population, soon became sectional. This was inevitable since the different regions developed different interests: the rice, tobacco and cotton of the South; the fishing, lumber, commerce of New England. National parties came into being when the Federalists succeeded at first in combining the large planters of the upper and lower South with the commercial interests of the North Atlantic region, and when Jefferson challenged this combination by uniting the grain growers and other small farmers both North and South into a rival party. Since then, the national parties have been strange alliances of heterogeneous sectional groups: Midwest farmers with the populist, Democratic and Republican parties; the urban immigrant North with the backward, nativist South. Ethnic and functional groups have, often by historic accident, flowed into one of the two parties: the Negroes, because of the Civil War, for sixty years or so voted Republican; the Irish, because of their original relation to Tammany Hall, became Democrats; the Germans, settling in the Midwest, became Republican; the urban Italians, in reaction to their exclusion by the Irish, became Republican.

Within the sectionalism of American political life, arose

the narrower, more flexible tactic of the pressure group standing outside the particular party, committed to neither, giving support or winning support on the basis of allegiance to the single issue alone. One of the first skillful innovators of this tactic was George Henry Evans, a confrère of Robert Owen and a leading figure for a time in the reform politics of the 1830s and '40s. Evans had been one of the leaders of the Workingmen's Party in 1829, a New York party that began with moderate success but which faded when ideological differences inflamed a latent factionalism, and when the Democrats "stole their thunder" by adopting some of their immediate demands. Evans who believed that free land would solve the class tensions and plight of the propertyless workers, organized an Agrarian League in the 1840s. His experience had taught him that a minority party could not win by its own votes and that politicians, interested primarily in "deals not ideals," would endorse any measure advocated by a group that could hold the balance of power. Evans "therefore asked all candidates to support his 'sliding measures.' In exchange for such a pledge, the candidate would receive the votes of the workingmen."[7] While the Agrarian League itself met with middling success, its tactics paid off in the later passage of the Homestead acts.

In 1933, with the arrival of the New Deal, the feeling arose that a new era was emerging. In a widely-quoted book, Professor Arthur N. Holcombe of Harvard wrote: "The old party politics is visibly passing away. The character of the new party politics will be determined chiefly by the interests and attitudes of the urban population. . . . There will be less sectional politics and more class politics."[8] The emergence of "functional" groups, particularly labor, and the growing assertion of ethnic groups, seemed to underscore the shift. The fact that Franklin Roosevelt was able to weave together these groups, some of whom

like the farmers had been allied with the G.O.P., seemed
to indicate that some historic realignments were taking
place. Some have. The trade union movement, politically
articulate for the first time, is outspokenly Democratic;
but the working-class vote has usually been Democratic.
Ethnic groups which have played a role in politics have,
by and large, retained their loyalty to the Democratic
Party; but there are many indications that, as a result of
rising prosperity and higher social status, significant
chunks of these nationality and minority groups are beginning to shift their allegiance.[9] The farmers, despite the
enormous supports voted by the New Deal, have returned
to the Republican fold.

While sectional politics have somewhat diminished,
class politics have not jelled. Elements of both are reflected in the rise of pressure groups and the lobbies.
The most spectacular use of the seesaw pressure group
tactic was the Anti-Saloon League, which, starting in
1893, was able in two and a half decades to push through
a Constitutional amendment prohibiting the manufacture
and sale of liquor in the United States. Since then, the
pressure group device has been adopted by thousands of
organizations, whether it be for tariff reform, opposition
to Federal medical programs, or political aid to the state
of Israel. In 1949, the Department of Commerce estimated
that there were 4,000 national trade, professional, civic
and other associations. Including local and branch chap-
ters there were probably 16,000 businessmen's organizations, 70,000 local labor unions, 100,000 women's clubs
and 15,000 civic groups carrying on some political education. The enormous multiplication of such groups obviously cancels out many of the threats made to candidates
defying one or the other interests.[10] But it makes possible,
too, a dextrous art of logrolling, which itself makes it
possible for small interests to exert great political leverage.
Thus, when peanuts were eliminated from a farm subsidy

program in 1955, over one hundred Southern congressmen held up a crop support bill until the subsidy was restored. (Although Georgia peanuts account for less than one half of one percent of farm income, subsidizing this crop has cost the U.S. 100 million dollars in the past decade.)

The multiplication of interests and the fractioning of groups make it difficult to locate the sources of power in the United States.[11] This political fractioning, occurring simultaneously with the break-up of old property forms and the rise of new managerial groups to power within business enterprises, spells the break-up, too, of older ruling classes in the United States. A ruling class may be defined as a power-holding group that has both an established community of interest and continuity of interest. One can be a member of the "upper class" (i.e. have greater privilege and wealth and be able to transmit that wealth) without being a member of the *ruling group*. The modern ruling group is a coalition whose modes of continuity, other than the political route as such, are still ill-defined.[12] More than ever, government in the United States has become in John Chamberlain's early phrase, "the broker state." To say this is a broker state, however, does not mean that all interests have equal power. This is a business society. But within the general acceptance of corporate capitalism, modified by union power and checked by government control, the deals and interest-group trading proceed.

Granting the usefulness of these frames of political analysis—the role of electoral structure in limiting social movements and social clashes; the tradition of popular appeal; and the force of interest-groups in shaping and modifying legislative policy—in understanding "traditional" political problems, they leave us somewhat ill-equipped to understand the issues which have dominated political dispute in the last decade. These categories do not help us understand the Communist issue, the forces behind the new nationalism of say Bricker and Knowland, and the momentary range of support and the intense emotional heat generated by Senator McCarthy.

For Europeans, particularly, the Communist issue must be a puzzle. After all, there are no mass Communist parties in the U.S. such as one finds in France and Italy; the Communist Party in the U.S. never, at any single moment, had more than 100,000 members. In the last five years, when the Communist issue appeared on the national scene, the Communists had already lost considerable political influence and were on the decline—the Communists had been expelled from C.I.O.;[13] the Progressive Party, repudiated by Henry Wallace, had fizzled; the Communists were losing strength in the intellectual community.

It is true that liberals have tended to play down the issue.[14] And some rational basis for its existence was present. There was the surprise of the aggression in Korea and the emotional reaction against the Chinese and Russian Communists which carried over to domestic Communists. The disclosures, particularly by Whittaker Chambers, of the infiltration of Communists into high posts in government and the existence of espionage rings, produced a tremendous shock in a nation which hitherto had been unaware of such machinations. People began realizing, too, that numbers alone were no criteria of Communist strength; in fact, thinking of Communist influence on the basis of statistical calculation itself betrayed an ignorance of Communist methods; in the United States the Communists by operating among intellectual groups and opinion leaders have had an influence far out of proportion to their actual numbers. And, finally, the revelations in the Canadian spy investigations, in the Allan Nunn May trial in Britain and in the Rosenberg case that the Soviets had stolen United States atom secrets,

themselves added fuel to the emotional heat against the
Communists.

When all of this is said, it still fails to account for the
extensive damage to the democratic fabric that McCarthy
and others were able to cause on the Communist issue—
and for the reckless methods disproportionate to the
problem: the loyalty oaths on the campus, the compulsive
Americanism which saw threats to the country in the
wording of a Girl Scout handbook, the violent clubbing
of the Voice of America (which under the ideological
leadership of such anti-Communists as Foy Kohler and
Bertram Wolfe had conducted intelligent propaganda in
Europe), the wild headlines and the senseless damaging
of the Signal Corps radar research program at Fort Monmouth—in short the suspicion and the miasma of fear that
played so large a role in American politics. Nor does it
explain the unchallenged position held so long by Senator
McCarthy.

McCarthy himself must be a puzzle to conventional
political analysis. Calling him a demagogue explains little;
the relevant questions are, to whom was he a demagogue,
and about what. McCarthy's targets were indeed strange.
Huey Long, the last major demagogue, had vaguely attacked the rich and sought to "share the wealth." Mc-
Carthy's targets were intellectuals, Harvard, Anglophiles,
internationalists, the Army.

His targets and his language do, indeed, provide important clues to the "radical right" that supported him, and
the reasons for that support. These groups constituted a
strange mélange: a thin stratum of soured patricians like
Archibald Roosevelt, the last surviving son of Teddy
Roosevelt, whose emotional stake lay in a vanishing image
of a muscular America defying a decadent Europe; the
"new rich"—the automobile dealers, real estate manipulators, oil wildcatters—who needed the psychological assur-
ance that they, like their forebears, had earned their own

wealth, rather than accumulated it through government aid, and who feared that "taxes" would rob them of that wealth; the rising middle class strata of the ethnic groups, the Irish and the Germans, who sought to prove their Americanism, the Germans particularly because of the implied taint of disloyalty during World War II; and finally, unique in American cultural history, a small group of intellectuals, many of them cankered ex-Communists, who, pivoting on McCarthy, opened up an attack on liberalism in general.

This strange coalition, bearing the "sword of the Lord and Gideon," cannot be explained in conventional political terms. These essays do provide some frame, particularly one to explain the "new rich" and the "rising ethnic" groups. One key concept is the idea of "status politics" advanced by Richard Hofstadter. His central idea is that groups that are upwardly mobile (i.e. that are advancing in wealth and social position), are often as anxious and as politically febrile as groups that have become déclassé. Many observers have noted that groups which have lost their social position seek more violently than ever to impose on all groups the older values of a society which they once bore. Hofstadter demonstrates that groups on the rise may insist on a similar conformity in order to establish themselves. This rise takes place in periods of prosperity, when class or economic interest group conflicts have lost much of their force.[15] The new, patriotic issues proposed by the status groups are amorphous and ideological. This theme is elaborated in the essay by Riesman and Glazer, with particular reference to the new rich. But these groups are able to assert themselves, the two sociologists point out, largely because of the exhaustion of liberal ideology—a collapse not from defeat but from "victory." The essay by Peter Viereck traces some of the historical roots of the peculiar rhetoric of the right, showing the sources of the anti-intellectualism and Anglophobia in the egalitarian populism of the last century. Professor Parsons, discussing the nature of social change in the United States, demonstrates how the resultant social strains foster the emergence of the new right. Glazer and Lipset, analyzing the recent study by Professor Stouffer on "Communism, Conformity and Civil Liberties," deal with limitations of "survey methods" in elucidating social attitudes. The long concluding essay by Professor Lipset provides a detailed analysis of the social groups identified with the new right and assesses their strength.

These essays were not written for this volume. All but the reviews of the Stouffer book appeared about the same time, and quite independently. And yet they showed a remarkable convergence in point of view. This convergence itself indicates that some of the recent concepts of sociology and social psychology—the role of status groups as a major entity in American life and status resentments as a real force in politics—were being applied fruitfully to political analysis.

Whether the groups analyzed in this volume form a political force depends upon many factors. Certainly McCarthy himself is, at the moment, at the nadir. By the logic of his own political position, and by the nature of his personality, he had to go to an extreme. And he ended, finally, by challenging Eisenhower. It was McCarthy's great gamble. And he lost, for the challenge to a Republican President by a Republican minority could only have split the party. Faced with this threat, the party rallied behind Eisenhower, and McCarthy himself was isolated. In this respect, the events prove the soundness of the thesis of Walter Lippmann and the Alsops in 1952 that only a Republican President could provide the necessary continuity of foreign and domestic policy initiated and maintained by the Fair Deal. A Democratic President would only have polarized the parties, and given the extreme Republican wing the license to lead the attack;

the administration of a moderate Republican could act as a damper on the extreme right.

The lessening of international tensions may confirm McCarthy's defeat, just as a flare-up of war in Asia, particularly Chinese Communist action over Formosa, might give him a platform to come back. Yet McCarthy has to be understood in relation to the people behind him and the changed political temper which these groups have brought. He was the catalyst, not the explosive force. These forces still remain.

The essays in this volume identify and deal with the emergence of the "status groups." Their emergence raises some further questions regarding the political theory and political temper of American democracy.

Throughout our history, Americans have had an extraordinary talent for compromise in politics and extremism in morality. The most shameless political deals (and "steals") have been rationalized as expedient and realistically necessary; yet in no other country were there such spectacular attempts to curb human appetites and brand them as illicit—and nowhere else such glaring failures. From the start America was at one and the same time the frontier community where "everything goes," and the fair country of the restrictive Blue Laws (to the extent, for example, of barring theatrical performances on Sunday). At the turn of the century the cleavage developed between the big city and the small town conscience: crime as a growing business was fed by the revenues from prostitution, liquor and gambling that a cynical urban society encouraged, and which a middle-class Protestant ethos sought to suppress with a ferocity unmatched in any other civilized country. Even in prim and proper Anglican England, prostitution is a commonplace of Piccadilly night life, and gambling one of the largest and most popular industries. But in America, the enforcement of public morals has been a continuing feature of our history.

The sources of this moralism are varied. This has been a middle-class culture, and there may be considerable truth to the generalization of Svend Ranulf that moral indignation is a peculiar fact of middle-class psychology and represents a disguised form of repressed envy.[16] One does not find moral indignation a feature of the temper of aristocratic cultures. Moralism and moral indignation are characteristic of religions that have largely abandoned other-worldly preoccupations and have concentrated on this-worldly concerns. Religions, like Catholicism, which are focused on heaven are often quite tolerant of man's foibles, weaknesses, and cruelties on earth; theft, after all, is only a venial sin, while pride bears the stain of venality. This is a country, and Protestantism a religion, in which piety has given way to moralism, and theology to ethics. Becoming respectable represents "moral" advancement, and regulating conduct, i.e. being "moral" about it, is a great concern of the Protestant churches in America.

This moralism, itself not unique to America, is linked to an evangelicalism that was largely unique. There has long been a legend, fostered for the most part by literary people, and compounded by sociologists, that America's has been a "puritan" culture. For the sociologists this has arisen out of a mistaken identification of the Protestant ethic with puritan code. The literary critics have been seduced by the myth of New England, and the literary revolt initiated by Van Wyck Brooks which sought to break the hold of puritanism in literature. While puritanism, and the "New England mind," have indeed played a large intellectual role in American life, in the habits and mores of the masses of people, the peculiar evangelicalism of Methodism and Baptism, with its high emotionalism, its fervor, enthusiasm and excitement, its revivalism, its excesses of sinning and of high-voltage confessing, has played a much more important role in coloring the moral temper of America. Baptism and Methodism have been the American religious creed because they were the rustic and frontier religions. In his page on "Why Americans Manifest a Sort of Fanatical Spiritualism," de Tocqueville observes: "In all states of the Union, but especially in the half-peopled country of the Far West, itinerant preachers may be met with who hawk about the word of God from place to place. Whole families, old men, women and children, cross rough passes and untrodden wilds, coming from a great distance, to join a camp-meeting, where, in listening to these discourses, they totally forget for several days and nights the cares of business and even the most urgent wants of the body."[17]

The Baptist and Methodist churches grew while the more "respectable" Protestant bodies remained static, precisely because their preachers went on with the advancing frontier and reflected its spirit. "In the camp meeting and in the political gathering logical discourse was of no avail, while the 'language of excitement' called forth an enthusiastic response," observed H. Richard Niebuhr.[18]

This revivalist spirit was egalitarian and anti-intellectual. It shook off the vestments and the formal liturgies and preached instead the gospel and roaring hymn. This evangelicalism was reflected in the moralism of a William Jennings Bryan, a religious as well as an economic champion of the West, and in the urban revivalism of a Dwight Moody and the Y.M.C.A. movement that grew out of his gospel fervor.[19] In their espousal of social reform, the evangelical churches reflected the peculiar influence of moralism. They were the supreme champions of prohibition legislation and Sabbath observance. Reform, in their terms, meant, not as in the New Deal, a belief in welfare legislation, but the redemption of those who had fallen prey to sin—and sin meant drink, loose women and gambling.

This moralism, so characteristic of American temper, had a peculiar schizoid character: it would be imposed with vehemence in areas of culture and conduct—in the censorship of books, the attacks on "immoral art," etc., and in the realm of private habits; yet it was heard only sporadically regarding the depredations of business or the corruption of politics. And yet, this has had its positive side. To the extent that moral indignation—apart from its rhetorical use in political campaigns—played so small a role in the actual political arena, the United States has been able to escape the intense ideological fanaticism—the conflicts of clericalism and class—which has been so characteristic of Europe.

The singular fact about the Communist problem is that an ideological issue was raised in American political life, with a compulsive moral fervor only possible because of the equation of Communism with sin. A peculiar change, in fact, seems to be coming over American life. While we are becoming more relaxed in the area of traditional morals (viz., the Supreme Court ruling against censorship in the case of the movie, *The Miracle*), we are becoming moralistic and extreme in politics. The fact that Senator McCarthy could seek to pin a Communist label on the Democratic Party, and tie it with a tag of "treason"—and be abetted for a time by Attorney General Brownell and the Republican Party is a reflection of a new political temper in America.

The tendency to convert politics into "moral" issues is reinforced by a second fact, the activities of the McCarthy-ite intellectuals—James Burnham, William Schlamm, Max Eastman, and their minor epigoni. The rise of intellectual apologists for a reactionary right is, too, a new phase in American life. The quixotic fact is that many of these men, ex-Communists, repudiated at first not the utopian vision of Communism, but its methods. In the thirties, the crucial intellectual fight was to emphasize, against the liberal piddlers who sought to excuse the harshness of Stalinism by reference to the historic backwardness of Russia, or the grandeur of the Soviet dream, that in social action there is an inextricable relation between "ends and means," and that consistently amoral means could only warp and hideously distort an end. Yet these men have forgotten this basic point in their defense of McCarthy. Schlamm, the author of a fine book about Stalinism, *Die Diktatur der Luge* (The Dictatorship of the Lie) applauds McCarthy as a man who is seriously interested in ideas. John T. Flynn, the old muckraker, denies McCarthy has ever made use of the lie. Max Eastman, slightly critical at times, worries most not about McCarthy but that the liberals by attacking McCarthy might be playing "the Communist game"; as if all politics were only two-sided, in this case McCarthy or the Communists.

How explain this reversal? Motivations are difficult to plumb. Some of these men, as George Orwell once pointed out in a devastating analysis of James Burnham,[20] slavishly worship power images. *The Freeman,* the old-maidish house organ of the intellectual right, coyly applauded McCarthy as a tough hombre.

Yet one significant fact emerges from this bile: the hatred of the ex-Communist is not so much of the Communist, but of the "liberals," and the root of the problem goes back to the political situation of the Thirties. In recent years there has been a growing myth that in the 1930s the Communist dominated the cultural life of America, its publishing houses, Broadway, Hollywood, and the colleges. The myth is a seductive one which grows more plausible with the revelation of different "name" personages who the public now discover were once open or covert fellow-travelers. Yet, as Granville Hicks points out, only one anti-Communist book is ever cited as having been suppressed in those years, while anti-Communist authors such as Eugene Lyons, Max Eastman, Freda

Utley, Jan Valtin all published anti-Soviet books.[21] The
Communists, in fact, felt that the shoe at times was on
the other foot. "In the autumn of 1934," says Hicks, "I
wrote an article for the *New Masses* in which I argued
that the *New York Times* book review assigned almost
all books on Russia to anti-Communists." The *Nation*
book section under Margaret Marshall in those years was
anti-Communist. The Communist cells in universities were
small; at Harvard in 1938, at the height of the popular
front, there were fourteen faculty Communists in all.
While the Communists were able to enlist a sizable
number of well-known names for their fronts, the Committee for Cultural Freedom, in issuing a statement in
1939 bracketing the Soviet and Nazi states as equally
immoral, displayed a more distinguished roster of intellectuals than any statement issued by a Communist front.

How explain these contrasting images of the Red
Decade—the anti-Communists who regarded the Communists as dominating the cultural life and the Communists who complained that they had little influence?
The evidence, I would say, lies on Hicks' side.[22] The
Communists did not dominate the cultural field, though
they wielded an influence far out of proportion to their
numbers. What is true, and here I feel Hicks missed the
subtle edge of the problem, is that the official institutions
of the cultural community—because of the Spanish Civil
War, the shock of Fascism, and the aura of New Deal
reform—did look at the Communist with some sympathy;
they regarded him as ultimately, philosophically wrong,
but still as a respectable member of the community. But
the vocal anti-Communists (many of them Trotskyites at
the time), with their quarrelsome ways, their esoteric
knowledge of Bolshevik history (most of the intellectuals
were completely ignorant of the names of the Bolsheviks
in the dock at the Moscow trials, Zinoviev, Kamenev,
Bukharin, Piatakov, Sokolnikov, Rakovsky) seemed ex-

treme and bizarre—and were regarded with suspicion. The anti-Stalinists, by raising "extraneous" issues of a "sectarian" nature, were "sabotaging" the fight against Fascism. Hence, in the thirties, one found the Communist possessing a place in the intellectual world, while the anti-Communists were isolated and thwarted.

Here, in a sense, is the source of the present-day resentment against "the liberals." If one looks for formal or ideological definition "the liberal" is difficult to pin down. To a McCarthyite, "the liberals" dominate the intellectual and publishing community—and define the canons of respectability and acceptance. And once again the knot of ex-Communists, now, as in the thirties, finds itself outside the pale. At stake is an attitude toward the Communists. *The Freeman* intellectuals want the Communists shriven or driven out of all areas of public or community life. The "liberal" says the effort is not worth the price, since there are few Communists, and the drive against them only encourages reactionaries to exact a conformity of opinion. By refusing to sanction these measures, the liberals find themselves under attack as "soft."

In these strange times, new polar terms have been introduced into political discourse, but surely none so strange as the division into "hard" and "soft." Certainly in attitudes towards the rights of Communists, there are many gradations of opinion among genuine anti-Communists, as the debates in the Committee for Cultural Freedom have demonstrated. But for the *Freeman* intellectuals, there are only two attributes—hard or soft. Even the *New York Post*, whose editor, James A. Wechsler has fought Communists for years, and the Americans for Democratic Action, whose initiating spirit was Reinhold Niebuhr, and whose co-chairman, Arthur Schlesinger, Jr., was one of the early intellectual antagonists of the Communists, before McCarthy ever spoke up on the subject, have been denounced as "soft."

What does the term mean? Presumably one is "soft" if one insists that the danger from domestic Communists is small. But the "hard" anti-Communists insist that no distinction can be made between international and domestic Communism. This may be true regarding intent and methods, but is it equally so regarding their power; is the strength of domestic Communists as great as that of international Communism? It is said, that many liberals refused to recognize that Communists constituted a security problem or that planned infiltration existed. This is rather a blanket charge, but even if largely true, the "hard" anti-Communists refuse to recognize the dimension of time. The question is: *what is the degree of the present-day Communist infiltration?* Pressed at this point some "hard" anti-Communists admit that the number of actual Communists may be small, but that the real problem arises because the liberals, especially in the large Eastern universities, are predominantly "anti-anti Communists." But what is the content of this "anti-anti Communism?" That it won't admit that the Communists constitute a present danger. And so we are back where we started.

The polarization of images reflects itself in a strange set, too, of contrasting conceptions about power position. The liberals, particularly in the universities, have felt themselves subject to attack by powerful groups; the pro-McCarthy intellectuals see themselves as a persecuted group, discriminated against in the major opinion forming centers in the land. A personal incident is relevant here. A few years ago I encountered Robert Morris, the counsel then for the Jenner Committee on internal subversion. He complained of the "terrible press" his committee was receiving. What press, he was asked; after all, the great Hearst and Scripps-Howard and Gannett chains, as well as an overwhelming number of newspaper dailies, had enthusiastically supported and reported the work of the Committee. I wasn't thinking of them, he replied. I was thinking of the *New York Times,* the *Washington Post,* the *St. Louis Post-Dispatch.*

The paradoxical fact is that on traditional economic issues, these "liberal" papers are conservative.[23] All three supported Eisenhower. Yet, traditional conservative issues no longer count in dividing "liberals" from "anti-Communists." The only issue is whether one is "hard" or "soft." And so, an amorphous, ideological issue, rather than an interest-group issue, has become a major dividing line in the political community.

The "ideologizing" of politics gains reinforcement from a third, somewhat independent tendency in American life, the emergence of what may be called the "symbolic groups." These are the inchoate, often ill-coordinated entities, known generally, in capital letters, as "Labor," "Business," the "Farmers," *et al.* The assumption is made that these entities have a coherent philosophy and a defined purpose and represent actual forces. But is this true in a society so multi-fractioned and interest-divided?

The utilitarians, the first to give politics a calculus, and thus begin an experimental social science, made a distinction between a social decision (the common purpose) and the sum total of individual self-interest decisions. Adam Smith assumed a natural harmony, if not identity, between the two. But Jeremy Bentham knew that such identity was artificial, although he felt that they could be reconciled by an intelligent legislator through "a well-regulated application of punishments."[24] The distinction between the self-interest and social decisions might be reworked in modern idiom as one between "market" and "ideological" decisions. The first represents a series of choices based on the rational self-interest of the individual or organization, with the aim of maximizing profit or the survival or enhancement of the organization. The second represents decisions, based on some purpose clothed in moral terms, in which the goal is deemed so important as to override when necessary the individual self-interest.[25]

In modern society, the clash between ideological and market decisions is often as intense within groups, as between groups. The "labor movement," for example, has strongly favored lower tariffs and broader international trade; yet the seamen's union has urged that U.S. government aid be shipped in American, not foreign bottoms, while the textile unions have fought for quotas on foreign imports. Politically minded unionists, like Mike Quill in New York, have had to choose between a wage increase for their members against a rise in transit fares for the public at large. Interest rivalries are often more direct. The teamsters' unions have lobbied against the railroad unions and the coal miners against the oil workers. In every broad group these interest conflicts have taken place, within industry, farm, and every other functional group in the society.

The tendency to convert interest groups into "symbolic groups" derives from varied sources. Much of it comes from "vulgar" Marxist thinking, with its image of a self-conscious, coordinated Business class (as in Jack London's image of "the oligarchs" in his *The Iron Heel,* and the stereotypes of "Wall Street"). Some of this was taken over by the New Dealers with their image of "America's Sixty Families." But the biggest impetus has come from the changing nature of political decision-making and the mode of opinion formation in modern society. The fact that decision-making has been centralized into the narrow cockpit of Washington, rather than the impersonal market, leads groups like the National Association of Manufacturers, the Farm Bureau, the A.F. of L., *et al,* to speak for *"Business,"* for the *"Farmers,"* for *"Labor."* At the same time, with the increased sensitivity to "public opinion," heightened by the introduction of the mass polling technique, the "citizen" (not the specific-interest individual) is asked what "Business" or "Labor" or the "Farmer" should do. In effect, these groups are often forced to assume an identity and greater coherence beyond their normal intra-mural interest conflicts. A result again is that political debate moves from specific interest clashes, in which issues can be identified and possibly compromised, to ideologically-tinged conflicts which polarize the groups and divide the society.

The essays in this book are primarily analytical. Yet they also point implicitly to a dangerous situation. The tendency to convert issues into ideologies, to invest them with moral color and high emotional charge, invites conflicts which can only damage a society. "A nation, divided irreconcilably on 'principle,' each party believing itself pure white and the other pitch black, cannot govern itself," wrote a younger Walter Lippmann.

The saving glory of the United States is that politics has always been a pragmatic give-and-take rather than a series of wars-to-the-death. One ultimately comes to admire the "practical politics" of a Theodore Roosevelt and his scorn for the intransigents, like Godkin and Villard, who, refusing to yield to expediency, could never put through their reforms. Politics, as Edmund Wilson has described T.R.'s attitude, "is a matter of adapting oneself to all sorts of people and situations, a game in which one may score but only by accepting the rules and recognizing one's opponents, rather than a moral crusade in which one's stainless standard must mow the enemy down."[26]

Democratic politics is bargaining and consensus because the historic contribution of liberalism was to separate law from morality. The thought that the two should be separate often comes as a shock. Yet, in the older Catholic societies, ruled by the doctrine of "two swords," the state was the secular arm of the Church, and enforced in civil life the moral decrees of the Church. This was possible, in political theory, if not in practice, because the society was homogeneous and everyone accepted the same religious values. But the religious wars that followed the Reformation proved that a plural society could only survive if it respected the principles of toleration. No group, be it Catholic or Protestant, could use the state to impose its moral conceptions on all the people. As the party of the *Politiques* put it, the "civil society must not perish for conscience's sake."[27]

These theoretical foundations of modern liberal society were completed by Kant, who, separating legality and morality, defined the former as the "rules of the game" so to speak; law dealt with procedural, not substantive issues. The latter were private matters of conscience with which the state could not interfere.

This distinction has been at the root of the American democracy. For Madison, factions (or interests) were inevitable and the function of the republic was to protect the causes of faction, i.e., liberty and "the diversity in the faculties of men." As an interpreter of Madison writes, "free men, 'diverse' man, fallible, heterogeneous, heterodox, opinionated, quarrelsome man was the raw material of faction."[28] Since faction was inevitable, one could only deal with its effects, and not smother its causes. One curbed these effects by a federal form of government, by separation of powers, *et al.* But for Madison two answers were central: first, an *extensive republic,* since a larger geographical area, and therefore a larger number of interests, would "lessen the insecurity of private rights," and second, the guarantee of representative government.

Representative government, as John Stuart Mill has so cogently pointed out, means representation of all interests, "since the interest of the excluded is always in danger of being overlooked." And being overlooked, as Calhoun pointed out, constitutes a threat to civil order. But representative government is important for the deeper reason that by including all representative interests one can keep up "the antagonism of influences which is the only real security for continued progress."[29] It is the only way of providing the "concurrent majorities" which, as Calhoun knew so well, were the solid basis for providing a check on the tyrannical "popular" majority. Only through representative government can one achieve consensus and conciliation.

This is not to say that the Communist "interest" is a legitimate one, or that the Communist issue is irrelevant. As a conspiracy, rather than as a legitimate dissenting group, the Communist movement is a threat to any democratic society. And, within the definition of "clear and present danger," a democratic society may have to act against that conspiracy. But these are questions to be handled by law. The tendency to use the Communist issue as a political club against other parties or groups (i.e. to provide an ideological guilt by association), or the tendency to convert questions of law into issues of morality (and thus shift the source of sanctions from courts and legitimate authority to private individuals), imposes a great strain on democratic society.

In almost 170 years since its founding American democracy has been rent only once by civil war. We have learned since then, not without strain, to include the "excluded interests," the populist farmers and the organized workers. These economic interest groups take a legitimate place in the society and the ideological conflicts that once threatened to disrupt the society, particularly in the New Deal period, have been mitigated. The new divisions created by the status anxieties of new middle class groups pose a new threat. The rancor of McCarthyism was one of its ugly excesses. Yet, the United States, so huge and complex that no single political boss or any single political grouping has ever been able to dominate it, may in time diminish these divisions. This

is an open society, and these status anxieties are part of
the price we pay for that openness.

[1] For an elaboration of the role of political contexts affecting attitudes,
see the remarks following by Glazer and Lipset, on page 141; also, S. M.
Lipset, *Agrarian Socialism* (University of California Press), pp. 224
passim.

[2] Charles A. Beard, *An Economic Interpretation of the Constitution*
(New York, 1935 edition), page 324.

[3] See Dixon Ryan Fox, *The Decline of the Aristocracy in the Politics
of New York.*

[4] Cited in Charles A. Beard, *The Rise of American Civilization* (1940
edition), Vol. 1, page 574.

[5] Cited in "American Individualism: Fact and Fiction," by A. T.
Mason. *American Political Science Review,* March, 1952. Professor
Mason's paper is the most concise account I know of the struggle be-
tween private economic power and popular political control in the
United States.

[6] A. T. Mason, *ibid.,* page 5.

[7] John R. Commons and associates, *History of Labour in the United
States,* Vol. 1, page 531.

[8] A. N. Holcombe, *The New Party Politics* (New York, 1933), page 11.

[9] See Samuel Lubell, *The Future of American Politics* (New York,
1952); Louis Harris, *Is There a Republican Majority?* (New York, 1955).

[10] For an extended discussion of the role of interest groups in American politics, see David Truman, *The Governmental Process* (New York,
1951).

[11] See David Riesman, *The Lonely Crowd* (Anchor edition, pp.
246-259).

[12] The amorphousness of power in contemporary United States and its
relationship to the break-up of "family capitalism," in the United States
is developed by the writer in a paper on "The Ambiguities of the Mass
Society and the Complexities of American Life," presented at a conference in Milan, Italy, in September, 1955 on "The Future of Freedom."
This paper will be included in the proceedings of the conference, to be
published in 1956 by Beacon Press.

[13] By 1952 they controlled unions with fewer than five percent of
United States labor membership as against a peak control of unions with
20 percent of union membership in 1944.

[14] The contradictory stand of the Truman administration compounded
these confusions and increased the alarums. On the one hand, leading
members of the administration, including Truman himself, sought to
minimize the degree of past Communist infiltration, on the other hand,
the administration let loose a buckshot security program which itself
inflamed the problems. This included the turning of the Attorney-Gen-
eral's list of subversive organizations into a blank check-list to deny
individuals passports and even non-government jobs; an unfair loyalty
program in which individuals could not even face their accusers; and the
prosecution of the Communist Party leaders under the Smith Act.

[15] Before the Civil War and immigration, discrimination in America

was almost solely on religious grounds. In the decades that followed, the rising social classes began to create status demarcations. For an excellent account of the turning-point in social discrimination in America, i.e., its emergence in an egalitarian society, see the essay by Oscar Handlin, "The Acquisition of Political and Social Rights by the Jews in the United States," in the *American Jewish Yearbook,* 1955.

In the expansion and prosperity of the 1870's and 1880's, Professor Handlin points out, "many a man having earned a fortune, even a modest one, thereafter found himself laboring under the burden of complex anxieties. He knew that success was by its nature evanescent. Fortunes were made only to be lost; what was earned in one generation would disappear in the next. Such a man, therefore, wished not only to retain that which he had gained; he was also eager for the social recognition that would permit him to enjoy his possessions; and he sought to extend these on in time through his family. . . . The last decades of the nineteenth century therefore witnessed a succession of attempts to set up areas of exclusiveness that would mark off the favored groups and protect them against excessive contact with outsiders. In imitation of the English model, there was an effort to create a 'high society' with its own protocol and conventions, with suitable residences in suitable districts, with distinctive clubs and media of entertainment, all of which would mark off and preserve the wealth of the fortunate families."

For an account of a parallel development in England, see the essay by Miriam Beard in the volume by Graeber and Britt, *Jews in a Gentile World.* For the sources of discrimination in American traditions and populism, see Daniel Bell, "The Grassroots of Jew Hatred in America," *The Jewish Frontier,* June 1944.

[16] Svend Ranulf, *Moral Indignation and Middle Class Psychology,* Copenhagen, 1938.

[17] De Tocqueville, *Democracy in America.* New York, 1945, volume II, page 134.

[18] H. Richard Niebuhr, *Social Sources of Denominationalism,* New York, 1929, page 141.

[19] See W. W. Sweet, *Revivalism in America,* New York, 1944.

[20] *Shooting an Elephant and Other Essays,* New York, 1950.

[21] Granville Hicks, *Where We Came Out,* New York, 1954.

[22] I have attempted to assemble some of that evidence in my essay on the history of American Marxist parties in the volume *Socialism and American Life,* edited by Egbert and Persons, Princeton, 1952.

[23] The sense of being a hunted, isolated minority is reflected quite vividly in an editorial note in *The Freeman*—June, 1955: "Since the advent of the New Deal (An Americanized version of Fabian socialism) the mass circulation media in this country have virtually closed their columns to opposition articles. For this they can hardly be blamed; their business is to sell paper at so much a pound and advertising space at so much a line. They must give the masses what they believe the masses want, if they are to maintain their mass circulation business; and there is no doubt that the promises of socialism reiterated by the propaganda machine of the government, have made it popular and dulled the public mind to the verities of freedom."

[24] Jeremy Bentham, *Principles of Morals and Legislation,* Oxford edi-

tion, page 3; see also, Elie Halevy, *Growth of Philosophical Radicalism,* New York, 1928; pp. 14–18.

25 The distinction, thus, is more than one between opinion and behavior. Quite often an ideological decision will have greater weight for a group than immediate self-interest (defined in rational market terms), and the group will act on the basis of ideology. The task of a realistic social psychology is to identify under what circumstances the ideological or market conditions will prevail.

26 Edmund Wilson, in *Eight Essays,* New York, 1954 (Anchor Books), page 213.

27 See Harold J. Laski, *The Rise of Liberalism,* New York, 1938, pp. 43–51. Also, Franz Neumann, *Behemoth,* New York, pp. 442–447.

28 See Neal Riemer, "James Madison's Theory of the Self-Destructive Features of Republican Government," *Ethics.*

29 See John Stuart Mill, *Representative Government* (Everyman edition, 1936), pp. 209, 201.

2

The Pseudo-Conservative Revolt

RICHARD HOFSTADTER

TWENTY YEARS ago the dynamic force in American political life came from the side of liberal dissent, from the impulse to reform the inequities of our economic and social system and to change our ways of doing things, to the end that the sufferings of the Great Depression would never be repeated. Today the dynamic force in our political life no longer comes from the liberals who made the New Deal possible. By 1952 the liberals had had at least the trappings of power for twenty years. They could look back to a brief, exciting period in the mid-thirties when they had held power itself and had been able to transform the economic and administrative life of the nation. After twenty years the

New Deal liberals have quite unconsciously taken on the psychology of those who have entered into possession. Moreover, a large part of the New Deal public, the jobless, distracted and bewildered men of 1933, have in the course of the years found substantial places in society for themselves, have become home-owners, suburbanites and solid citizens. Many of them still keep the emotional commitments to the liberal dissent with which they grew up politically, but their social position is one of solid comfort. Among them the dominant tone has become one of satisfaction, even of a kind of conservatism. Insofar as Adlai Stevenson won their enthusiasm in 1952, it was not in spite of, but in part because of the air of poised and reliable conservatism that he brought to the Democratic convention. By comparison, Harry Truman's impassioned rhetoric, with its occasional thrusts at "Wall Street," seemed passé and rather embarrassing. The change did not escape Stevenson himself. "The strange alchemy of time," he said in a speech at Columbus, "has somehow converted the Democrats into the truly conservative party of this country—the party dedicated to conserving all that is best, and building solidly and safely on these foundations." The most that the old liberals can now envisage is not to carry on with some ambitious new program, but simply to defend as much as possible of the old achievements and to try to keep traditional liberties of expression that are threatened.

There is, however, a dynamic of dissent in America today. Representing no more than a modest fraction of the electorate, it is not so powerful as the liberal dissent of the New Deal era, but it is powerful enough to set the tone of our political life and to establish throughout the country a kind of punitive reaction. The new dissent is certainly not radical—there are hardly any radicals of any sort left—nor is it precisely conservative. Unlike most of the liberal dissent of the past, the new dissent not only has no respect for non-conformism, but is based upon a relentless demand for conformity. It can most accurately be called pseudo-conservative—I borrow the term from the study of *The Authoritarian Personality* published five years ago by Theodore W. Adorno and his associates—because its exponents, although they believe themselves to be conservatives and usually employ the rhetoric of conservatism, show signs of a serious and restless dissatisfaction with American life, traditions and institutions. They have little in common with the temperate and compromising spirit of true conservatism in the classical sense of the word, and they are far from pleased with the dominant practical conservatism of the moment as it is represented by the Eisenhower Administration. Their political reactions express rather a profound if largely unconscious hatred of our society and its ways—a hatred which one would hesitate to impute to them if one did not have suggestive clinical evidence.

From clinical interviews and thematic apperception tests, Adorno and his co-workers found that their pseudo-conservative subjects, although given to a form of political expression that combines a curious mixture of largely conservative with occasional radical notions, succeed in concealing from themselves impulsive tendencies that, if released in action, would be very far from conservative. The pseudo-conservative, Adorno writes, shows "conventionality and authoritarian submissiveness" in his conscious thinking and "violence, anarchic impulses, and chaotic destructiveness in the unconscious sphere. . . . The pseudo conservative is a man who, in the name of upholding traditional American values and institutions and defending them against more or less fictitious dangers, consciously or unconsciously aims at their abolition."[1]

Who is the pseudo-conservative, and what does he want? It is impossible to identify him by class, for the

pseudo-conservative impulse can be found in practically
all classes in society, although its power probably rests
largely upon its appeal to the less educated members of
the middle classes. The ideology of pseudo-conservatism
can be characterized but not defined, because the pseudo-
conservative tends to be more than ordinarily incoherent
about politics. The lady who, when General Eisenhower's
victory over Senator Taft had finally become official,
stalked out of the Hilton Hotel declaiming, "This means
eight more years of socialism" was probably a fairly good
representative of the pseudo-conservative mentality. So
also were the gentlemen who, at the Freedom Congress
held at Omaha over a year ago by some "patriotic" organizations, objected to Earl Warren's appointment to the
Supreme Court with the assertion: "Middle-of-the-road
thinking can and will destroy us"; the general who spoke
to the same group, demanding "an Air Force capable of
wiping out the Russian Air Force and industry in one
sweep," but also "a material reduction in military expenditures";[2] the people who a few years ago believed simultaneously that we had no business to be fighting communism in Korea, but that the war should immediately
be extended to an Asia-wide crusade against communism;
and the most ardent supporters of the Bricker Amendment. Many of the most zealous followers of Senator
McCarthy are also pseudo-conservatives, although there
are presumably a great many others who are not.

The restlessness, suspicion and fear manifested in various phases of the pseudo-conservative revolt give evidence
of the real suffering which the pseudo-conservative ex-
periences in his capacity as a citizen. He believes himself
to be living in a world in which he is spied upon, plotted
against, betrayed, and very likely destined for total ruin.
He feels that his liberties have been arbitrarily and out-
rageously invaded. He is opposed to almost everything
that has happened in American politics for the past twenty

years. He hates the very thought of Franklin D. Roosevelt. He is disturbed deeply by American participation in the United Nations, which he can see only as a sinister organization. He sees his own country as being so weak that it is constantly about to fall victim to subversion; and yet he feels that it is so all-powerful that any failure it may experience in getting its way in the world—for instance, in the Orient—cannot possibly be due to its limitations but must be attributed to its having been betrayed.[3] He is the most bitter of all our citizens about our involvement in the wars of the past, but seems the least concerned about avoiding the next one. While he naturally does not like Soviet communism, what distinguishes him from the rest of us who also dislike it is that he shows little interest in, is often indeed bitterly hostile to such realistic measures as might actually strengthen the United States vis-à-vis Russia. He would much rather concern himself with the domestic scene, where communism is weak, than with those areas of the world where it is really strong and threatening. He wants to have nothing to do with the democratic nations of Western Europe, which seem to draw more of his ire than the Soviet Communists, and he is opposed to all "give-away programs" designed to aid and strengthen these nations. Indeed, he is likely to be antagonistic to most of the operations of our federal government except Congressional investigations, and to almost all of its expenditures. Not always, however, does he go so far as the speaker at the Freedom Congress who attributed the greater part of our national difficulties to "this nasty, stinking 16th [income tax] Amendment."

A great deal of pseudo-conservative thinking takes the form of trying to devise means of absolute protection against that betrayal by our own officialdom which the pseudo-conservative feels is always imminent. The Bricker Amendment, indeed, might be taken as one of the primary symptoms of pseudo-conservatism. Every dissenting movement brings its demand for Constitutional changes; and the pseudo-conservative revolt, far from being an exception to this principle, seems to specialize in Constitutional revision, at least as a speculative enterprise. The widespread latent hostility toward American institutions takes the form, among other things, of a flood of proposals to write drastic changes into the body of our fundamental law. Last summer, in a characteristically astute piece, Richard Rovere pointed out that Constitution-amending had become almost a major diversion in the Eighty-third Congress.[4] About a hundred amendments were introduced and referred to committee. Several of these called for the repeal of the income tax. Several embodied formulas of various kinds to limit non-military expenditures to some fixed portion of the national income. One proposed to bar all federal expenditures on "the general welfare"; another, to prohibit American troops from serving in any foreign country except on the soil of the potential enemy; another, to redefine treason to embrace not only persons trying to overthrow the government but also those trying to "weaken" it, even by peaceful means. The last proposal might bring the pseudo-conservative rebels themselves under the ban of treason: for the sum total of these amendments might easily serve to bring the whole structure of American society crashing to the ground.

As Mr. Rovere points out, it is not unusual for a large number of Constitutional amendments to be lying about somewhere in the Congressional hoppers. What is unusual is the readiness the Senate has shown to give them respectful consideration, and the peculiar populistic arguments some of its leading members have used to justify referring them to the state legislatures. While the ordinary Congress hardly ever has occasion to consider more than one amendment, the Eighty-third Congress saw six Constitutional amendments brought to the floor of the Senate,

all summoning simple majorities, and four winning the
two-thirds majority necessary before they can be sent to
the House and ultimately to the state legislatures. It must
be added that, with the possible exception of the Bricker
Amendment itself, none of the six amendments so honored
can be classed with the most extreme proposals. But the
pliability of the senators, the eagerness of some of them
to pass the buck and defer to "the people of the country,"
suggests how strong they feel the pressure to be for some
kind of change that will give expression to that vague
desire to repudiate the past that underlies the pseudo-
conservative revolt.

One of the most urgent questions we can ask about
the United States in our time is the question of where all
this sentiment arose. The readiest answer is that the new
pseudo-conservatism is simply the old ultra-conservatism
and the old isolationism heightened by the extraordinary
pressures of the contemporary world. This answer, true
though it may be, gives a deceptive sense of familiarity
without much deepening our understanding, for the particular patterns of American isolationism and extreme
right-wing thinking have themselves not been very satis-
factorily explored. It will not do, to take but one example,
to say that some people want the income tax amendment
repealed because taxes have become very heavy in the
past twenty years: for this will not explain why, of three
people in the same tax bracket, one will grin and bear it
and continue to support social welfare legislation as well
as an adequate defense, while another responds by supporting in a matter-of-fact way the practical conservative
leadership of the moment, and the third finds his feelings
satisfied only by the angry conspiratorial accusations and
extreme demands of the pseudo-conservative.

No doubt the circumstances determining the political
style of any individual are complex. Although I am concerned here to discuss some of the neglected social-

psychological elements in pseudo-conservatism, I do not
wish to appear to deny the presence of important economic and political causes. I am aware, for instance, that
wealthy reactionaries try to use pseudo-conservative organizers, spokesmen and groups to propagate their notions
of public policy, and that some organizers of pseudo-
conservative and "patriotic" groups often find in this work
a means of making a living—thus turning a tendency
toward paranoia into a vocational asset, probably one of
the most perverse forms of occupational therapy known
to man. A number of other circumstances—the drastic
inflation and heavy taxes of our time, the dissolution of
American urban life, considerations of partisan political
expediency—also play a part. But none of these things
seem to explain the broad appeal of pseudo-conservatism,
its emotional intensity, its dense and massive irrationality,
or some of the peculiar ideas it generates. Nor will they
explain why those who profit by the organized movements
find such a ready following among a large number of
people, and why the rank-and-file janizaries of pseudo-
conservatism are so eager to hurl accusations, write letters
to congressmen and editors, and expend so much emotional energy and crusading idealism upon causes that
plainly bring them no material reward.

Elmer Davis, seeking to account for such sentiment in
his recent book, *But We Were Born Free,* ventures a
psychological hypothesis. He concludes, if I understand
him correctly, that the genuine difficulties of our situation
in the face of the power of international communism have
inspired a widespread feeling of fear and frustration, and
that those who cannot face these problems in a more
rational way "take it out on their less influential neigh-
bors, in the mood of a man who, being afraid to stand
up to his wife in a domestic argument, relieves his feelings
by kicking the cat."[5] This suggestion has the merit of
both simplicity and plausibility, and it may begin to
account for a portion of the pseudo-conservative public.

But while we may dismiss our curiosity about the man who kicks the cat by remarking that some idiosyncrasy in his personal development has brought him to this pass, we can hardly help but wonder whether there are not, in the backgrounds of the hundreds of thousands of persons who are moved by the pseudo-conservative impulse, some commonly shared circumstances that will help to account for their all kicking the cat in unison.

All of us have reason to fear the power of international communism, and all our lives are profoundly affected by it. Why do some Americans try to face this threat for what it is, a problem that exists in a world-wide theater of action, while others try to reduce it largely to a matter of domestic conformity? Why do some of us prefer to look for allies in the democratic world, while others seem to prefer authoritarian allies or none at all? Why do the pseudo-conservatives express such a persistent fear and suspicion of *their own government*, whether its leadership rests in the hands of Roosevelt, Truman or Eisenhower? Why is the pseudo-conservative impelled to go beyond the more or less routine partisan argument that we have been the victims of considerable misgovernment during the past twenty years to the disquieting accusation that we have actually been the victims of persistent conspiracy and betrayal—"twenty years of treason"? Is it not true, moreover, that political types very similar to the pseudo-conservative have had a long history in the United States, and that this history goes back to a time when the Soviet power did not loom nearly so large on our mental horizons? Was the Ku Klux Klan, for instance, which was responsibly estimated to have had a membership of from 4,000,000 to 4,500,000 persons at its peak in the 1920's, a phenomenon totally dissimilar to the pseudo-conservative revolt?

What I wish to suggest—and I do so in the spirit of one setting forth nothing more than a speculative hypothesis —is that pseudo-conservatism is in good part a product of the rootlessness and heterogeneity of American life, and above all, of its peculiar scramble for status and its peculiar search for secure identity. Normally there is a world of difference between one's sense of national identity or cultural belonging and one's social status. However, in American historical development, these two things, so easily distinguishable in analysis, have been jumbled together in reality, and it is precisely this that has given such a special poignancy and urgency to our status-strivings. In this country a person's status—that is, his relative place in the prestige hierarchy of his community—and his rudimentary sense of belonging to the community—that is, what we call his "Americanism"—have been intimately joined. Because, as a people extremely democratic in our social institutions, we have had no clear, consistent and recognizable system of status, our personal status problems have an unusual intensity. Because we no longer have the relative ethnic homogeneity we had up to about eighty years ago, our sense of belonging has long had about it a high degree of uncertainty. We boast of "the melting pot," but we are not quite sure what it is that will remain when we have been melted down.

We have always been proud of the high degree of occupational mobility in our country—of the greater readiness, as compared with other countries, with which a person starting in a very humble place in our social structure could rise to a position of moderate wealth and status, and with which a person starting with a middling position could rise to great eminence. We have looked upon this as laudable in principle, for it is democratic, and as pragmatically desirable, for it has served many a man as a stimulus to effort and has, no doubt, a great deal to do with the energetic and effectual tone of our economic life. The American pattern of occupational mobility, while often much exaggerated, as in the Horatio

Alger stories and a great deal of the rest of our mythology, may properly be credited with many of the virtues and beneficial effects that are usually attributed to it. But this occupational and social mobility, compounded by our extraordinary mobility from place to place, has also had its less frequently recognized drawbacks. Not the least of them is that this has become a country in which so many people do not know who they are or what they are or what they belong to or what belongs to them. It is a country of people whose status expectations are random and uncertain, and yet whose status aspirations have been whipped up to a high pitch by our democratic ethos and our rags-to-riches mythology.[6]

In a country where physical needs have been, by the scale of the world's living standards, on the whole well met, the luxury of questing after status has assumed an unusually prominent place in our civic consciousness. Political life is not simply an arena in which the conflicting interests of various social groups in concrete material gains are fought out; it is also an arena into which status aspirations and frustrations are, as the psychologists would say, projected. It is at this point that the issues of politics, or the pretended issues of politics, become interwoven with and dependent upon the personal problems of individuals. We have, at all times, two kinds of processes going on in inextricable connection with each other: *interest politics*, the clash of material aims and needs among various groups and blocs; and *status politics*, the clash of various projective rationalizations arising from status aspirations and other personal motives. In times of depression and economic discontent —and by and large in times of acute national emergency —politics is more clearly a matter of interests, although of course status considerations are still present. In times of prosperity and general well-being on the material plane, status considerations among the masses can become

much more influential in our politics. The two periods in
our recent history in which status politics has been particularly prominent, the present era and the 1920's, have
both been periods of prosperity.

During depressions, the dominant motif in dissent takes
expression in proposals for reform or in panaceas. Dissent
then tends to be highly programmatic—that is, it gets
itself embodied in many kinds of concrete legislative proposals. It is also future-oriented and forward-looking, in
the sense that it looks to a time when the adoption of
this or that program will materially alleviate or eliminate
certain discontents. In prosperity, however, when status
politics becomes relatively more important, there is a tendency to embody discontent not so much in legislative
proposals as in grousing. For the basic aspirations that
underlie status discontent are only partially conscious;
and, even so far as they are conscious, it is difficult to give
them a programmatic expression. It is more difficult for
the old lady who belongs to the D.A.R. and who sees her
ancestral home swamped by new working-class dwellings
to express her animus in concrete proposals of any degree
of reality than it is, say, for the jobless worker during a
slump to rally to a relief program. Therefore, it is the
tendency of status politics to be expressed more in vindictiveness, in sour memories, in the search for scapegoats, than in realistic proposals for positive action.[7]

Paradoxically the intense status concerns of present-day
politics are shared by two types of persons who arrive
at them, in a sense, from opposite directions. The first are
found among some types of old-family, Anglo-Saxon
Protestants, and the second are found among many types
of immigrant families, most notably among the Germans
and Irish, who are very frequently Catholic. The Anglo-
Saxons are most disposed toward pseudo-conservatism
when they are losing caste, the immigrants when they are
gaining.[8]

Consider first the old-family Americans. These people, whose stocks were once far more unequivocally dominant in America than they are today, feel that their ancestors made and settled and fought for this country. They have a certain inherited sense of proprietorship in it. Since America has always accorded a certain special deference to old families—so many of our families are *new*—these people have considerable claims to status by descent, which they celebrate by membership in such organizations as the D.A.R. and the S.A.R. But large numbers of them are actually losing their other claims to status. For there are among them a considerable number of the shabby genteel, of those who for one reason or another have lost their old objective positions in the life of business and politics and the professions, and who therefore cling with exceptional desperation to such remnants of their prestige as they can muster from their ancestors. These people, although very often quite well-to-do, feel that they have been pushed out of their rightful place in American life, even out of their neighborhoods. Most of them have been traditional Republicans by family inheritance, and they have felt themselves edged aside by the immigrants, the trade unions, and the urban machines in the past thirty years. When the immigrants were weak, these native elements used to indulge themselves in ethnic and religious snobberies at their expense.[9] Now the immigrant groups have developed ample means, political and economic, of self-defense, and the second and third generations have become considerably more capable of looking out for themselves. Some of the old-family Americans have turned to find new objects for their resentment among liberals, left-wingers, intellectuals and the like—for in true pseudo-conservative fashion they relish weak victims and shrink from asserting themselves against the strong.

New-family Americans have had their own peculiar

status problem. From 1881 to 1900 over 8,800,000 immigrants came here, during the next twenty years another
14,500,000. These immigrants, together with their descendants, constitute such a large portion of the population
that Margaret Mead, in a stimulating analysis of our
national character, has persuasively urged that the characteristic American outlook is now a third-generation
point of view.[10] In their search for new lives and new
nationality, these immigrants have suffered much, and
they have been rebuffed and made to feel inferior by the
"native stock," commonly being excluded from the better
occupations and even from what has bitterly been called
"first-class citizenship." Insecurity over social status has
thus been mixed with insecurity over one's very identity
and sense of belonging. Achieving a better type of job or
a better social status and becoming "more American" have
become practically synonymous, and the passions that
ordinarily attach to social position have been vastly
heightened by being associated with the need to belong.

The problems raised by the tasks of keeping the family
together, disciplining children for the American race for
success, trying to conform to unfamiliar standards, pro-
tecting economic and social status won at the cost of
much sacrifice, holding the respect of children who grow
American more rapidly than their parents, have thrown
heavy burdens on the internal relationships of many new
American families. Both new and old American families
have been troubled by the changes of the past thirty
years—the new because of their striving for middle-class
respectability and American identity, the old because of
their efforts to maintain an inherited social position and
to realize under increasingly unfavorable social conditions
imperatives of character and personal conduct deriving
from nineteenth-century, Yankee-Protestant-rural backgrounds. The relations between generations, being cast
in no stable mold, have been disordered, and the status

anxieties of parents have been inflicted upon children.[11] Often parents entertain status aspirations that they are unable to gratify, or that they can gratify only at exceptional psychic cost. Their children are expected to relieve their frustrations and redeem their lives. They become objects to be manipulated to that end. An extraordinarily high level of achievement is expected of them, and along with it a tremendous effort to conform and be respectable. From the standpoint of the children these expectations often appear in the form of an exorbitantly demanding authority that one dare not question or defy. Resistance and hostility, finding no moderate outlet in give-and-take, have to be suppressed, and reappear in the form of an internal destructive rage. An enormous hostility to authority, which cannot be admitted to consciousness, calls forth a massive overcompensation which is manifest in the form of extravagant submissiveness to strong power. Among those found by Adorno and his colleagues to have strong ethnic prejudices and pseudo-conservative tendencies, there is a high proportion of persons who have been unable to develop the capacity to criticize justly and in moderation the failings of parents and who are profoundly intolerant of the ambiguities of thought and feeling that one is so likely to find in real-life situations. For pseudo-conservatism is among other things a disorder in relation to authority, characterized by an inability to find other modes for human relationship than those of more or less complete domination or submission. The pseudo-conservative always imagines himself to be dominated and imposed upon because he feels that he is not dominant, and knows of no other way of interpreting his position. He imagines that his own government and his own leadership are engaged in a more or less continuous conspiracy against him because he has come to think of authority only as something that aims to manipulate and deprive him. It is for this reason, among others, that he

enjoys seeing outstanding generals, distinguished secre-
taries of state, and prominent scholars browbeaten and
humiliated.

Status problems take on a special importance in American life because a very large part of the population suffers
from one of the most troublesome of all status questions:
unable to enjoy the simple luxury of assuming their own
nationality as a natural event, they are tormented by a
nagging doubt as to whether they are really and truly and
fully American. Since their forebears voluntarily left one
country and embraced another, they cannot, as people do
elsewhere, think of nationality as something that comes
with birth; for them it is a matter of *choice,* and an object
of striving. This is one reason why problems of "loyalty"
arouse such an emotional response in many Americans
and why it is so hard in the American climate of opinion
to make any clear distinction between the problem of
national security and the question of personal loyalty. Of
course there is no real reason to doubt the loyalty to
America of the immigrants and their descendants, or
their willingness to serve the country as fully as if their
ancestors had lived here for three centuries. None the
less, they have been thrown on the defensive by those
who have in the past cast doubts upon the fullness of
their Americanism. Possibly they are also, consciously or
unconsciously, troubled by the thought that since their
forebears have already abandoned one country, one allegiance, their own national allegiance might be considered
fickle. For this I believe there is some evidence in our
national practices. What other country finds it so necessary to create institutional rituals for the sole purpose of
guaranteeing to its people the genuineness of their nationality? Does the Frenchman or the Englishman or the
Italian find it necessary to speak of himself as "one hundred per cent" English, French or Italian? Do they find
it necessary to have their equivalents of "I Am an Ameri-

can Day"? When they disagree with one another over national policies, do they find it necessary to call one another un-English, un-French or un-Italian? No doubt they too are troubled by subversive activities and espionage, but are their countermeasures taken under the name of committees on un-English, un-French or un-Italian activities?

The primary value of patriotic societies and anti-subversive ideologies to their exponents can be found here. They provide additional and continued reassurance both to those who are of old American ancestry and have other status grievances and to those who are of recent American ancestry and therefore feel in need of reassurance about their nationality. Veterans' organizations offer the same satisfaction—what better evidence can there be of the genuineness of nationality and of *earned* citizenship than military service under the flag of one's country? Of course such organizations, once they exist, are liable to exploitation by vested interests that can use them as pressure groups on behalf of particular measures and interests. (Veterans' groups, since they lobby for the concrete interests of veterans, have a double role in this respect.) But the cement that holds them together is the status motivation and the desire for an identity.

Sociological studies have shown that there is a close relation between social mobility and ethnic prejudice. Persons moving downward, and even upward under many circumstances, in the social scale tend to show greater prejudice against such ethnic minorities as the Jews and Negroes than commonly prevails in the social strata they have left or are entering.[12] While the existing studies in this field have been focused upon prejudice rather than the kind of hyper-patriotism and hyper-conformism that I am most concerned with, I believe that the typical prejudiced person and the typical pseudo-conservative dissenter are usually the same person, that the mechanisms at work in both complexes are quite the same,[13] and that it is merely the expediencies and the strategy of the situation today that cause groups that once stressed racial discrimination to find other scapegoats. Both the displaced old-American type and the new ethnic elements that are so desperately eager for reassurance of their fundamental Americanism can conveniently converge upon liberals, critics, and nonconformists of various sorts, as well as Communists and suspected Communists. To proclaim themselves vigilant in the pursuit of those who are even so much as accused of "disloyalty" to the United States is a way not only of reasserting but of advertising their own loyalty—and one of the chief characteristics of American super-patriotism is its constant inner urge toward self-advertisement. One notable quality in this new wave of conformism is that its advocates are much happier to have as their objects of hatred the Anglo-Saxon, Eastern, Ivy League intellectual gentlemen than they are with such bedraggled souls as, say, the Rosenbergs. The reason, I believe, is that in the minds of the status-driven it is no special virtue to be more American than the Rosenbergs, but it is really something to be more American than Dean Acheson or John Foster Dulles—or Franklin Delano Roosevelt.[14] The status aspirations of some of the ethnic groups are actually higher than they were twenty years ago—which suggests one reason (there are others) why, in the ideology of the authoritarian right-wing, anti-Semitism and such blatant forms of prejudice have recently been soft-pedaled. Anti-Semitism, it has been said, is the poor man's snobbery. We Americans are always trying to raise the standard of living, and the same principle now seems to apply to standards of hating. So during the past fifteen years or so, the authoritarians have moved on from anti-Negroism and anti-Semitism to anti-Achesonianism, anti-intellectualism, anti-nonconformism, and other variants of the same idea, much in the same way as the average American, if he can manage it, will move on from a Ford to a Buick.

Such status-strivings may help us to understand some of the otherwise unintelligible figments of the pseudo-conservative ideology—the incredibly bitter feeling against the United Nations, for instance. Is it not understandable that such a feeling might be, paradoxically, shared at one and the same time by an old Yankee-Protestant American, who feels that his social position is not what it ought to be and that these foreigners are crowding in on his country and diluting its sovereignty just as "foreigners" have crowded into his neighborhood, and by a second- or third-generation immigrant who has been trying so hard to de-Europeanize himself, to get Europe out of his personal heritage, and who finds his own government mocking him by its complicity in these Old-World schemes?

Similarly, is it not status aspiration that in good part spurs the pseudo-conservative on toward his demand for conformity in a wide variety of spheres of life? Conformity is a way of guaranteeing and manifesting respectability among those who are not sure that they are respectable enough. The nonconformity of others appears to such persons as a frivolous challenge to the whole order of things they are trying so hard to become part of. Naturally it is resented, and the demand for conformity in public becomes at once an expression of such resentment and a means of displaying one's own soundness. This habit has a tendency to spread from politics into intellectual and social spheres, where it can be made to challenge almost anyone whose pattern of life is different and who is imagined to enjoy a superior social position—notably, as one agitator put it, the "parlors of the sophisticated, the intellectuals, the so-called academic minds."

Why has this tide of pseudo-conservative dissent risen to such heights in our time? To a considerable degree, we must remember, it is a response, however unrealistic, to realities. We do live in a disordered world, threatened by a great power and a powerful ideology. It is a world of enormous potential violence, that has already shown us the ugliest capacities of the human spirit. In our own country there has indeed been espionage, and laxity over security has in fact allowed some spies to reach high places. There is just enough reality at most points along the line to give a touch of credibility to the melodramatics of the pseudo-conservative imagination.

However, a number of developments in our recent history make this pseudo-conservative uprising more intelligible. For two hundred years and more, various conditions of American development—the process of continental settlement, the continuous establishment in new areas of new status patterns, the arrival of continuous waves of new immigrants, each pushing the preceding waves upward in the ethnic hierarchy—made it possible to satisfy a remarkably large part of the extravagant status aspirations that were aroused. There was a sort of automatic built-in status-elevator in the American social edifice. Today that elevator no longer operates automatically, or at least no longer operates in the same way.

Secondly, the growth of the mass media of communication and their use in politics have brought politics closer to the people than ever before and have made politics a form of entertainment in which the spectators feel themselves involved. Thus it has become, more than ever before, an arena into which private emotions and personal problems can be readily projected. Mass communications have aroused the mass man.

Thirdly, the long tenure in power of the liberal elements to which the pseudo-conservatives are most opposed and the wide variety of changes that have been introduced into our social, economic and administrative life have intensified the sense of powerlessness and victimization among the opponents of these changes and have widened the area of social issues over which they feel discontent.

There has been, among other things, the emergence of a wholly new struggle: the conflict between businessmen of certain types and the New Deal bureaucracy, which has spilled over into a resentment of intellectuals and experts.

Finally, unlike our previous postwar periods, ours has been a period of continued crisis, from which the future promises no relief. In no foreign war of our history did we fight so long or make such sacrifices as in World War II. When it was over, instead of being able to resume our peacetime preoccupations, we were very promptly confronted with another war. It is hard for a certain type of American, who does not think much about the world outside and does not want to have to do so, to understand why we must become involved in such an unremitting struggle. It will be the fate of those in power for a long time to come to have to conduct the delicate diplomacy of the cold peace without the sympathy or understanding of a large part of their own people. From bitter experience, Eisenhower and Dulles are learning today what Truman and Acheson learned yesterday.

These considerations suggest that the pseudo-conservative political style, while it may already have passed the peak of its influence, is one of the long waves of twentieth-century American history and not a momentary mood. I do not share the widespread foreboding among liberals that this form of dissent will grow until it overwhelms our liberties altogether and plunges us into a totalitarian nightmare. Indeed, the idea that it is purely and simply fascist or totalitarian, as we have known these things in recent European history, is to my mind a false conception, based upon the failure to read American developments in terms of our peculiar American constellation of political realities. (It reminds me of the people who, because they found several close parallels between the NRA and Mussolini's corporate state, were once deeply troubled at the thought that the NRA was the beginning of American fascism.) However, in a populistic culture like ours, which seems to lack a responsible elite with political and moral autonomy, and in which it is possible to exploit the wildest currents of public sentiment for private purposes, it is at least conceivable that a highly organized, vocal, active and well-financed minority could create a political climate in which the rational pursuit of our well-being and safety would become impossible.

[1] Theodore W. Adorno et al., *The Authoritarian Personality* (New York, 1950), pp. 675–76. While I have drawn heavily upon this enlightening study, I have some reservations about its methods and conclusions. For a critical review, see Richard Christie and Marie Jahoda, eds., *Studies in the Scope and Method of "The Authoritarian Personality"* (Glencoe, Illinois, 1954), particularly the penetrating comments by Edward Shils.

[2] On the Omaha Freedom Congress see Leonard Boasberg, "Radical Reactionaries," *The Progressive,* December, 1953.

[3] See the comments of D. W. Brogan in "The Illusion of American Omnipotence," *Harper's,* December, 1952.

[4] Richard Rovere, "Letter from Washington," *New Yorker,* June 19, 1954, pp. 67–72.

[5] Elmer Davis, *But We Were Born Free* (New York, 1954), pp. 35–36; cf. pp. 21–22 and *passim.*

[6] Cf. in this respect the observation of Tocqueville: "It cannot be denied that democratic institutions strongly tend to promote the feeling of envy in the human heart; not so much because they afford to everyone the means of rising to the same level with others as because these means perpetually disappoint the persons who employ them. Democratic institutions awaken and foster a passion for equality which they can never entirely satisfy." Alexis de Tocqueville, *Democracy in America,* ed. by Phillips Bradley (New York, 1945), Vol. I, p. 201.

[7] Cf. Samuel Lubell's characterization of isolationism as a vengeful memory. *The Future of American Politics* (New York, 1952), Chapter VII. See also the comments of Leo Lowenthal and Norbert Guterman on the right-wing agitator: "The agitator seems to steer clear of the area of material needs on which liberal and democratic movements concentrate; his main concern is a sphere of frustration that is usually ignored in traditional politics. The programs that concentrate on material needs seem to overlook that area of moral uncertainties and emotional frustrations that are the immediate manifestations of malaise. It may therefore be conjectured that his followers find the agitator's statements attractive not because he occasionally promises to 'maintain the American standards of living' or to provide a job for everyone, but because he intimates that he will give them the emotional satisfactions that are denied them in the contemporary social and economic set-up. He offers attitudes, not bread." *Prophets of Deceit* (New York, 1949), pp. 91–92.

[8] Every ethnic group has its own peculiar status history, and I am well aware that my remarks in the text slur over many important differences.

The status history of the older immigrant groups like the Germans and the Irish is quite different from that of ethnic elements like the Italians, Poles and Czechs, who have more recently arrived at the point at which they are bidding for wide acceptance in the professional and white-collar classes, or at least for the middle-class standards of housing and consumption enjoyed by these classes. The case of the Irish is of special interest, because the Irish, with their long-standing prominence in municipal politics, qualified as it has been by their relative non-acceptance in many other spheres, have an unusually ambiguous status. In many ways they have gained, while in others, particularly insofar as their municipal power has recently been challenged by other groups, especially the Italians, they have lost some status and power. The election of 1928, with its religious bigotry and social snobbery, inflicted upon them a status trauma from which they have never fully recovered, for it was a symbol of the Protestant majority's rejection of their ablest leadership on grounds quite irrelevant to merit. This feeling was kept alive by the breach between Al Smith and FDR, followed by the rejection of Jim Farley from the New Deal succession. A study of the Germans would perhaps emphasize the effects of uneasiness over national loyalties arising from the Hitler era and World War II, but extending back even to World War I.

[9] One of the noteworthy features of the current situation is that fundamentalist Protestants and fundamentalist Catholics have so commonly subordinated their old feuds (and for the first time in our history) to unite in opposition to what they usually describe as "godless" elements.

[10] Margaret Mead, *And Keep Your Powder Dry* (New York, 1942), Chapter III.

[11] See Else Frenkel-Brunswik's "Parents and Childhood as seen through the Interviews," *The Authoritarian Personality*, Chapter X. The author remarks (pp. 387–88) concerning subjects who were relatively *free* from ethnic prejudice that in their families "less obedience is expected of the children. Parents are less status-ridden and thus show less anxiety with respect to conformity and are less intolerant toward manifestations of socially unaccepted behavior. . . . Comparatively less pronounced statusconcern often goes hand in hand with greater richness and liberation of emotional life. There is, on the whole, more affection, or more unconditional affection, in the families of unprejudiced subjects. There is less surrender to conventional rules. . . ."

[12] Cf. Joseph Greenblum and Leonard I. Pearlin, "Vertical Mobility and Prejudice" in Reinhard Bendix and Seymour M. Lipset, eds., *Class, Status and Power* (Glencoe, Illinois, 1953), pp. 480–91; Bruno Bettelheim and Morris Janowitz, "Ethnic Tolerance: A Function of Personal and Social Control," *American Journal of Sociology*, Vol. IV (1949), pp. 137–45.

[13] The similarity is also posited by Adorno, *op. cit.*, pp. 152 ff., and by others (see the studies cited by him, p. 152).

[14] I refer to such men to make the point that this animosity extends to those who are guilty of no wrongdoing. Of course a person like Alger Hiss, who has been guilty, suits much better. Hiss is the hostage the pseudo-conservatives hold from the New Deal generation. He is a heaven-sent gift. If he did not exist, the pseudo-conservatives would not have been able to invent him.

3

The Intellectuals
and the Discontented Classes

DAVID RIESMAN AND
NATHAN GLAZER

IN THE nineteen-thirties Maury Maverick, who died in 1954, was a quite exceptional but far from untypical representative of the Texas political outlook: free-swinging, red-tape cutting, "a man's a man for a' that." Born to a famous Texas name which had entered the common speech, he enjoyed living up to it by defending the downtrodden: the Spanish-Americans of San Antonio; the small businessmen; and, most courageously, the Communists and their right to be heard in the municipal auditorium. In the Maverick era Texas was reputed to be the most interventionist state in the Union, providing some of the firmest support to Roosevelt's foreign policy. Its influential Congressional delegation, which included Sam Rayburn as well as Senator Tom

Connally and a less cautious Lyndon Johnson, were Roosevelt's stalwarts as often in domestic as in foreign policy. But not many years later Maverick had turned into a political untouchable, and Texas competed with the North Central isolationist belt in violent opposition to the old Roosevelt policies no less than to the policies of Truman, his successor and legitimate heir.

Texas demonstrates in extreme form the great shift in the character of American politics and political thinking since the Second World War. We can date the change more precisely than that. In the election of 1948, Harry Truman, more unequivocally and guilelessly committed to many New Deal policies and attitudes than F.D.R., won an election against a candidate far more liberal and capable, if less appealingly homespun, than Eisenhower. Even as late as the beginning of 1950, the special political tone of the Roosevelt era continued to influence public life. We need only recall the mood of the Democratic Senators investigating McCarthy's charges of Communist infiltration into the State Department early that year. The transcript shows them at ease, laughing away McCarthy's charges, taking it for granted that the country was with them, and that McCarthy was another Martin Dies. Four years later, another group of Democratic Senators sat in judgment on McCarthy. They were tense and anxious, seeking the protective cover of J. Edgar Hoover, trying to seem just as good Communist-hunters—indeed, better Republicans—than any of their colleagues. In the last years of Truman's term, while many demagogic anti-Communist steps were taken by a reluctant administration —as well as many effective ones under Acheson's bedeviled auspices—the general climate of Washington still remained comparatively easygoing. Congress was a partially manageable menace and General Vaughan still could get along without knowing the difference between Harry Dexter White and Adolf Berle.

Many explanations have been offered for what appears
to be a decisive shift in the American mentality. Fear of
the Soviet Union is alleged by some to be the cause;
others blame McCarthy, his allies, and his victims; others
look for cynical explanations, while still others think that
Americans have abandoned liberal traditions for good and
all. In this essay we attempt to estimate the real extent
of the shift, to delineate some factors, previously neglected, which may be relevant, and to offer some very
tentative interpretations pointing toward the revival of a
liberal political imagination.

1

Detectable and decisive shifts of political mood can
occur, of course, without affecting the majority. And this
seems to be what has happened in this country. The less
educated part of the population takes a long time learning
to form an opinion about any international matter and
even more time to change it. It is not easily accessible to
new information and is not trained to alter its opinions
under exposure to the public interpretation of events.[1]
Thus, the World War II alliance with the Soviet Union
did little to change the suspicion and distrust with which
(apart from sheer apathy) the poor and less educated in
this country have always regarded Russia—indeed, all
foreign countries; these people were "protected" by their
fatalism, generalized suspiciousness, and apathy from
the wartime messages of the movies, the OWI, and like
agencies. Consequently, the worsening of relations with
the Soviet Union found the "backward" strata already
holding the appropriate attitudes toward Russia—no
change was demanded of them, and little change occurred.

The less educated of whom we speak are of course

literate; they have radios and TV and buy newspapers; and to an Asiatic they must appear to move with fabulous speed. Certainly, in non-political matters (where the "voter" has at hand the ready mechanism of a retail store) fashions spread with ever faster waves, and the "backward" buy "modern" in furniture long before they will buy it in elections. Yet it is the educated, the readers of editorial pages, who have customarily been responsible for the major changes in American political position. For example, the shift of this group from neutrality to intervention in 1940 and 1941 allowed the Lend Lease Act to slip through. It also supplied the cadre under Averell Harriman which then energetically did the actual "lending."

The odd situation today, however, is that such a change does not suffice to explain what happened between 1950 and 1952. Many of the intelligent (i.e., college-educated) and articulate minority still in the main are not unsympathetic to Roosevelt's and Truman's foreign policies. They believe that the alliances with Britain and France must be maintained; they do not regard Communist infiltration as a serious problem; they do regard the threat to civil liberties by Communist hunters as a serious problem. If they do not always say so, this is partly for protective coloration, partly because, as we shall see, they have been put on the defensive not only strategically but also within themselves. (There are of course others of the college-educated who have always hated Truman and Roosevelt, largely for domestic "that man" reasons; they are not averse to using foreign policy as a heaven-sent means of vindication.)

As we have seen, the shift has not been among the inarticulate—they have always held their present attitudes. The decisive factors, we suggest, have been twofold, and interconnected. On the one hand, the opinion leaders among the educated strata—the intellectuals and those who take cues from them—have been silenced, rather more by their own feelings of inadequacy and failure than by direct intimidation. On the other hand, many who were once among the inarticulate masses are no longer silent: an unacknowledged social revolution has transformed their situation. Rejecting the liberal intellectuals as guides, they have echoed and reinforced the stridency of right-wing demi-intellectuals—themselves often arising from those we shall, until we can find a less clumsy name, call the ex-masses.

2

During the New Deal days a group of intellectuals led and played lawyer for classes of discontented people who had tasted prosperity and lost it, and for a mass of underprivileged people who had been promised prosperity and seen enough mobility around them to believe in it. Today, both sources of discontent have virtually disappeared as a result of fifteen years of prosperity.[2] This same prosperity, and its attendant inflation, has hit many elderly and retired people who cannot adjust financially, politically, or psychologically to the altered value of a dollar—people, who, though they have the money, cannot bring themselves to repair their homes because they have not been brought up to "do it yourself" nor to pay three dollars an hour to someone else for doing it. Among the youth, too, are many people who are at once the beneficiaries and the victims of prosperity, people made ill-at-ease by an affluence not preceded by imagining its reality, nor preceded by a change to a character-structure more attuned to amenity than to hardship. The raw-rich Texas millionaire appears often to be obsessed by fears that "they" will take his money away—almost as if he were fascinated by a fatality which would bring him, as it were, back to earth.

These people, whether suddenly affluent or simply better off, form a new middle class, called out of the city tenements and the marginal small towns by the uneven hand of national prosperity; many have moved to the fringes of urban centers, large and small. This has been described in *Fortune* as a new middle-class market, which will play a great role in keeping the economy prosperous. But in politics, these former masses do not have so benign an influence—we shall call them the *discontented classes*.

Their discontent is only partially rooted in relative economic deprivation. Many of them, it is true, forgetting their condition of fifteen years ago, see only that the salaries and income they would once have thought prince-ly do not add up to much. Politically, such people, think-ing in terms of a relatively fixed income (in this case, of course, not from capital, save occasional rentals, but from salaries and wages) against a standard of variable ex-penses, are generally conservative. And their conservatism is of a pinched and narrow sort, less interested in the preservation of ancient principles than in the current reduction of government expenditures and taxes. It is the conservatism we usually associate with provincial France rather than with the small-town venture capitalist of the older Yankee sort. This conservatism helps create the particular posture of the discontented classes vis-à-vis America's foreign role: they are mad at the rest of the world for bothering them, hate to waste money in spank-ings and cannot stand wasting money in rewards.

But more significant, and more difficult to understand and grapple with, is a discontent which arises from the mental discomforts that come with belonging to a class rather than a mass—discomforts founded less on economic than on intellectual uncertainty. If one belongs to the middle class one is supposed to have an opinion, to cope with the world as well as with one's job and immediate surroundings. But these new members have entered a realm where the interpretations of the world put forth

by intellectuals in recent decades, and widely held among
the educated, are unsatisfying, even threatening. Having
precariously won respectability in paycheck and consumption style, they find this achievement menaced by a political and more broadly cultural outlook tending to lower
barriers of any sort—between this nation and other nations,
between groups in this nation (as in the constant appeals
to inter-ethnic amity), between housing projects reserved
for Negroes and suburbs reserved for whites; many families also cannot stand the pressure to lower barriers between men and women, or between parents and children.

When this barrier-destroying outlook of the intellectuals
promised economic advance as well as racial equality,
many of the impoverished could accept the former and
ignore the latter. Now, having achieved a modicum of
prosperity, the political philosophy of the intellectuals,
which always requires government spending, taxes, and
inflation, is a threat—and the racial equality, which could
be viewed with indifference in the city tenement or
homogeneous small town, is a formidable reality in the
new suburbs. When the intellectuals were developing the
ideology justifying cutting in the masses on the bounties
of American productivity, they were less apt to be called
do-gooders and bleeding hearts—the grown-up version of
that unendurable taunt of being a sissy—than now when
the greater part of the masses needing help are outside
the nation's boundaries.[3]

Very often, moreover, the individuals making up the
discontented classes have come, not to the large civilizing
cities, but to the new or expanding industrial frontiers—
to Wichita and Rock Island, to Jacksonville or the Gulf
Coast, to Houston or San Diego, to Tacoma or Tona-
wanda. Even those who become very rich no longer head
automatically for New York and Newport. Whereas the
Baptist Rockefeller, coming from Cleveland where he was
educated, allowed Easterners to help civilize him by

giving away his money, as Carnegie and Frick also did, these new rich lack such centralized opportunities for gratuitous benevolence, being constrained by the income tax and the institutionalization of philanthropy. And their wives (whatever their secret and suppressed yearnings) no longer seem to want the approval of Eastern women of culture and fashion; they choose to remain within their provincial orbits, rather than to become immigrants to an alien cosmopolitan center. Indeed, the airplane has made it possible for the men—and *Vogue* and Neiman-Marcus for the women—to share in the advantages of New York without the miseries, expenses, and contaminations of living there. Howard Hughes, for example, can do business operating from a plane, yacht, or hotel room.

All this, however, puts some complex processes too simply. New big money in America has always tended to unsettle its possessors and the society at large. For one thing, the absence of an aristocracy means that there is no single, time-approved course of buying land, being deferential to the values of those already on the land, and earning a title by good behavior. Though Rockefeller tried philanthropy, he was still hated, still needed the services of Ivy Lee. Yet he lived at a time when the aristocratic model, in Europe if not here, provided certain guide-posts. Today, the enormously wealthy new men of Texas have not even the promise of an assured well-traveled road, at the end of which stand duchesses, Newport, and gate-keepers like Ward McAllister. Instead, such men may prefer to buy a television program for McCarthy, or to acquire the publishing firm of Henry Holt, or, on behalf of an anti-Wall Street business demagogue, the very railroad which once helped cement New York "Society."

Moreover, the partial and uneven spread of cosmopolitan values to the lower strata and to the hinterland has as one consequence the fact that rich men can no longer simply spend their way to salvation. Conspicuous underconsumption has replaced conspicuous consumption as the visible sign of status, with the result that men who have made enough money to indulge the gaudy dreams of their underprivileged youth learn all too fast that they must not be flamboyant. This is a trick that the older centers of culture have played on the newer centers of wealth. The latter can try to catch up; Baylor and Houston Universities, and the Dallas Symphony, have not done too badly. Or they can enter the still gaudy forum of politics to get back at those they suspect of ridiculing their efforts. Perhaps there was something of this in Hearst, as there is in some of the newer magnates of the media. Senator McCarthy, with his gruff charm and his Populist roots, seems made to order for such men; and he has attracted some of the political plungers among the new underprivileged rich,[4] a task made easier by the fact that they have too few intellectuals and idea men to divide and distract them.

Furthermore, a great many Americans, newly risen from poverty or the catastrophe of the Depression, are much more fearful of losing their wealth than are scions of more established families already accustomed to paying taxes, to giving to charity, and to the practice of *noblesse oblige*. We know many men who made their money in war orders, or through buying government-financed plants, or through price supports, who hate the federal government with the ferocity of beneficiaries—and doubtless want to cut off aid from the ungrateful French or British! Such men cannot admit that they did not make "their" money by their own efforts; they would like to abolish the income tax, and with it the whole nexus of defense and international relations, if only to assert their own anachronistic individualism the more firmly. They are likely to be clients, not only of lawyers who specialize in the capital gains tax, but also of prophets and politicians specializing in the bogeys of adults.

The rapid and unanticipated acquisition of power seems to produce a sense of unreality—people are "up in the air." We face the paradox that many Americans are more fearful today though more prosperous than ever before and though America is in some ways more powerful.

3

It is the professional business of politicians, as of other promoters and organizers, to find in the electorate or other constituency organizable blocs who will shift their allegiance to them, who will respond with passion in the midst of indifference, and with identification in the midst of diffuse and plural ties. In the pre-World War I days of the great outcry against the Trusts, it was possible to find a few old and dislocated middle-class elements which resented the new dominance by big and baronial business —in some respects, these were precursors of the present discontented classes, though with more to hope for and less to fear. In the thirties, the way had already in large measure been prepared for an appeal to unemployed factory workers and Southern and Western farmers on the basis of Wilsonian and Populist rhetoric, made into a heady brew by more recent infusions of radicalism, native and imported. These discontented masses showed in their voting behavior (in NLRB and Agricultural Adjustment Act elections as well as at the polls) that the appeal, whatever it meant to those who made it, hit home in terms of the listeners' wants and situation.

How can the discontented classes of today be welded into a political bloc? This is the question that haunts and tempts politicians. The uncertainty of the Democrats faced with Stevenson and of the Republicans faced with McCarthy signifies not only disagreements of principle but also doubts as to whether a proper appeal has as yet

been found on which a ruling or controlling coalition can
be built. As geologists cover the earth prospecting for
oil, so politicians cover the electorate prospecting for
hidden hatreds and identities.

In local elections campaigns can be waged on the
promise to hold down taxes and build no more schools.
And many people in national affairs will respond to a
promise to hold down inflation or to create more jobs.
But when voters feel insecure in the midst of prosperity,
it is not an economic appeal that will really arouse them.
For it is not the jobs or goods they do not have that
worry them; indeed, what worries them is often that they
do not know what worries them, or why, having reached
the promised land, they still suffer. Sharply felt needs
have been replaced by vague discontents; and at such a
time programs or clear-cut ideas of any kind are worse
than useless, politically speaking. This is one reason why
the appeal to the discontented classes is so often more a
matter of tone than of substance—why a gesture of retro-
active vindictiveness like the Bricker Amendment can
arouse angry Minute Women and small-town lawyers,
why on the whole the pseudo-conservative right has so
small a program and so belligerent a stance. In this
situation, ideology tends to become more important than
economics.[5]

And when one must resort to ideology in a prosperous
America, one must fall back on the vaguely recalled,
half-dreamlike allegiances and prejudices serving most
people for ideology. Americanism, of course, will play a
major role; but, paradoxically enough, so do those underground half-conscious ethnic allegiances and prejudices
which, as Samuel Lubell has shown, still play a large part
in American politics. In much that passes for anti-Communism these strands are combined, as for instance for
many Irish or Polish Catholics whose avid anti-Communism enables them to feel more solidly American than

some less fanatical Protestants who, as earlier arrivals, once looked down on them; similarly, a good deal of McCarthy's support represents the comeback of the German-Americans after two world wars. A haunting doubt about Americanism and disloyalty, however, affects not only those of recent enemy or socially devalued stocks but also those many businessmen forced to operate under government regulations of price and materials control, or under defense contracts. As Talcott Parsons has observed (see Chapter 5), these men are constantly being asked, on grounds of patriotism, to obey government norms which they are as constantly opposing and evading; for them it is convenient to discover that it is not they who are ambivalent toward defense, but those others, the Reds or the State Department or the Democrats. Many of these men, especially perhaps in small business, are victims of a prosperity which has made them rich but neither as enlightened as many big business managers nor as independent as their ideology expects them to be.

Not all members of the discontented classes come from similar backgrounds or arrive at similar destinations; nevertheless, mobility—a fast rise from humble origins, or a transplantation to the city, or a move from the factory class to the white-collar class—is a general characteristic. They or their parents are likely to have voted Democratic sometime between 1930 and 1948, and such a memory makes them more susceptible to ideological appeals, for in rising above their impoverished or ethnically "un-American" beginnings, they have found it "time for a change" in identification: they would like to rise "above" economic appeals ("don't let them take it away") to ideological ones—or, in more amiable terms, "above" self-interest to patriotism. Such people could not be brought in one move into the Republican Party, which would seem too much like a betrayal of origins, but they could be brought to take a stand "above party"—and to vote for a non-partisan general whom the Democrats had also sought. According to a recent study reported by Professor Malcolm Moos, in two counties outside Boston the self-declared "independent" voters now outnumber the Republicans and Democrats combined—a reflection of this roving background of discontented classes which has become the most dynamic force in American political life.[6] Recently, a woman who had campaigned for Eisenhower (while her husband voted for Stevenson) told one of us how much she admired Ike's sincerity, adding, "Actually I don't know enough about politics to identify myself with either one [major party], and I am a—what do you call it—an independent." Of course, not all independents stand in this sort of proud ignorance above parties and above the politicians who may have helped their parents with jobs or visas or the warmth of recognition.

Just as many among the newly prosperous tend at present to reject the traditional party labels (while others seek, perhaps after a split ticket or two, the protective coloration of the GOP), so they also reject the traditional cultural and educational leadership of the enlightened upper and upper-middle classes. They have sent their children to college as one way of maintaining the family's social and occupational mobility. Some of these children have become eager strivers for cosmopolitanism and culture, rejecting the values now held by the discontented classes. But many of those who have swamped the colleges have acquired there, and helped their families learn, a half-educated resentment for the traditional intellectual values some of their teachers and schoolmates represented. While their humbler parents may have maintained in many cases a certain reverence for education, their children have gained enough familiarity to feel contempt. (Tragically, the high schools and colleges have often felt compelled at the same time to lower their standards to meet the still lower level of aspiration of these youngsters, no eager beavers for learning, but too well off to enter the labor force.) In many local school board fights, the old conservative and hence intellectually libertarian elites have been routed by lower-middle-class pressure groups who, often to their surprise, discovered the weakness of the schools and their defenders—in many of these fights, much as on the national scene, ethnic elements helped identify the combatants. Once having seen the political weakness, combined with social prestige, of the traditional cultural values, the discontented classes, trained to despise weakness, became still less impressed by the intellectual cadres furnishing much of the leadership in the Thirties.

The high school and college training has had a further effect of strengthening the desire of the graduates to take some part in political life, at least by voting: we know that non-voting and non-participation generally is far more common among the uneducated. Even more, it has strengthened their need for an intellectual position to give a name, an identity, to their malaise. Whatever they think of intellectuals as such, they cannot do without them, and sustenance rejected in the form of the adult education work of the Ford Foundation is sought or accepted from mentors like Hunt's Facts Forum whose tone reflects their own uneasiness and yet gives it a factual, "scientific" cast. Thus they repay their "education for citizenship."

We have spoken earlier of the xenophobia and slowness in altering opinions characteristic of the lower classes. If in a survey people are asked, "Do you think it wise to trust others?" the less educated are always the more suspicious; they have in the course of life gained a peasant-like guile, the sort of sloganized cynicism so beautifully described by Richard Wright in Black Boy. In an hierarchical society, this distrust does not become a dynamic social and political factor; except insofar as it prevents the organization of the masses it remains a problem only for individuals in their relations with other individuals. But when the mistrustful, with prosperity, are suddenly pushed into positions of leverage, attitudes previously channeled within the family and neighborhood are projected upon the national and international scene.

Recent psychoanalytically-oriented work on ethnic prejudice provides possible clues as to why overt anti-Semitism has declined at the same time that attacks on Harvard and other symbols of Eastern seaboard culture seem to have increased. In their valuable book, *The Dynamics of Prejudice,* Bruno Bettelheim and Morris Janowitz make the point that in America Jews and Negroes divide between them the hostilities which spring from internal conflict: The super-ego is involved in anti-Semitism, since the Jew is felt to represent the valued but unachieved goals of ambition, money, and group loyalty ("clannishness"), whereas fear and hatred of the Negro spring from id tendencies which the individual cannot manage, his repressed desires for promiscuity, destruction of property, and general looseness of living. (In Europe, the Jews must do double duty, as the outlet for both id and super-ego dynamisms.) Today, on the one hand, the increasing sexual emancipation of Americans has made the Negro a less fearsome image in terms of sexuality (though he remains a realistic threat to neighborhood real estate and communal values) and, on the other hand, prosperity has meant that the Jew is no longer a salient emblem of enviable financial success. Thus, while the KKK declines the former "racial" bigot finds a new threat: the older educated classes of the East, with their culture and refinement, with "softness" and other amenities he does not yet feel able to afford.[7]

Furthermore, the sexual emancipation which has made the Negro less of a feared and admired symbol of potency has presented men with a much more difficult problem: the fear of homosexuality. Indeed, homosexuality becomes a much more feared enemy than the Negro. (It may also be that homosexuality is itself spreading or news of it is spreading, so that people are presented with an issue which formerly was kept under cover—another consequence of enlightenment.) How powerful, then, is the political consequence of combining the image of the homosexual with the image of the intellectual—the State Department cooky-pusher Harvard-trained sissy thus becomes the focus of social hatred and the Jew becomes merely one variant of the intellectual sissy—actually less important than the Eastern-educated snob! Many people say of McCarthy that they approve of his ends but not of his methods. We think this statement should be reversed to read that they approve of his methods, which are so obviously not sissified, but care little about his ends, which are irrelevant provided that the targets are drawn with the foregoing constellation in mind.

As a result of all this, the left-wing and liberal intellectuals, who came forward during the New Deal and who played so effective a role in the fight against Nazism and in "prematurely" delineating the nature of the Communist as an enemy, today find themselves without an audience, their tone deprecated, their slogans ineffectual.

4

Apart from this central social change, much has happened to reduce the intellectuals to a silence only temporarily broken by such a clamor as that over McCarthy.

For one thing, the success of the New Deal has silenced them. The New Deal as a triumphant movement at once of the "folk," liberal government officials, and the intellectuals, came to an end in 1937. By this time the major reforms, such as the NLRB and Social Security, had already been institutionalized, and many of the remaining unspent energies of the movement were dissipated in the Court-packing fight—nominally waged to preserve the reforms. After this, the crusading spirit could only work on modifications and defenses of an extant structure (for instance, the last major New Deal bill, the Wages and Hours Act of 1938). This vacuum of goals was concealed by affairs in Europe; Fascism in Spain and Germany, and its repercussions in this country, absorbed many New Dealers, the intellectuals, and their allies among the cultivated, and provided them with an agenda. But it was assumed that, once the war was over, the New Dealers and their allies could return to the unending problem of controlling the business cycle and reforming the economy. The business cycle, however, refused to turn down, or did not turn down very far. The one postwar victory based on something like the old New Deal approach and coalition—that of 1948—owed more to the anger of well-to-do farmers at the sag in agricultural prices than it did to the self-interested voting of the city workers. Had the depression come, the alliance forged by Roosevelt might have emerged unimpaired from the war-time National Unity front. But it turned out to be "too easy" to control the business cycle: Keynesianism was no longer esoteric knowledge but the normal working doctrine of administrators, liberal or conservative, and even the Republicans, as was demonstrated in 1953-4, could keep a down-turn in the business cycle under control.

What was left on the home front? One could raise the floor under wages, but in a time of prosperity and inflation that could not excite many beyond those, like the Textile Workers Union, who spoke for the worst-paid workers. One could press for socialized medicine, but this had little of the force of the old New Deal campaigns.

One could denounce Wall Street and the interests, but it looked old-fashioned, and more, it divided the liberal intellectuals from those who, on the issues that still counted, were natural allies. For Wall Street was closer to the liberal intellectuals on the two domestic issues that were still alive—civil rights and civil liberties—and on the whole range of issues related to foreign policy than were the former allies of the liberal intellectuals, the farmers and the lower classes of the city, both in their old form as factory workers and in their new form as white-collar workers.

Indeed, what has happened is that the old issues died, and on the new issues former friends or allies have become enemies, and former enemies have become friends. Thus: the liberal intellectuals have had to switch their attitudes toward Wall Street—as symbolizing both the great financiers and the giant corporations they organize —and toward "small business." By 1940, one could no longer speak of Wall Street as "the enemy." Demographic shifts and the Depression, along with the increasing ability of industry to finance expansion from reserves, had already weakened the hegemony of Eastern capital. The New Deal, by rhetoric and by such legislation as the SEC and the Holding Company Act, weakened it further, in comparison with the growing power of mid-continent businessmen (not to speak of tax-privileged oil and gas men). And the war had the same effect, for the small businessmen and tougher big businessmen of the Midwest paid less taxes and less attention to OPA and WPB. Wall Street lawyers Stimson and McCloy (perhaps Wendell Willkie might be added), Wall Street bankers Forrestal, Lovett, and Harriman, all have had a far greater cosmopolitanism and tolerance for intellectuals than do, for example, the big and little car dealers and other "small businessmen" of the Eisenhower Administration.[8] In general, Wall Streeters, like the British Tories, are a chastened lot—and an easy symbol of abuse for pastoral and Populist simplifications. But, while Harry Hopkins and Tommy Corcoran recruited such men for Roosevelt, many New Dealers and their journalist and intellectual supporters resented their entrance.

They also resented the military, who were frequently similarly chastened men, sensitive to the limits of "free enterprise." The liberal political imagination in America, with its tendency to consider generals and admirals hopeless conservatives, and its tendency to consider war an outmoded barbarity that serious thinkers should not concern themselves with, was incapable of seeing that military men, like Wall Streeters, might be natural allies in the new epoch, and that military issues would become at least as important as the domestic economic issues of the New Deal era. What could be more crucial today than the outcome of the struggle between the Strategic Air Command and the Army Ground Forces? Yet who concerns himself with it? (The self-styled conservatives, being so often isolationists with overtones of manifest-destiny jingoism, have been on the whole even less well prepared to consider such issues.)

When the comments on policy of intellectuals and academic people are dated by ignorance, the military man who might be guided by thoughtful civilians—and there are many such—feels the hopelessness of communication; he must, in spite of himself, resort to pressure and public relations to defend his service and with it his country. Aside from a few journalists like the Alsops, several able magazine editors, and a handful of academic people like Bernard Brodie and the late Edward Mead Earle, only atomic scientists (and their occasional sociological counselors such as Edward A. Shils) have made serious efforts to grapple with such factors.

Today, the Federal defense budget is so large as to

leave little room for major socio-cultural argument; in Washington, at least, anything outside of it can be no more than a fringe benefit. As Eliot Janeway has pointed out, we are now in a defense cycle rather than a business cycle; and Daniel Bell, tracing this out in terms of the capital expansion consequences of military commitments, has emphasized how many of the conventional areas of business and social decision are foreclosed. If a depression permitting reshaping of political thinking is unlikely, so also is a huge surplus the spending of which could lead to a healthy controversy outside the warring military services and their highly placed civilian partisans. Everywhere we look, then, there is room for change only within a narrow margin, if we interpret change in terms traditional among intellectuals.

At home, indeed, only the cause of racial emancipation remains to arouse enthusiasm. And this cause differs politically from the old New Deal causes in that it represents for many liberals and intellectuals a withdrawal from the larger statist concerns—it is a cause which is carried into personal life and into the field of culture where it attracts many reflective young people who appear apathetic to civic and electoral politics. By its nature, the field of race is one in which everyone can have a hand: institutionalization has not proceeded nearly so far as it has with economic underprivilege. Thus, every state has some form of social security, but only a few have an FEPC; and, as many Americans become more sensitive to interpersonal considerations, they feel it imperative to work for the amelioration of racial slights that would not have troubled an earlier generation. But as we have indicated, the demand for tolerance of Negroes cannot replace, politically, the demand for "economic equality": it is a very great and aggravating demand to make on children of white immigrants who are paying off the mortgage on their first suburban house.

5

Thus, for liberal intellectuals in the postwar era the home front could not be the arena for major policies, mobilizing a majority coalition, that it was in the 1930's; the focus had shifted to foreign policy. But for this the New Dealers and the intellectuals were generally unprepared. In particular, they were not prepared to view the Communists and the Soviet Union as the enemy in the way they had earlier recognized Fascism as the enemy, and for this failure they were to suffer seriously. Not many New Dealers had actually been pro-Soviet: the liberal politicians, lawyers, and civil servants had little in common with Popular Front writers, who were contemptuous of reform and addicted to slogans about Marx, the proletariat, and the Revolution. Indeed, the New Dealers were almost too ready to dismiss both the Stalinists and their left-wing sectarian critics; preoccupied with domestic reforms and anti-fascism, they formed no clear-cut image of Communism. They did not sympathize with it, let alone accept it, but they did not see it as a major enemy.

Understandably, they could not be as ebullient in carrying on a policy in which Communism was the major enemy as they could be in attacking depression and the interests. True, they did what was necessary: Truman's Point IV program and the Marshall Plan were the major postwar achievements of the American political imagination. However, these brilliant anti-Communist measures have not succeeded in saving the New Dealers from the taint of fellow-traveling. Moreover, these measures were not able to arouse among intellectuals, and sensitive young people, very much enthusiasm, even in the hearts of those active in administration of the aid program. For one thing, with the whole planet sending in distress signals, Point IV seems a drop of milk in a rusty Malthusian bucket—to be defended more for what it symbolizes at home than for its often ambiguous blessings (lowered death rates and uncontrollable population growth) abroad. For another thing, all these measures of international hope and help have been launched and caught up in the spirit of cold-war public relations. Thus, no one knows any longer whether he supports a program because it is worthwhile and an expression of humaneness, or because it is necessary to harry Soviet satellites or win over neutralists in Europe and Asia, or because it is necessary to appear tough-minded vis-à-vis congressmen and Philistines generally. A military "angle" has been discovered in, for instance, the work of anthropologists seeking to mediate the coming of industry to Indonesia. While such practical compromises and dual motives are always involved in reform, in this case they have often served to confuse the reformers, who deny, even to themselves, that they are motivated by anything visionary; hence the intellectual climate becomes less and less open to political imagination.[9]

As the hope of solving our foreign problems by indiscriminately and rapidly raising the standard of living of the rest of the world has waned, the more informed critics of contemporary politics have had to fall back on an austerity program—a program promising less and requiring more: more money, more soldiers, more arms, more aid, hence more taxes. All this is required, of course, not for redistribution within America, though a good deal of this does ensue, but to provide a new carrier (it costs as much as a Valley Authority) or a radar early-warning defense (as costly as socialized medicine). This program divides the intellectuals among themselves—many still agitate for socialized medicine—but divides them still more grievously from the poor and uneducated—for the latter, whatever the bellicose consequences of their xenophobia and love of verbal violence, always oppose war and sacrifice.

It is perhaps in reaction to these dilemmas that one new issue—that of the protection of traditional civil liberties—has risen in recent years to monopolize almost completely the intellectuals' attention. But this, too, is an issue which demands sacrifice from the uneducated masses—not financial sacrifice but the practice of deference and restraint which is understood and appreciated only among the well-to-do and highly educated strata.[10] Thus, a focus on civil liberties and on foreign policy tends, as we have seen, to make intellectuals seek allies among the rich and well-born, rather than among the working-men and farmers they had earlier courted and cared about; indeed, it tends to make them conservative, once it becomes clear that civil liberties are protected, not by majority vote (which is overwhelmingly unsympathetic), but by traditional institutions, class prerogatives, and judicial life-tenure.

At the same time, the protection of civil liberties has had to cope with the Communist issue, much as other liberal causes have. The Sacco-Vanzetti case united the liberals; the Rosenberg case divided them. The great civil liberties cases of the post-Enlightenment era were not fought to save the Czar's spies and police from detection and punishment; they were fought for anarchists, for socialists and liberals, for professors teaching evolution or economics; and it takes either a case-hardened and sometimes disingenuous naïveté about Communists or a subtle strategic decision about where to draw the line to muster much enthusiasm for the defense of intellectuals who plead the Fifth Amendment. In this situation, the defense becomes at best a rear-guard action, but cannot hope to be a "positive" program—a demand on the basis of which political identities can be reshaped.

Where do the college-bred young stand in all this? In

the late Thirties they were offered blood, sweat, and tears in the fight against Nazism. Some sought and accepted the agenda. But the fight against Nazism was made real by its domestic opponents: one saw almost all that was despicable—anti-Semites, fascists, Europe-haters, the bigoted and the crack-pot—lined up on the pro-Nazi side. Today, the pathetic passel of domestic Communists cannot be compared with these fascists who organized street gangs or shook down businessmen; and many of the Communists' allies are decent, if misguided, "liberals who haven't learned." In international politics, we must accept alliances with despots no more savory than our erstwhile domestic fascists. Thus, the young are asked to fight international Communism not on the basis of street experience but of what they are taught. Cool in spirit generally, they can hardly be expected to show enthusiasm. Indeed, a holding game against the Communists is a reality and a prospect to sober the most enthusiastic. The question of appeasement that most thoughtful people could reject offhand in the pre-atom-bomb era now becomes more insistent intellectually even while it becomes outlawed politically.

If we leave substance aside, and consider the tone of politics, we realize that the loss of initiative by intellectuals is coupled with a change of emotional accent. The conservative and ascetic program just sketched is not avant-garde; it is dull; there is no hope in it of saving the world; it assumes the world is well enough and only wishes the Communists thought so too.

Demands are the basis of politics: the demands of a group or class, formulated by its intellectual leaders—or, more accurately, the demands create and identify the group or class which then is led. When a group is either satisfied or exhausted, when for whatever reason it no longer makes demands, then it has lost the élan which can attract new forces. It can only hope that the institu-

tions and battalions that have been built up by the vanished élan of the past are large enough to withstand the
onslaught of those who do make new demands.

6

It is not only the dilemmas of policy that have been
responsible for the decline of enthusiasm and vitality
among the liberal intellectuals in the last decade or so.
Another factor is hard to discuss without sounding like
E. A. Ross, Henry Pratt Fairchild, and other pre-World
War I opponents of immigration from Eastern and Southern Europe; yet it seems evident to us that the American
crusading spirit has been sustained in considerable measure by the non-conformist conscience of New England
and its offshoots in the Western Reserve and the Far
West.[11] As long as the new immigrants looked up to this
model, they tended to imitate the benign as well as the
sharp-shooting doctrines and practices of the Yankees, but
in a cumulative process which is only now reaching its
end, the New Englanders themselves have run out of
confidence and prestige: their land is now Vacationland,
rather than the source of Abolitionist and other gospel; in
the home territory, surrounded by Irish, Italians, Poles,
French Canadians, Portuguese whom they have influenced
more than either party will admit, they feel defeated and
out of control in the charter institutions.[12]

This is not the place to trace the complex relations
between the New England conscience and pragmatic
reform. The remaining possessors of that conscience are
still a national asset, but there are fewer of them proportionately; their wealth is smaller proportionately; and,
scattered throughout the country, they are more remote
from the centers of ideas. New ideas have their head-
quarters in New York. They often originate with, or are

mediated by, Jews who have more reasons for hesitation and are perhaps psychologically as well as sociologically more vulnerable to pressure than the New Englanders—just as the newer media (movies and broadcasting) in which they are influential are weaker in the face of censorship than the older media (book publishing and the press) in which they play less part than the Yankees do. To be sure, there are many affinities between Jews and Puritans—both are people of the Book—and a political and intellectual alliance of the sort that Holmes and Brandeis once typified is still to be found, especially in smaller communities.

On the whole, as Americanization spreads, the old Puritan families have been slowly losing status. Some have responded by eccentricity, leadership, intellectuality, and liberalism; others have joined angry "pro-America" movements—where, ironically enough (save in the DAR), they meet the very Irish or Italian or other newer elements who have displaced or jostled them.[13] Since they can no longer safely snub these ex-Wops, ex-Shanty Irish, and ex-Hunkies, they displace their animus onto the weak targets provided by intellectuals, "left-wingers," "one-worlders," and so on.[14] And they can blame these latter people for the very social changes that have brought the descendants of lowly immigrants into the top councils of what was once, in some areas, the ethnically rather exclusive club of the Republican Party. Their blame, moreover, is not entirely misplaced, for the New Deal, along with the war, did help bring prosperity and mobility and reputability to Catholics and Jews.

After the war, the recognition of the Communist menace still further boosted the status of Catholics by making them almost automatically charter members of the anti-Communist crusade. By the same token, the intellectuals, their limited links with Communism continuously and extravagantly exposed, became more vulnerable. We be-

lieve that Granville Hicks in *Where We Came Out* presents a reasonably just picture of the actual extent of
Communist influence in the Thirties—an influence much
less than is now often supposed even among intellectuals;
indeed, his picture does not take sufficient account of the
infinitesimal extent of Party effectiveness outside the
major seaboard cities. The New Dealers, as we have
already said, were even less affected than the intellectuals,
but they shared with the latter some personal and journal-
istic ties; this, plus some dramatic cases like those of
Harry Dexter White and Alger Hiss and the belated
fellow-traveling of Henry Wallace, made it politically
possible—though fantastic—to damn the New Deal as a
Communist-front organization. This has created a situation obviously quite different from that of earlier decades,
when though liberal intellectuals and New Dealers were
also called Communists, they only became as a result
firmer and angrier. Today such libel is not only a disaster
for public relations but cause for an anxious inner
scrutiny. For as it becomes clear that few of the causes
liberals have espoused have been immune to exploitation
by the Communists, the liberal intellectuals lose their
former sure conviction about their causes and are put,
inside as well as out, on the defensive. One evidence of
this is the strategy of continuous balancing so many of
us engage in: if one day we defend Negroes (one of the
few causes which, though taken up by Communists, still
gets relatively unambiguous attention from intellectuals),
then the next day we set the record straight by calling
for more aid to Indo-China—not, let us repeat, merely for
protective coloration but to make clear to ourselves that
we are not fools or dupes of fellow-traveler rhetoric.

The intellectuals themselves are further weakened—in
their own minds, at least—by the fact that their ideas,
even where relevant to contemporary discontent, are
quickly taken over by the mass media and transmuted

into the common stock of middlebrow conceptions. They can no longer control, even by intentional opacity, the pace of distribution. Thus, what they produce soon becomes dissociated from them and their immediate coteries; in the division of labor, the middlebrows take over the function of dissemination and translation, and this alienation from their "product" leaves the intellectuals, even when they may reach a wider audience with more dispatch than ever before in history, with a feeling of impotence and isolation.

And, finally, the self-confidence of the liberal intellectuals is weakened by their own egalitarian ideology, which has led them not only to attack ethnic and class barriers but to defer to the manners and mores of the lower classes generally. Whereas in the days of Eastern seaboard hegemony the masses sought to imitate the classes, if they sought to rise at all, today imitation is a two-way process, and intellectuals are no longer protected by class and elite arrogance (and the strategic ignorances arrogance protects) against the attitudes of their enemies.[15] We find, for example, the cynicism of the lower strata reflected in the desire of the intellectuals to appear tough-minded and in their fear to be thought naive. Such tough-mindedness in turn may then require acceptance of belligerent and vindictive attitudes in domestic and foreign affairs, and a further weakening of any visionary hopes and motives.

What the left has lost in tone and initiative, the right has gained. The right has believed, ever since "that man" entered the White House, in the utter deviltry of the New Deal. But what was once a domestic misanthropy has now been writ large upon the globe: the right has hit on what it regards as an unquestioned truth, which needs only to be spread (the utter sinfulness, the total evil, of the idea of Communism and the total perfection of the idea of Americanism); it maintains the zeal of missionaries in propagating this truth; it feels today it possesses a newer, better, altogether more avant-garde knowledge, even though about so limited a subject as the influence of Communists on American culture and politics (look at *The Freeman* and *The American Mercury,* or at *McCarthy and His Enemies* for illustration). Moreover, this new right possesses that convenient and perhaps essential feeling of martyrdom which its very presence gives to many liberal intellectuals: it sees itself as a minority suffering for its desire to enlighten the people (Peter Viereck has referred to the "bleeding hearts of the right").[16]

But the parallel is far from complete. For the left and the liberals in their days of influence really wanted something: they had specific reforms in mind, and specific legislation. The new right, with its few intellectuals trying to create a program for it, wants at best an atmosphere: it really has no desire to change the face of the nation; it is much more interested in changing the past, in rewriting the history of the New Deal, of the Second World War and its aftermath, or in more ambitious efforts, of the whole modern movement. Here again the comparison of the new right with the Communists is instructive, for the latter, too, in this country have been preoccupied with a state of mind: they have aimed, if not to make Americans sympathetic to the Soviet Union, at least unsympathetic toward its enemies here and overseas. To this end, their greatest efforts have been in rewriting recent and current history, in presenting a certain picture of the world in which big business, on the one side, supported fascism and anti-Semitism, while the Soviet Union, on the other side, fostered Negroes, Jews, and other minorities, and defended the working class. American domestic politics have been useful to the Communists in providing object-lessons for this general theory and in recruiting stalwarts for its further propagation. In the same way, one can read or listen to the organs of the new right and find nothing that amounts to a legislative program: the bills they want passed are those which give expression to their feelings about the past, such as the Bricker Amendment,[17] or withdrawing Hiss's pension and otherwise harrassing Communists (often in ways that such veteran Communist-hunters as Governor Dewey think unjust and unwise)—the fight for these measures is an educative fight in re-interpreting the past. When it comes to coping with world Communism, this group has nothing to propose in the way of strengthening anti-Communists abroad —nothing but withdrawal or muted quasi-suicidal hints of preventive war. In fact, the hatred this group feels for the modern world, as manifested at home, in America, is so huge that there is little energy left over for the rest of the globe—rather, there is an aimless destructiveness in which legislative and local battles simply focus and dramatize resentment.

Nevertheless, this group now possesses the enthusiasm and momentum previously held by liberals. Its leaders cannot channel discontent; they can interpret it: they can explain why everything has gone wrong—for the while, that is enough. Thus, the picture today in American politics is of intelligence without force or enthusiasm facing force and enthusiasm without intelligence.

How much longer can this pattern last? International developments will probably be determinative—the belligerence coupled with isolationism of this rightist group may tempt or frighten the Soviet Union into further adventures and incidents, finally touching off a war of annihilation (we think this most unlikely, and assuredly not inevitable). But the present leadership of the discontented classes has to do more than symbolize their disorientation and lack of satisfying political loyalties if it is to solidify new allegiances. For this, no intellectual reserve of demands appears in the offing. Instead, the leadership

is continually subject to the temptation to fall back on
the more developed intellectual positions of laissez-faire
or of various brands of fascism—but these, it knows, will
lose them much of their potential following, which is
neither conservative in the older free enterprise sense nor
on the lookout for, though tempted by, civil commotion
and foreign adventure. It is not surprising that Congress
represents the peak of strength of this group, since Congress is a sounding-board for mood—and an extraordinarily democratic one—as much as it is a machine for
pork-processing and bill-passing. A tone, however, soon
becomes monotonous and, if not institutionalized when
at its shrillest, fades away.

In sum, the earlier leadership by the intellectuals of
the underprivileged came about through a program of
economic changes; and this program demonstrated an
ability in the leaders to interpret the situation of the
unorganized workers, of minority groups, and of marginal
farmers. Today, a different group of classes (including
many of these former underprivileged groups, now risen
to middle-income status) wants something, but their
wants (partly for the very reason that these people are
now above subsistence or disfranchisement) are much less
easily formulated. These new groups want an interpretation of the world; they want, or rather might be prepared
to want, a more satisfying life.

It is the unsatisfying quality of life as they find it in
America that mostly feeds the discontent of the discontented classes. Their wealth, their partial access to education and fuller exposure to the mass media—indeed, their
possession of many of the insignia they have been taught
to associate with the good life—these leave them restless,
ill at ease in Zion. They must continually seek for reasons
explaining their unrest—and the reasons developed by
intellectuals for the benefit of previous proletariats are of
course quite irrelevant.

Is it conceivable that the intellectuals, rather than their enemies, can have a share in providing new interpretations and in dissipating, through creative leadership, some of the resentment of the discontented classes? What kind of life, indeed, is appropriate to a society whose lower classes are being devoured faster by prosperity than Puerto Rican immigration can replenish? We have almost no idea about the forms the answers might take, if there are answers. But we do recognize that one obstacle to any rapprochement between the discontented classes and the intellectuals is the fact that many of the latter are themselves of lower-middle-class origin, and detest the values they have left behind—the dislike is not just one way. They espouse a snobbery of topic which makes the interests of the semi-educated wholly alien to them—more alien than the interests of the lower classes. Only in the great new melting pot of the Army would there appear to be instances where intellectuals discover that individuals in the discontented classes are "not so bad," despite their poisonous tastes in politics and culture—instances where the great camaraderie of the male sex and the even greater one of the brass-haters bridge the gap created by the uneven development of social mobility and cultural status. Of course, to suppose that the intellectuals can do very much to guide the discontented classes by winning friends and influencing people among them is as ridiculous as supposing that Jews can do much to combat political anti-Semitism by amiability to non-Jews. Nevertheless, there is only one side from which understanding is likely to come, and that is their own.

[1] For data on the negligible influence of political campaigns, see Paul Lazarsfeld, Bernard Berelson, and Hazel Gaudet, *The People's Choice* (Harpers, New York, 1948).

[2] To be sure, there are enclaves where the underprivileged can still be found, as in the Southern Alleghenies or the rural Deep South. And, as we shall see, the fact that "everyone" has moved up means that mobility may not have kept pace with aspiration, one reason why the slogan "you never had it so good" is a poor campaign weapon.

[3] The concept of "intolerance of ambiguity," developed by Else

Frenkel-Brunswik and co-workers, is relevant here: these newly prosperous ones want to see the world clearly bounded, in blacks and whites;
they have been brought up conventionally, to make use of conventional
categories, and fluidity of boundaries threatens their self-assurance and
their very hold on reality.

4 It is at this point that the lack of connection between the small cadre
of truly conservative intellectuals and any sizable anti-liberal audience
becomes a major factor in the present political scene. For patronage
politics and for the untutored businessman, writers like Allen Tate or
Russell Kirk have nothing but contempt; their "conservatism" (as some
critics have pointed out) is based on an irrelevant landed-gentry and
professional-class model. With a few exceptions, the pseudo-conservatives
who have a radical and nihilistic message for the untutored have to face
little intellectual competition, save from occasional socially conscious
clergymen and priests.

5 Strictly speaking, there is no such thing as an "economic" appeal,
nor is a well-paying job a "natural" need of mankind. Rather, the present
insistence of the American workingman that he is entitled to such a job
is the outgrowth of recent experience, clarified and interpreted for him
by his leaders. These combine into a demonstration that depressions are
not necessary (though perhaps wars are), and that therefore jobs and
all that goes with them are necessary.

6 According to a study of the 1952 election by the Survey Research
Center of the University of Michigan, only two groupings in the population were resistant to these appeals and went more strongly Democratic
than in 1948: these were the Negroes on the one extreme of the social
spectrum and the college-educated, upper income, and professional and
managerial strata at the other extreme—the latter also produced more
Republican votes, as the result of a decline in the non-voters. See Angus
Campbell, Gerald Gurin, and Warren E. Miller, *The Voter Decides*
(Row, Peterson and Co., Evanston, 1954), Table 5.1.

7 Professor Richard Hofstadter, to whose work we are indebted, reminds us of the status gain involved in being able to bait old-family
Anglo-Saxons on the ground they are un-American—a greater gain than
is to be won by demonstrating superiority simply to the Jews. (See
Chapter 2.)

8 In the perspective employed here, "Engine Charlie" Wilson's Detroit
provides a smaller and less cosmopolitan environment than Secretary
Humphrey's Cleveland.

9 Commenting on an earlier draft of this paper—and we are indebted
to such comments for many important revisions—Arthur Schlesinger, Jr.,
reminds us of utopian thinkers still alive and kicking, such as Stringfellow Barr, Clarence Streit, and the United World Federalists. We feel
that the spectrum here is not wide or the proposals terribly imaginative;
moreover, many of the proposals are counsels of despair, to avoid world
catastrophe, rather than of hope, to improve American or planetary life.

10 It was evident in the first opinion polls of the thirties that the conventional notion of the rich as conservative and the poor as radical was
correct in the realm of government, labor, and distributive policy—thus,
the poor have no objection to government ownership—but false in the
realm of civil liberties and foreign policy where the greater impact of

mistrust and fear of the strange and the stranger among the poor came to light.

[11] In addition, the Southern Scotch-Irish Presbyterians, such as Woodrow Wilson, have played a great role, especially in the Democratic and in splinter parties.

[12] On the whole, the English settlements over the globe indicate that the non-conformist conscience needs to be surrounded by other such consciences if it is to remain effective. The English Methodist who goes to Kenya or Australia to make his fortune is likely to retain the values he went out with, and not be prodded towards wider social sympathies, so that eventually his descendants will be estranged from Colonial Office officials representing his cousins who have stayed, and moved intellectually and morally forward in the Old Country. Similarly, the New Englanders who have left New England, the Quakers who have left Pennsylvania, may not—despite relative ease of intranational movement—keep up with developments in the original centers of cultivated morality. Indeed, New Englanders marooned in the Midwest (the late Robert Taft came of such stock) have been the source of much soured high-principled reaction—the "colonial" conscience at its worst.

[13] The Jews, so largely beneficiaries of inflation and gainers of middle-class and professional status, have overwhelmingly remained Roosevelt Democrats, though a kind of "leakage" has provided some of the leadership and newspaper support for the new right.

[14] See Richard Hofstadter's excellent essay, "The Pseudo-Conservative Revolt" (Chapter 2).

[15] We ourselves had an experience of this when we undertook to write a criticism of Norman Dodd's report as Staff Director of the Reece Committee investigating foundations. We criticized not only the crackpot notions that socialists and the great foundations had plotted to take America over on behalf of education and the Federal government—a plot somehow connected with "empiricism" and the prestige-laden "name" universities—but we also ridiculed the illiteracy, the demi-educated vein in which the report was written. Then we had misgivings about pulling the rank of our own education and relative fluency, and withdrew our comments on the style of the report. It is no longer comfortable (or expedient) to bait the hillbilly, the hick, the Negro preacher, or the night-school lawyer—so, too, with the political arriviste. The ridicule that greeted Bryan in Tennessee did not greet Congressman Reece.

[16] When not long ago we heard Frank Chodorov, a leading organizer and publicist of the right, speak to a businessmen's luncheon, we felt that he bore much the same relation to his audience that, for instance, a speaker sent out by the American League for Peace and Democracy might have borne to a meeting of a Unitarian Sunday evening forum: he was more extreme, and therefore seemed more daring, but he shared enough of the values and verbal tags of the group to disguise somewhat the extent to which he was pushing their logics and rhetorics to fanatical limits. Indeed, Communist organizing tactics have often given lessons to rightists, and the little library in a New Hampshire town that might have received, from an anonymous donor, a copy of a novel by Howard Fast or a subscription to *The National Guardian* will now get the Buckley and Bozell book or *The Freeman*.

[17] The Minute Women of America who buttonholed Senators on behalf of the Bricker Amendment are of course quite different in social position from the lower-class women who, in a few interviews a student supervised by one of us conducted by telephone, praised Senator McCarthy as the only one in Washington who was cleaning out the crooks and the Commies: they saw him as a kind of Lone Ranger, bravely fighting an all-powerful "they." Throughout this paper, we have had to collapse such distinctions to form general categories; we hope to stimulate further discussion of the coalitions—and the contradictions—that we lump as the discontented classes.

4

The Revolt Against the Elite

PETER VIERECK

Defeat of western silver.
Defeat of the wheat.
Victory of letterfiles
And plutocrats in miles
With dollar signs upon their coats
And spats on their feet.
Victory of custodians,
Plymouth Rock,
And all that inbred landlord stock.
Victory of the neat. . . .
Defeat of the Pacific and the long Mississippi. . . .
And all these in their helpless days
By the dour East oppressed, . . .

Crucifying half the West,
Till the whole Atlantic coast
Seemed a giant spiders' nest....
And all the way to frightened Maine the old East
    heard them call, ...
Prairie avenger, mountain lion,
Bryan, Bryan, Bryan, Bryan,
Smashing Plymouth Rock with his boulders from the
    West.

—from Vachel Lindsay's "higher vaudeville" imitation of how a sixteen-year-old Bryanite Populist
radical in 1896 would have viewed the revolt of
western mass egalitarianism against Atlantic coast
traditionalism and aristocracy. Note the stress on revenge ("avenger, mountain lion") for having been
humiliated and patronized intellectually or socially
by "that inbred landlord stock" of Plymouth Rock;
this emotion of revenge for humiliation is often
shared by recent immigrants in Boston and the east
as well as by the Populist older stock in Wisconsin
and the west.

DURING THE Jacobin Revolution of
1793, in those quaint days when the lower classes still
thought of themselves as the lower classes, it was for
upper-class sympathies and for *not* reading "subversive
leftist literature" that aristocrats got in trouble.

Note the reversal in America. Here the lower classes
seem to be the upper classes—they have automobiles, lace
curtains and votes. Here, in consequence, it is for alleged
lower-class sympathies—for "leftist" sympathies—that the
aristocrats are purged by the lower class.

In reality those lower-class sympathies are microscopic
in most of that social register (Lodge, Bohlen, Acheson,
Stevenson, and Harvard presidents) which McCarthy is

trying to purge; even so, leftist sympathies are the pretext given for the purge. Why is it necessary to allege those lower-class sympathies as pretext? Why the pretext in the first place? Because in America the suddenly enthroned lower classes cannot prove to themselves psychologically that they are now upper-class unless they can indict for pro-proletariat subversion those whom they know in their hearts to be America's real intellectual and social aristocracy.

Ostensibly our aristocrats are being metaphorically guillotined for having signed, twenty years ago, some pinko-front petition by that egghead Voltaire (a typical reversal of the 1793 pretext) and for having said, not "Let them eat cake," but "Let them read books" (violation of loyalty oath to TV). Behind these ostensible pretexts, the aristocratic pro-proletarian conspirators are actually being guillotined for having been too exclusive socially—and, even worse, intellectually—at those fancy parties at Versailles-sur-Hudson. McCarthyism is the revenge of the noses that for twenty years of fancy parties were pressed against the outside window pane.

In Populist-Progressive days and in New Deal days, those same noses were pressed with openly radical, openly lower-class resentment. During 1953 and 1954, the same noses snorted triumphantly with right-wing Republicanism. This demagogue's spree of symbolically decapitating America's intellectual and social upper class, but doing so while shouting a two hundred per cent upperclass ideology, suggests that McCarthyism is actually a leftist instinct behind a *self-deceptive* rightist veneer. This combination bolsters the self-esteem of sons of Democratic urban day laborers whose status rose into stuffy Republican suburbia. Their status rose thanks to the Communism-preventing social reforms of Roosevelt. Here for once is a radicalism expressing not poverty but sudden prosperity, biting the New Deal hand that fed it.

What figure represents the transition, the missing link, between the often noble, idealistic Populist-Progressives (like that truly noble idealist, La Follette) and the degeneration of that movement into something so different, so bigoted as McCarthyism? According to my hypothesis, that transition, that missing link is Father Charles Coughlin. All liberals know that Coughlin ended by defending Hitler in World War II and preaching the vilest anti-Semitism. They sometimes forget that Coughlin began his career by preaching social reforms to the left of the New Deal; his link with Populism and western Progressivism emerges from the fact that Coughlin's chief panacea was the old Populist panacea of "free silver," as a weapon against Wall Street bankers, eastern seaboard intellectuals, and internationalists, three groups hated alike by democratic Populists and by semi-fascist Coughlinites. And Coughlin's right-wing fascist anti-Semitism sounds word for word the same as the vile tirades against "Jewish international bankers" by the left-wing egalitarian Populist, Ignatius Donnelly.

On the surface, Senators like Wheeler and Nye (originally Progressives and campaigners for La Follette) seemed to reverse themselves completely when they shifted—in a shift partly similar to Coughlin's—from "liberal" Progressives to "reactionary" America Firsters. But basically they never changed at all; throughout, they remained passionately Anglophobe, Germanophile, isolationist, and anti-eastern-seaboard, first under leftist and then under rightist pretexts. Another example is Senator McCarran, who died in 1954. McCarran ended as a McCarthyite Democrat, hating the New Deal more than did any Republican. This same McCarran had been an eager New Dealer in 1933, voting for the Wagner Act and even for the NRA. Yet throughout these changes, he remained consistently anti-internationalist, anti-British, anti-eastern-intellectual.

Broadening the generalization, we may tentatively conclude: the entire midwest Old Guard Republican wing of today, journalistically or vulgarly referred to as "conservative," does not merit that word at all. Theirs is not the traditional conservatism of a Winston Churchill or of a Burke or of our own *Federalist* papers. Theirs is not true American conservatism in the sense in which Irving Babbitt defines indirect democracy (in his great book *Democracy and Leadership*), as opposed to plebiscitarian, Tom Painean direct democracy. "Conservative" is no proper label for western Old Guard Republicans, nor for their incongruous allies among the status-craving, increasingly prosperous, but socially insecure immigrants in South Boston and the non-elite part of the east. What all these groups are at heart is the same old isolationist, Anglophobe, Germanophile revolt of radical Populist lunatic-fringers against the eastern, educated, Anglicized elite. Only this time it is a Populism gone sour; this time it lacks the generous, idealistic, social reformist instincts which partly justified the original Populists.

Many of our intellectual aristocrats have helped to make the McCarthyite attack on themselves a success by denouncing McCarthyism as a rightist movement, a conservative movement. At first they even denounced it as a Red-baiting, anti-Communist movement, which is exactly what it wanted to be denounced as. By now they have at least caught on to the fact that it is not anti-Communist, has not trapped a single Red spy—whether at Fort Monmouth, the Voice of America, or the State Department—and is a major cause of the increased neutralism in Europe, McCarthy being the "Typhoid Mary" of anti-Americanism.

But although American liberals have now realized that McCarthyism is not anti-Communist (which is more than many American businessmen and Republicans have realized), they have still not caught on to the full and deep-rooted extent of its radical anti-conservatism. That is because they are steeped in misleading analogies with the very different context of Europe and of the European kind of fascism. Partly they still overlook the special situation in America, where the masses are more bourgeois than the bourgeoisie. I am speaking in terms of psychology, not only of economics. A lot more is involved psychologically in the American ideal of the mass man than the old economic boast (a smug and shallow boast) that simply "everybody" is "so prosperous" in America. "Every man a king" is not true of America today. Rather, every man is a king except the kings.

The real kings (the cultural elite that would rank first in any traditional hierarchy of the Hellenic-Roman West) are now becoming declassed scapegoats: the eggheads. The fact that they partly brought that fate on themselves by fumbling the Communist issue does not justify their fate, especially as the sacred civil liberties of everybody, the innocent as much as the guilty, must suffer for that retribution.

America is the country where the masses won't admit they are masses. Consequently America is the country where the thought-controllers can self-deceptively "make like" patriotic pillars of respectability instead of admitting what they are: revolutionaries of savage direct democracy (Napoleon plus Rousseau plus Tom Paine plus the Wild West frontier) against the traditional, aristocratic courts and Constitution and against the protection of minority intellectual elites by the anti-majoritarian Bill of Rights. The McCarthyites threaten liberty precisely because they are so egalitarian, ruling foreign policy by mass telegrams to the Executive Branch and by radio speeches and Gallup Poll. The spread of democratic equal rights facilitates, as Nietzsche prophesied, the equal violation of rights.

Is *liberté* incompatible with sudden *égalité?* It was, as people used to say in the Thirties, "no accident that" an

American Legion meeting in New York in July, 1954, passed two resolutions side by side—the first condemning another Legion branch for racial discrimination (the "Forty and Eight" society) and the second endorsing McCarthyism. This juxtaposition is noted not in order to disparage the long overdue anti-bigotry of the first resolution. Rather, the juxtaposition is noted in order to caution the oversimplifying optimism of many liberal reformers who have been assuming that the fight for free speech and the fight for racial tolerance were synonymous.

Admittedly not all nationalist bigots have yet "caught on" to the more lucrative new trend of their own racket. Many will continue to persecute racial minorities as viciously as in the past, though surely decreasingly and with less profit. Because of the Southern atmosphere of Washington, the anti-segregation resolution could not be repeated when the Legion met there a month later.

Often untypical or tardy about new trends, the South is more opposed to the good cause of Negro rights and to the bad cause of McCarthyism than the rest of the nation. One Southerner (I am not implying that he represents the majority of the South) told me he regards as Communistic the defenders of the civil liberties of any of our several racial minorities; then he went on to reproach the North for "not fighting for its civil liberties against that fascist McCarthy."

The same day I heard that statement, I read an account of a McCarthy mass meeting in the North at which racial discrimination was denounced as un-American and in which anyone defending civil liberties against McCarthy was called Communistic. At the same meeting, a rabbi accused the opposition to Roy Cohn of anti-Semitic intolerance. Next, Cohn's was called "the American Dreyfus Case" by a representative of a student McCarthyite organization, Students for America. This young representative of both McCarythism and racial brotherhood con-

cluded amid loud applause: "Roy Cohn and Joe McCarthy
will be redeemed when the people have taken back their
government from the criminal alliance of Communists,
Socialists, New Dealers, and the Eisenhower-Dewey Republicans."

This outburst of direct democracy[1] comes straight from
the leftist rhetoric of the old Populists and Progressives,
a rhetoric forever urging the People to take back "their"
government from the conspiring Powers That Be. What
else remained but for Rabbi Schultz, at a second Cohn-
McCarthy dinner, to appeal to "the plain people of
America" to "march on Washington" in order to save, with
direct democracy, their tribune McCarthy from the big
bosses of the Senate censure committee?

Bigotry's New Look is perhaps best evidenced by
McCarthy's abstention, so far, from anti-Semitic and
anti-Negro propaganda and, more important, by countless
similar items totally unconnected with the ephemeral
McCarthy. A similar juxtaposition occurs in a typical
New York *Times* headline of September 4, 1954, page
ONE: PRESIDENT SIGNS BILL TO EXECUTE PEACETIME SPIES;
ALSO BOLSTERS BAN ON BIAS. Moving beyond that relatively
middle-of-the-road area to the extremist fringe, note the
significant change in "For America." This nationalist
group is a xenophobic and isolationist revival of the old
America First Committee. But instead of appeasing the
open Nazis who then still ruled Germany, as in the old-
fashioned and blunter days of Father Coughlin, "For
America" began greatly expanding its mass base in 1954
by "quietly canvassing Jewish and Negro prospects."

And so it goes. From these multiplying examples we
may tentatively generalize: Manifestations of ethnic intolerance today tend to decrease in proportion as ideological
intolerance increases. In sharp contrast, both bigotries
previously used to increase together.

If sociologists require a new term for this change (as if there were not enough jargon already), then at least let it be a brief, unponderous term. I would suggest the word "transtolerance" for this curious interplay between the new tolerance and the new intolerance. Transtolerance is ready to give all minorities their glorious democratic freedom—provided they accept McCarthyism or some other mob conformism of Right or Left. I add "or Left" because liberals sometimes assume conformism is inevitably of the Right. Yet "Right" and "Left" are mere fluctuating pretexts, mere fluid surfaces for the deeper anti-individualism (anti-aristocracy) of the mass man, who ten years ago was trying to thought-control our premature anti-Communists as "warmongers" and who today damns them as "Reds" and who ten years from now, in a new appeasement of Russia, may again be damning them as "Wall Street warmongers" and "disloyal internationalist bankers."

Transtolerance is the form that xenophobia takes when practiced by a "xeno." Transtolerant McCarthyism is partly a movement of recent immigrants who present themselves (not so much to the world as to themselves) as a two hundred per cent hate-the-foreigner movement. And by extension: Hate "alien" ideas. Transtolerance is also a sublimated Jim Crow: against "wrong" thinkers, not "wrong" races. As such, it is a Jim Crow that can be participated in with a clear conscience by the new, non-segregated flag-waving Negro, who will be increasingly emerging from the increased egalitarian laws in housing and education. In the same way it is the Irishman's version of Mick-baiting and a strictly kosher anti-Semitism. It very sincerely champions against anti-Semites "that American Dreyfus, Roy Cohn"; simultaneously it glows with the same mob emotions that in all previous or comparable movements have been anti-Semitic.

The final surrealist culmination of this new development would be for the Ku Klux Klan to hold non-segregated lynching bees.

At the same moment when America fortunately is nearer racial equality than ever before (an exciting gain, insufficiently noted by American-baiters in Europe and India), America is moving further from liberty of opinion. "Now remember, boys, tolerance and equality," my very progressive schoolma'am in high school used to preach, "come from cooperation in some common task." If Orwell's 1984 should ever come to America, you can guess what "some common task" will turn out to be. Won't it be a "team" (as they will obviously call it) of "buddies" from "all three religions" plus the significantly increasing number of Negro McCarthyites, all "cooperating" in the "common task" of burning books on civil liberties or segregating all individualists of "all three" religions?

It required Robespierre to teach French intellectuals that *égalité* is not synonymous with *liberté*. Similarly, Joseph McCarthy is the educator of the educators; by his threat to our lawful liberties, he is educating America intellectuals out of a kind of liberalism and back to a kind of conservatism. The intellectual liberals who twenty years ago wanted to pack the Supreme Court as frustrating the will of the masses (which is exactly what it ought to frustrate) and who were quoting Charles Beard to show that the Constitution is a mere rationalization of economic loot—those same liberals today are hugging for dear life that same court and that same Constitution, including its Fifth Amendment. They are hugging those two most conservative of "outdated" institutions as their last life preservers against the McCarthyite version of what their Henry Wallaces used to call "the century of the common man."

Our right to civil liberties, our right to an unlimited

non-violent dissent, is as ruggedly conservative and traditional as Senator Flanders and the mountains of Vermont.
It is a right so aristocratic that it enables one lonely
individual, sustained by nine non-elected nobles in black
robes, to think differently from 99.9 per cent of the
nation, even if a majority of "all races, creeds, and
colors," in an honest democratic election, votes to suppress the thinking of that one individual.

But what will happen to that individual and his liberties
if ever the 99.9 per cent unite in direct democracy to
substitute, as final arbiter of law, the white sheets for the
black robes?

2

Asians and Europeans ought never to confuse genuine
American anti-Communism, a necessary shield for peace
and freedom against aggression, with the pseudo-anti-
Communism of the demagogues, which is not anti-
Communism at all but a racket. American anti-Communism, in the proper sense of the term, usually turns
out to be a surprisingly sober and reasonable movement,
fair-minded and sincerely dedicated to civil liberties.
Indeed, when you consider the disappointed hopes and
the murderous provocations suffered by an unprepared
public opinion in the five years between Yalta illusions
and Korean casualty lists, there emerges a reality more
typical and impressive than the not-to-be-minimized
existence of racketeers and thought-controllers; and that
impressive reality is the sobriety, the reasonableness of
America's genuine anti-Communists, whether Eisenhower,
Stevenson or Norman Thomas.

Pro-Communist periodicals in Europe have been linking American anti-Communists and McCarthy, as if there
were some necessary connection. The zany rumor that

McCarthyism is anti-Communism may be spread by honest ignorance, but it may also be spread maliciously: to give anti-Communism a bad name abroad, to make anti-Communism as intellectually disreputable as it seemed during the Popular Front era. But the fact that pro-Communists find it strategic to link the McCarthy methods with American anti-Communism is no reason for our American anti-Communists to do so, or to allow even the hint of such a linkage to continue.

To move to a different but overlapping problem: There is likewise no reason for philosophical conservatives (disciples of Burke, Coleridge, Tocqueville, Irving Babbitt and the Federalists, rather than of President McKinley or Neville Chamberlain) to condone even the hint of any linkage between our philosophical conservatism and that *rigor mortis* of Manchester liberalism known as the Old Guard of the Republican Party.

I now propose to develop the above two generalizations. First, if McCarthyism does not represent anti-Communism, what does it represent? Second, if the present Republican Party does not merit the support of philosophical (Burkean or Federalist) conservatives, then who does merit that support in 1956?

To a certain extent, the new nationalist toughness ("McCarthyism") is the revenge of those who felt snubbed in 1928, when the man with the brown derby lost the election, and who felt snubbed a second time in 1932, when the nomination went to his victorious rival from Groton and Harvard.

But even more important than that old wound (the Irish Catholic role in McCarthyism being intolerantly overstressed by its liberal foes) is the McCarthy-Dirksen-Bricker coalition of nationalism, Asia Firstism and Europe-Last isolationism; and what is this coalition but a Midwest hick-Protestant revenge against that same "fancy" and condescending east? That revenge is sufficiently emotional to unite a radical wing with a reactionary wing. The revenge-emotion of McCarthyism has united the old Midwest Populist instincts on the down-with-everybody Left (barn-burners from way back and distrusters of Anglicized highbrow city-slickers) with the rich Chicago *Tribune* nationalists on the authoritarian Right. Both these Midwest groups are Protestant, not Catholic. Both are against an east viewed as Europe First and Asia Last— shorthand for an east viewed as aristocratic, interna- tionalist, over-educated, and metaphorically (if rarely literally) Grotonian.

By itself and without allies, the resentment of lower- middle-class Celtic South Boston against Harvard (simul- taneous symbol of Reds and Wall Street plutocrats) was relatively powerless. (Note that no serious mass move- ment like McCarthy's was achieved by the earlier out- burst of that resentment in Coughlinism.) It was only when the South Boston resentment coalesced with the resentment of flag-waving Chicago isolationists and newly-rich Protestant Texans (still denied *entrée* into the *chicté* of Wall Street) that the American seaboard aristocracy was seriously threatened in its domination of both governmental and intellectual public opinion and in its domination of its special old-school-tie preserve, the Foreign Service. Against the latter, the old Populist and La Follette weapon against diplomats of "you inter- nationalist Anglophile snob" was replaced by the dead- lier weapon of "you egghead security-risk"—meaning, as the case might be, alleged unbeliever and subverter or alleged homosexual or alleged tippler and babbler. All of these allegations have been made for centuries by pseudo-wholesome, "pious" peasants against "effete" noblemen.

What is at stake in this revolt? Liberty or mere eco- nomic profit? Probably neither. Nobody in any mass movement on any side in any country is really willing to

bear the burden of liberty (which is why liberty is pre-
served not by mass-will nor by counting noses but by
tiny, heroic natural-aristocracies and by the majesty—
beyond mob majorities—of moral law). As for economic
profit, there is enough of *that* lying around in lavish
America to keep both sides happily glutted, in defiance
of both Marx and Adam Smith. Instead, the true goal
of both sides—the McCarthyite rebels and the seaboard
aristocracy—is the psychological satisfaction of determining the future value-pattern of American society.

As a pretext for its drive toward this true goal, the
first side uses "anti-Communism." (Falsely so, because
nothing would please the Communists more than a victory of the Bricker, McCarthy and Chicago *Tribune* side,
thereby isolating America from Western Europe.) As a
counter-pretext, the second side uses "civil liberties."

The latter is not solely a pretext but valid enough at
the moment, now that this side is seeing its own ox being
gored. But ultimately much of its oratory about civil
liberties rings as false as that of self-appointed anti-
Communism, if only you consider the silence of the second
side about "civil liberties" when the gored ox was not
their own pet Foreign Service aristocrats and professors
but the violated civil liberties of thousands of interned
Japanese-Americans during World War II or the Minneapolis Trotskyites jailed under the Smith Act (in both
cases under Roosevelt), not to mention the hair-raising
precedent of currently denying a passport to the anti-
Stalinist Marxist, Max Schachtman. With some honorable
exceptions, the internment of friendless Japanese-Americans, of un-"forward-looking" conscientious objectors and
of presumably un-chic Trotskyites has evoked fewer
decibels of "witch-hunt, witch-hunt!" from fashionable
liberals, fewer sonorous quotations of what Jefferson
wrote to Madison about free minds, than does the current
harassing of a more respectably bourgeois and *salonfähig*

ex-Stalinoid from the Institute of Pacific Relations. Thus does snobbism take precedence over ideology in the conformism known as "anti-conformism."

In every American community, picture some eagle scout of "anti-Communism" battling some village Hampden of "civil liberties." What a spectacle! Insincerity or self-deception on both sides.

Which of the two unattractive alternatives can be sufficiently improved and matured to become not merely a lesser evil but a positive good? Since the noble pretexts of both sides ring so hollow, why do I favor (while retaining an independent third position) a victory by the second of these two sides? Not for its *beaux yeux*—not, that is, for its comic snobbism, its mutually contradictory brands of "progressive" political chic, "*avant-garde*" cultural chic, and Eastern-college, country-club social chic. Even its trump card, namely, the ethical superiority to McCarthyism of its upper-class educated liberals, remains badly compromised by the 1930s—the silence, because of expediency, during the Moscow Trials and the business-baiting McCarthyism-of-the-Left of too many New Deal agitations and investigations. Still, despite everything, the heritage known as "New England" (a moral rather than sectional term and diffused through all sections) does inspiringly combine the two things that mean most to me in determining my choice: respect for the free mind and respect for the moral law.

This combination of moral duty and liberty may by 1956 have a new birth of nationwide appeal, owing to the providential emergence of the leadership of Adlai Stevenson, a blender of New England and Middle West, an intellectual uncompromised by Popular Frontist illusions or by the era of Yalta appeasement.

No "great man" theories, no determinism: Let us take Stevenson merely as symbolizing imperfectly a still potential goal, a new era that may or may not be attained by

his very diverse followers. For intellectuals, he symbolizes
the mature outgrowing and discarding of what in part
was their bad and silly era. A bad era insofar as they
sacrificed ethical means to a progress achieved by Machiavellian social engineering. (Defined metaphysically, the
ethical double standard of many toward Russia was a
logical consequence of the initial false step of seeking a
short-cut to material progress outside the moral framework.) A silly era insofar as they alternated this expediency with the opposite extreme, that of idealistic *a priori*
blueprints and abstractions; these lack the concrete context of any mature, organically evolved idealism. An
oscillation between these extremes was likewise characteristic of the eighteenth-century liberal intellectuals, oscil-
lating between impractical utopian yearnings and an all-
too-practical softness (double standard) toward Jacobin
social engineering.

Here is one extremely small but revealing example of
the new, maturer kind of intellectual leadership: Stevenson did not have his name listed to endorse the *Nation*
magazine (that Last Mohican from the liberal illusions
of the 1930s), even though such routine endorsements in
past years came automatically from the highest liberal
intellectuals and New Dealers. Today, most liberal intellectuals have learned to distinguish between the "liberalism" of certain double-standard *Nation* experts (even
while rightly defending their free speech against Mc-
Carthyism or thought control) and the valid liberalism
of, say, the *New Republic,* the *Progressive,* or the *Reporter.* Five years ago, when I began writing the chapter
about the *Nation* in *Shame and Glory of the Intellectuals,*
that ethical distinction was still unclear to most liberal
intellectuals. How much saner America would be today if
those businessmen who would like to be "conservatives"
had some Republican version of Mr. Stevenson to teach
them the comparable quality of distinguishing between

endorsing genuine anti-Communism and endorsing the
"anti-Communism" of the McCarthys, Jenners and Dirk-
sens!

What businessman today—whether in the New York-
Detroit axis or even in Chicago *Tribune*land—sees anything radical or even liberal about the SEC or insurance
of bank deposits? These and other New Deal cushionings
of capitalism have become so traditional, so built-in a
part of our eastern business communities that their old
feud with the New Deal becomes a fading anachronism,
a feud dangerous only if it still hampers their support of
Eisenhower's "New Deal Republicans" against the isolationist nationalist Republicans.

Though the partly unintentional effect of such New
Deal reforms has been conservative, this does not mean
we can go to the opposite extreme and call the New
Deal as a whole conservative. In contrast with its Communism-preventing social reforms, its *procedures* of agita-
tional direct democracy were occasionally as radical as
the business world alleged them to be, by-passing the
Supreme Court, the Constitution, and the rest of our
indirect democracy. Further, the Popular Front attitude
of expediency toward the sheer evil of Communism,
though it mesmerized New Deal talkers in New York
more than actual New Deal doers in Washington, was as
radical an anti-ethics on the Left as is—on the Right—the
similar anti-ethics of a Popular Front with McCarthyism.

It is the bad and silly aspects of the New Deal, the
procedural and unethical aspects, which have been rightly
outgrown in new leaders like Stevenson, who rightly
retain the valuable humane and conservative aspects.
This refreshing development, by which—unlike its nationalist Republican foes—a fallible movement outgrows its
own errors, is the decisive argument for supporting
Stevenson and the Democrats in the Presidential election
of 1956. The same support was actually earned by them

already in 1952, but less obviously then, owing to the then legitimate hope that Eisenhower could help the Republicans to similarly outgrow their errors.

Despite the magnificent personal intentions of our decent and kindly President, the present Republican Administration—when considered as a whole, Knowland, Nixon and all—has obviously failed to evoke a world-minded, responsible American conservatism. Instead, the Republican leadership has left to others (like the bipartisan Watkins Committee) its own plain duty of restraining its wild men of the Right, whose activity was defined by the ever perceptive Will Herberg (*New Leader*, January 18, 1954) as "government by rabble-rousing, the very opposite of a new conservatism." Such revolutionary agitators would never be tolerated in the more truly conservative party of Eden, Butler and Churchill.

A conservative kind of government would bring the following qualities: a return to established ways, relaxation of tension and calm confidence, reverence for the Constitution and every single one of its time-hallowed amendments and liberties, orderly gradualism, protection of the Executive Branch from outside mob pressure. The conservative kind of government would bring an increased respect—even to the point of pompous stuffiness—for time-honored authority and for venerable dignitaries. Specifically, that would mean an increased respect for such dignitaries as Justices of the Supreme Court, famous generals decorated for heroism or with a Nobel Prize for statesmanship, past Presidents (because of the impersonal dignity of that office and because of the traditionalist's need of historical continuity), and any present President and his top appointments, especially in such a snobbishly aristocratic preserve as the Foreign Service. The above qualities are the stodgier virtues. They are not invariably a good thing, nor is conservatism in every context a good thing. All I am saying is that these happen to be the

qualities of conservative rule, and the Republican Administration has not brought us a single one of them.

The Democrats were voted out of office partly because
the country was fed up (and rightly so) with certain of
the more radical notions and agitations of the New Deal
1930s. Yet, it now appears, by contrast, that those now-
nostalgic "twenty years of treason" gave America a bit
more of old-fashioned conservative virtues than the
present self-styled anti-soap-boxing of Republican soap-
boxers.

Unless one of two unexpected events occurs, the Republican Party has forfeited its claim to retain in 1956
those decisive votes of non-partisan independents which
gave it victory in 1952. The unexpected events are either
a far firmer assertion of presidential leadership over the
anti-Eisenhower barn-burners and wild men in the Senate,
or else their secession into a radical third party. If either
of these blessings occurs, there will again be good reason
for independents to vote for Eisenhower: on moral
grounds if he asserts his leadership, on strategic grounds
if there is a McCarthy third party. The latter would save
the Republicans in the same unexpected way that the
secession of pro-Communists into the Progressive Party
saved Truman in 1948.

If neither of these unlikely blessings occurs for the
Republicans, then the last remaining obstacle has been
cleared away for all thoughtful conservatives and independents, as well as liberals and Democrats, to support
Adlai Stevenson for President in 1956. Though neither
giddy optimism nor personal hero-worship is in order, at
least there is a good chance—in proportion to our own
efforts to make it a good chance—that a Stevenson party,
outgrowing the bad and the silly aspects of the 1930s,
will lead America beyond the two false alternatives of
Babbitt Senior Republicans and Babbitt Junior liberals.
Ahead potentially lies an American synthesis of Mill with

Burke, of liberal free dissent with conservative roots in historical continuity.

Of two American alternatives with bad records, the slanderous wild nationalists and the sometimes double-standard civil-libertarians, only the second alternative is capable of outgrowing a bad and silly past. The 1956 elections can bring it a better and wiser future under the better and wiser intellectualism of Stevenson. Here ends a cycle once partly symbolized by Alger Hiss ("a generation on trial"). Here, symbolized by Adlai Stevenson, begins potentially a new cycle of the glory, not the shame, of the eggheads.

3

In view of America's present mood of prosperous moderation, the McCarthy revolution and all other extremes of right and left will almost certainly lose. All that might rescue them is the emotionalism that would accompany a lost or costly war in China. But, luckily, the stakes are neither that high nor that desperate. America is no Weimar Republic, and McCarthyism tends to be more a racket than a conspiracy, more a cruel publicity hoax (played on Fort Monmouth, the Voice of America, the State Department) than a serious "fascist" or war party. Despite demagogic speeches ("speak loudly and carry a small stick"), the nationalist wing of the Republicans cares no more about really blockading and fighting the Red Chinese despotism than Hamlet's vehement player cared about Hecuba. Our indispensable European allies need not fear that Americans, even our nationalist wild men, will become preventive-warriors or trigger-happy. The struggle to be the new American ruling (taste-determining) class is a domestic struggle, in which foreign policy and Our Boys in China merely furnish heartless slogans to embarrass the older ruling class.

In this struggle, two points emerge about diction: First, "nationalism" is less often a synonym of "national interest" than an antonym; second, no alchemy has yet been invented by which a loud repetition of the word "anti-Communism" transforms a Yahoo into a Houyhnhnm.

That the McCarthy movement normally accuses only non-Communists of "Communism" is one of the main rules of the game. Why? Not because the Communist menace to America has decreased (it has increased since Malenkov), but because McCarthy is not after the scalps of Communists in the first place but after the scalps of all those traditionalists who, like Senators Watkins and Flanders, favor government by law. And the reason why emotional McCarthyism, more by instinct than design, simply *must* be against traditionalists, conservatives and government-by-law is explained by its unadmitted but basic revolutionary nature. It is a radical movement trying to overthrow an old ruling class and replace it from below by a new ruling class.

I use "ruling class" not in the rigid Marxist sense but to mean the determiners of culture patterns, taste patterns, value patterns. For in America classes are fluid, unhereditary, and more psychological than economic. As suggested earlier, our old ruling class includes eastern, educated, mellowed wealth—internationalist and at least superficially liberalized, like the Achesons of Wall Street or the Paul Hoffmans of the easternized fraction of Detroit industrialists. The new would-be rulers include unmellowed plebeian western wealth (Chicago, Texas, much of Detroit) and their enormous, gullible mass-base: the nationalist alliance between the sticks and the slums, between the hick-Protestant mentalities in the west (Populist-Progressive on the Left, Know-Nothing on the Right) and the South Boston mentalities in the east. The latter are, metaphorically, an unexplored underground cata-comb, long smoldering against the airy, oblivious palaces of both portions (liberal and Wall Street) of the eastern upper world.

Nobody except McCarthy personally can bridge this incongruous alliance of sticks and slums, and likewise span both sides of their respective religions. Too many commentators assume that the censured McCarthy, being increasingly discredited, will now be replaced by a smoother operator, by a more reliably Republican type like Nixon. To be sure, an Arrow collar ad like Nixon, eager-eyed, clean-shaven and grinning boyishly while he assesses the precise spot for the stiletto, is socially more acceptable in the station-wagons of all kinds of junior executives on the make. However, even though the Vice President's tamer version of the McCarthy drama would flutter more lorgnettes in respectable suburbia, that gain would be counterbalanced by the loss of the still more numerous South Boston mentalities. The latter would thereupon revert to the Democratic party, from which only a "proletarian," non-Protestant McCarthy, never a bourgeois Rotarian Nixon, can lure them.

A fact insufficiently stressed is that McCarthy himself was originally a member of the Wisconsin "Democrat Party." The otherwise similar Senator Pat McCarran pre-ferred to remain, at least nominally, a Democrat to the end. Here, clearly, is a function of voter-wooing—namely, wooing to Republicanism the slummier part of the thought-control bloc—which only a McCarthy and not even the most "glamorous" Nixon or Dirksen can perform for the wealthy, suburban, Republican anti-civil-liber-tarians. I would, therefore, disagree with Adlai Stevenson when he equates Nixon's appeal with McCarthy's.

No one but McCarthy can combine these incompatibles of Catholic slums and Protestant sticks into one movement, not to mention scooping up *en passant* the scattered lunatic fringes that emerged from anti-anti-Fascist isolationism during World War II. Therefore, it is premature to write McCarthy off as finished. What will indeed destroy him in the long run is the fact that his organizing ability does not keep pace with his publicizing ability, and that the left (New Deal) and right (Wall Street) wings of the old aristocracy can today partly team up whenever they need to protect their common interests. The wealthy Wall Street lawyer Acheson symbolized this team-up under Truman and was hated for it; his aristocratic, old-school-tie, Anglicized mannerisms were a Red flag to the McCarthyite plebeian revolution.

The New Deal and Wall Street battled in the 1930s when their imagined interests seemed irreconcilable. (I say "imagined" and "seemed" because it was hardly a threat to Wall Street when the New Deal reforms immunized workers against that lure of Communism to which French workers succumbed.) But the common Anglophilism of the internationalist, educated eastern seaboard united them (fortunately for the cause of liberty) on the interventionist, anti-Nazi side during World War II. And, by today, the New Deal reforms have become so deeply rooted and traditional a part of the *status quo,* so conservative in a relative (though not absolute) sense, that the new plebeian money from the Midwest can no longer count on a split between social chic (eastern money in New Canaan and Long Island) and progressive chic (clichés of "forward"-looking uplift). Whether under Eisenhower Republicans or Stevenson Democrats, there will be no such split. And, unless there is a lost war, this partial unity between the financial and the liberal wings of aristocracy will fortunately smash the McCarthyite plebeian insurrection of "direct democracy" (government by mass meetings and telegrams).

The partial *rapprochement* between Wall Street and a

now middle-aged New Deal is evidenced by the many
recent books by veteran New Dealers on the advantages
of enlightened "bigness" in business—books, for example,
by David Lilienthal, J. K. Galbraith and Adolf Berle.
These three valuable writers I profoundly admire on most
points, but I disagree on the following rhetorical question:
While fully recognizing the harmful snob-motives of the
medieval feudal mind, was there not, nevertheless, some
sound moral core within its "reactionary" distrust of the
cash-nexus bourgeois?

Are liberal intellectuals, in a mirror-image of their
former Left Bank stance, now suddenly to become joiners,
good sports, success-worshipers, members of The Team?
Will it next be a triumph of their adaptability to suffer in
silence, without the old "holy indignation," the spectacle
of a Republican auto dealer patronizing a great scientist
as if he were his clerk instead of approaching him cap in
hand? In that case, who on earth, if *not* the intellectuals,
will resist the periodic stampedes to entrust American
culture to the manipulators of gadgets? This resistance to
stampedes ought to express not the conformism of "non-
conformism," flaunted to pose as a devil of a fellow, but
the sensitivity of a deeper and finer grain, an ear conforming not to bandwagon-tunes but to the finer, older, deeper
rhythms of American culture.

A few years ago, liberal intellectuals were reproaching
me for refusing to bait Big Business—and today (in
several cases) for refusing to equate it with Santa Claus.
Why do either? Business-baiting was and is a cheap
bohemian flourish, a wearing of one's soulfulness on one's
sleeve, and no substitute for seriously analyzing the real
problem: namely, the compulsion of modern technics
(whether under capitalist bigness or a socialist bigness)
to put know-how before know-why.

When the alternative is the neo-Populist barn-burners
from Wisconsin and Texas, naturally I ardently prefer

Big Business, especially a *noblesse*-obligated and New Dealized Big Business. For its vanity (desire to seem sophisticated) makes a point of allowing a lot more elbow-room to the free mind. But what a choice! All America's great creative spirits of the past, like Melville (who spoke of "the impieties of Progress") and conservative Henry Adams, would turn in their graves, as indignantly as would liberal Abraham Lincoln, at even the hint that no noble third alternative remained for a nation boasting of itself as the freest on earth.

Insofar as they refute the old Stalinist lie about America's imaginary mass poverty and the imaginary prosperity of the Soviet slave kennels, let us welcome the belated liberal conversions to anti-business-baiting. But what when they go to the other extreme of whitewashing almost everything, from the old robber barons to the new "bigness"? What when the paeans to economic prosperity ignore the psychological starvation, the cultural starvation, the mechanized mediocrity of too-efficient bigness? At that point, the value-conserver must protest: Judge our American elephantiasis of know-how not solely in contrast with the unspeakably low values of Soviet Communism but also in contrast with our own high anti-commercial traditions of Hawthorne, Melville and Thoreau, all of whom knew well enough that the railroad rides upon us, not we on the railroad.

Where the Communist police state is the alternative, let us continue to emphasize that American Big Business is an incomparably lesser evil. But beyond that special situation no further concessions, least of all unnecessary ones. Let us frankly embrace as enjoyable conveniences the leisure and services resulting from IBM efficiency. But must the embrace be corybantic? Shall intellectuals positively wallow in abdicating before a bigness which admittedly gives Americans economic prosperity and, at present, a relative political freedom but which robotizes them into a tractable, pap-fed, Reader's-Digested and manipulated mass-culture?

Too utilitarian for a sense of tragic reverence or a sense of humor, and prone (behind "daring" progressive clichés) to an almost infinite smugness, one kind of bourgeois liberal is forever making quite unnecessary sacrifices of principle to expediency—first to the fellow-traveling Popular Front line in the 1930s, now to the opposite line in the 1950s. But there comes a time when lasting values are conserved not by matey back-slapping but by wayward walks in the drizzle, not by seemingly practical adjustments but by the ornery Unadjusted Man.

---

¹ What do we mean by "direct democracy" as contrasted with "indirect democracy"? Let us re-apply to today the conservative thesis of Madison's tenth *Federalist* paper and of Irving Babbitt's *Democracy and Leadership.*

Direct democracy (our mob tradition of Tom Paine, Jacobinism, and the Midwestern Populist parties) is government by referendum and mass petition, such as the McCarthyite Committee of Ten Million.

Indirect democracy (our semi-aristocratic and Constitutionalist tradition of Madison and the *Federalist*) likewise fulfills the will of the people but by *filtering* it through parliamentary Constitutional channels and traditional ethical restraints.

Both are ultimately majority rule, and ought to be. But direct democracy, being immediate and hotheaded, facilitates revolution, demagogy, and Robespierrian thought control, while indirect democracy, being calmed and canalized, facilitates evolution, a statesmanship of *noblesse oblige,* and civil liberties.

5

Social Strains in America

TALCOTT PARSONS

To THE relatively objective observer, whether American or foreign, it seems clear that the complex of phenomena that have come to be known as "McCarthyism" must be symptoms of a process in American society of some deep and general significance. Some interpret it simply as political reaction, even as a kind of neofascism. Some think of it as simply a manifestation of nationalism. The present paper proposes to bring to bear some theoretical perspectives of sociology in an attempt to work out an interpretation which goes beyond catchwords of this order.

McCarthyism can be understood as a relatively acute symptom of the strains which accompany a major change in the situation and structure of American society, a change which in this instance consists in the development of the attitudes and institutional machinery required to implement a greatly enhanced level of national political responsibility. The necessity for this development arises both from our own growth to an enormous potential of power, and from the changed relation to the rest of the world which this growth in itself, and other changes extraneous to American development, have entailed. The strains to which I refer derive primarily from conflicts between the demands imposed by the new situation and the inertia of those elements of our social structure which are most resistant to the necessary changes.

The situation I have in mind centers on the American position in international affairs. The main facts are familiar to all. It is not something that has come about suddenly, but the impact of its pressures has been cumulative.

The starting point is the relative geographical isolation of the United States in the "formative" period of its national history, down to, let us say, about the opening of the present century. The Spanish-American War extended our involvements into the Spanish-speaking areas of the Caribbean and to the Philippines, and the Boxer episode in China and our mediation of the Russo-Japanese War indicated rapidly growing interests in the Orient. Then the First World War brought us in as one of the major belligerents, with a brief possibility of taking a role of world leadership. From this advanced degree of international involvement, however, we recoiled with a violent reaction, repudiating the Treaty of Versailles and the League of Nations.

In the ensuing period of "normalcy," until the shock of Pearl Harbor settled the question, it could still be held that the "quarrels" of foreign powers beyond the Americas were none of our concern, unless some "arbitrary" disturbance impinged too closely on our national interests. By the end of the Second World War, however, this attitude could not again be revived by any body of opinion which pretended to depend upon a realistic appraisal of our situation. Our own strength, in spite of our massive disarmament and demobilization, had grown too great; the defeat of France and the disorganization of Germany destroyed such continental European balance of power as had existed; Britain, though victorious, was greatly weakened in the face of world-wide commitments; and Soviet Russia emerged as a victorious and expanding power, leading with a revolutionary ideology a movement which could readily destroy such elements of stability favorable to our own national values and interests as still remained in the world. Along with all this have come developments in military technology that have drastically neutralized the protections formerly conferred by geographical distance, so that even the elementary military security of the United States cannot now be taken for granted apart from world-wide political order.

The vicissitudes of American foreign policy and its relations to domestic politics over this period show the disturbing effect of this developing situation on our society. We have twice intervened militarily on a grand scale. With a notable difference of degree, we have both times recoiled from the implications of our intervention. In the second case the recoil did not last long, since the beginnings of the Cold War about 1947 made it clear that only American action was able to prevent Soviet domination of the whole continent of Europe. It can, however, be argued that this early and grand-scale resumption of responsibility imposed serious internal strains because it did not allow time for "digesting" the implications of our role in the war.

The outstanding characteristic of the society on which this greatly changed situation has impinged is that it had come to be the industrial society par excellence—partly because the settlement of the continental area coincided with the later industrial revolution, partly because of the immense area and natural resources of the country, but partly too because of certain important differences between American and European society. Since the United States did not have a class structure tightly integrated with a political organization that had developed its main forms before the industrial revolution, the economy has had a freedom to develop and to set the tone for the whole society in a way markedly different from any European country or Japan.

All highly industrialized societies exhibit many features in common which are independent of the particular historical paths by which their developments have taken place. These include the bureaucratic organization of the productive process itself, in the sense that the roles of individuals are of the occupational type and the organizations in which they are grouped are mainly "specific function" organizations. Under this arrangement the peasant type of agricultural holding, where farming is very closely bound up with a kinship unit, is minimized; so too of small family businesses; people tend to look to their productive function and to profit as a measure of success and hence of emancipation from conflicting ties and claims; the rights of property ownership are centered primarily in the organization which carries functional responsibility, and hence permits a high degree of segregation between private life and occupational roles for production purposes; contract plays a central part in the system of exchange, and para-economic elements tend to be reduced in importance.

Outside the sphere which touches the organization of the economy itself, industrialism means above all that the structures which would interfere with the free functioning of the economy, and of their adaptation to it, are minimized. The first of these is family and kinship. The

American family system, chiefly characterized by the isolation of the nuclear or conjugal family, has gone farther
than in any European society toward removing all inter-
ferences with the occupational roles of the breadwinning
members, and with occupational mobility. A second field
is religion. The American combination of federalism and
the separation of church and state has resulted in a
system of "denominational pluralism" which prevents organized religion from constituting a monolithic structure
standing in the way of secular social developments. The
third field concerns the matter of social stratification.
The United States of course has a class structure; but it
is one which has its primary roots in the system of occupational roles, and in contrast to the typical European
situation it acts as no more than a brake on the processes
of social mobility which are most important to an industrial type of occupational system. Under an effective
family system there must be some continuity of class
status from generation to generation, and there cannot
be complete "equality of opportunity." In America, however, it is clearly the occupational system rather than
kinship continuity that prevails.

Linked to this situation is our system of formal education. The United States was among the pioneers in developing publicly supported education; but this has taken
place in a notably decentralized way. Not only is there no
Department of Education in the Federal government,
but even the various state departments are to a large
extent service organizations for the locally controlled
school systems. Higher education further has been considerably more independent of class standards which
equate the "scholar" with the "gentleman" (in a class
sense) than has been the case in Europe. Also a far larger
proportion of each age-group attends institutions of
higher education than in European countries.

Politically the most important fact about American industrialism is that it has developed overwhelmingly under the aegis of free enterprise. Historically the center of gravity of the integration of American society has not rested in the political field. There came to be established a kind of "burden of proof" expectation that responsibilities should not be undertaken by government unless, first, the necessity for their being undertaken at all was clearly established, and second, there was no other obviously adequate way to get the job done. It is therefore not surprising that the opening up of vast new fields of governmental responsibility should meet with considerable resistance and conflict.

The impact of this problem on our orientation to foreign relations has been complicated by an important set of internal circumstances. It is a commonplace that industrialism creates on a large scale two sets of problems which uniformly in all industrialized countries have required modifications of any doctrinaire "laissez-faire" policy: the problems of controlling the processes of the economy itself, and of dealing with certain social repercussions of industrialization.

As the process of industrialization has developed in America there has been a steady increase in the amount of public control imposed on the economy, with the initiative mainly in the hands of the Federal government. This trend was accelerated in the latter years of the nineteenth century, and has continued, with interruptions, through the New Deal. The New Deal, however, was more concerned with the social repercussions of industrialization, rather than with more narrowly economic problems. The introduction of a national system of social security and legislation more favorable to labor are perhaps the most typical developments. This internal process of government intervention has not gone far enough to satisfy European socialists, but it certainly constitutes a great modification of the earlier situation. Moreover, in

broad lines it can be regarded as firmly established. It is
significant that the major political parties now tend to
vie with each other in promoting the extension of social
security benefits, that there is no likelihood of repeal of
the Federal Reserve Act, and that there is no strong
movement to place the unions under really severe legal
restraints.

On the whole, business groups have accepted the new
situation and cooperated to make it work with considerably more good faith than in Continental Europe.
Nevertheless, these internal changes have been sufficiently
recent and far-reaching to keep the strains attendant on
them from being fully resolved. Moreover they have
created an important part of the problems with which
this examination is chiefly concerned, problems touching
the composition of the higher strata of the society, where
the primary burden of responsibility must fall.

By contrast with European countries, perhaps in some
ways particularly Britain, the United States has been
conspicuous for the absence or relative weakness of two
types of elite elements. The first of these is a hereditary
upper class with a status continuous from pre-industrial
times, closely integrated with politics and public service.
The second is an occupational elite whose roots are essentially independent of the business world—in the independent professions, the universities, the church, or government, including civil and military services.

In America the businessmen have tended to be the
natural leaders of the general community. But, both for
the reasons just reviewed and for certain others, this
leadership has not remained undisputed. On the whole
the business community has, step by step, resisted the
processes of internal change necessitated by industrialization rather than taken the leadership in introducing them.
The leadership that has emerged has been miscellaneous
in social origin, including professional politicians, espe-

cially those in touch with the urban political machines, leaders in the labor union movement and elements in close touch with them. An important part has been played by men and women who may be said to exhibit a more or less "aristocratic" tinge, particularly in the Eastern cities, President Roosevelt of course having been among them. An important part has been played by lawyers who have made themselves more independent of the business connection than the typical corporation lawyer of a generation ago. Under the pressure of emergency, there has been a tendency for high military officers to play important roles in public life.

Another important group has been composed of "intellectuals"—again a rather miscellaneous assembly including writers, newspapermen, and members of university faculties. In general the importance of the universities has been steadily enhanced by the increasingly technical character of the operations of the economy; businessmen themselves have had to be more highly educated than their predecessors, and have become increasingly dependent on still more highly trained technicians of various kinds.

The important point is that the "natural" tendency for a relatively unequivocal business leadership of the general community has been frustrated, and the business group has had to give way at many points. Nevertheless, a clearly defined non-business component of the elite has not yet crystallized. In my opinion, the striking feature of the American elite is not what Soviet propaganda contends that it is—the clear-cut dominance by "capitalists" —but rather its fluid and relatively unstructured character. In particular, there is no clear determination of where political leadership, in the sense including both "politics" and "administration," is to center.

A further feature of the structure of American society is intimately related to the residual strains left by recent social changes. There is a continuing tendency for earlier economic developments to leave a "precipitate" of upper groups, the position of whose members is founded in the achievements of their ancestors, in this case relatively recent ones. By historical necessity these groups are strongest in the older parts of the country. Hence the cities of the Eastern seaboard have tended to develop groups that are the closest approach we have—though still very different from their European equivalent—to an aristocracy. They have generally originated in business interests, but have taken on a form somewhat similar to the mercantile aristocracies of some earlier European societies, such as the Hanseatic cities. In the perspective of popular democratic sentiments, these groups have tended to symbolize at the same time capitalistic interests and social snobbery. In certain circumstances they may be identified with "bohemianism" and related phenomena which are sources of uneasiness to traditional morality.

As the American social and economic center has shifted westward, such groups in the great Middle Western area and beyond have been progressively less prominent. There the elites have consisted of new men. In the nature of the case the proportional contribution to the economy and the society in general from the older and the newer parts of the country has shifted, with the newer progressively increasing their share. But at the same time there is the sense among them of having had to fight for this share against the "dominance" of the East. A similar feeling permeates the lower levels of the class structure. A major theme of the populist type of agrarian and other radicalism had combined class and sectional elements, locating the source of people's troubles in the bankers and railway magnates of the East and in Wall Street. It must not be forgotten that the isolationism of the between-the-wars period was intimately connected with this sectional and class sentiment. The elder La Follette, who was one of the principal destroyers of the League of Nations, was not a "conservative" or in any usual sense a reactionary, but a principal leader of the popular revolt against "the interests."

It must also not be forgotten that a large proportion of the American population are descendants of relatively recent immigrants whose cultural origins are different from the dominant Protestant Anglo-Saxon elements. A generation and more ago the bulk of the new immigration constituted an urban proletariat largely dominated by the political machines of the great cities. By now a great change has taken place. The children of these immigrants have been very much Americanized, but to a considerable degree they are still sensitive about their full acceptance. This sensitivity is if anything heightened by the fact that on the whole most of these elements have risen rapidly in the economic and social scale. They are no longer the inhabitants of the scandalous slums; many have climbed to lower middle class status and higher. They have a certain susceptibility to "democratic" appeals which are directed against the alleged snobbery of the older dominant elements.

Finally, the effect of the great depression of the 1930's on the leading business groups must not be forgotten. Such a collapse of the economy could not fail to be felt as a major failure of the expectation that business leaders should bear the major responsibility for the welfare of the economy as a whole and thus of the community. In general it was not the businessmen but the government, under leadership which was broadly antagonistic to business, which came to the rescue. Similarly, the other great class of American proprietors, the farmers, had to accept governmental help of a sort that entailed controls, which in turn inevitably entailed severe conflicts with the individualistic traditions of their history. The fact that the strains of the war and postwar periods have been piled so immediately on those of depression has much to do with the severity of the tensions with which this analysis is concerned.

My thesis, then, is that the strains of the international situation have impinged on a society undergoing important internal changes which have themselves been sources of strain, with the effect of superimposing one kind of strain on another. What responses to this compound strain are to be expected?

It is a generalization well established in social science that neither individuals nor societies can undergo major structural changes without the likelihood of producing a considerable element of "irrational" behavior. There will tend to be conspicuous distortions of the patterns of value and of the normal beliefs about the facts of situations. These distorted beliefs and promptings to irrational action will also tend to be heavily weighted with emotion, to be "overdetermined" as the psychologists say.

The psychology of such reactions is complex, but for present purposes it will suffice to distinguish two main components. On the negative side, there will tend to be high levels of anxiety and aggression, focused on what rightly or wrongly are felt to be the sources of strain and difficulty. On the positive side there will tend to be wishful patterns of belief with a strong "regressive" flavor, whose chief function is to wish away the disturbing situation and establish a situation in phantasy where "everything will be all right," preferably as it was before the disturbing situation came about. Very generally then the psychological formula tends to prescribe a set of beliefs that certain specific, symbolic agencies are responsible for the present state of distress; they have "arbitrarily" upset a satisfactory state of affairs. If only they could be eliminated the trouble would disappear and a satisfactory state restored. The role of this type of mechanism in primitive magic is quite well known.

In a normal process of learning in the individual, or of developmental change in the social system, such irrational phenomena are temporary, and tend to subside as capacity to deal with the new situation grows. This may be more or less easily achieved of course, and resolution of the conflicts and strains may fail to be achieved for a long period or may even be permanently unsuccessful. But under favorable circumstances these reactions are superseded by an increasingly realistic facing of the situation by institutionalized means.

Our present problem therefore centers on the need to mobilize American society to cope with a dangerous and threatening situation which is also intrinsically difficult. It can clearly only be coped with at the governmental level; and hence the problem is in essence a matter of political action, involving both questions of leadership— of who, promoting what policies, shall take the primary responsibility—and of the commitment of the many heterogeneous elements of our population to the national interest.

Consequently there has come to be an enormous increase in pressure to subordinate private interests to the public interest, and this in a society where the presumptions have been more strongly in favor of the private interest than in most. Readiness to make commitments to a collective interest is the focus of what we ordinarily mean by "loyalty." It seems to me that the problem of loyalty at its core is a genuine and realistic one; but attitudes toward it shade all the way from a reasonable concern with getting the necessary degree of loyal cooperation by legitimate appeals, to a grossly irrational set of anxieties about the prevalence of disloyalty, and a readiness to vent the accompanying aggression on innocent scapegoats.

Underlying the concern for loyalty in general, and explaining a good deal of the reaction to it, is the ambivalence of our approach to the situation: The people in the most "exposed" positions are on the one hand pulled by patriotic motives toward fulfillment of the expectations inherent in the new situation; they want to "do their bit." But at the same time their established attitudes and orientations resist fulfillment of the obligation. In the conflict of motives which ensues it is a natural consequence for the resistance to be displaced or projected on to other objects which function as scapegoats. In the present situation it is precisely those parts of our population where individualistic traditions are strongest that are placed under the greatest strain, and that produce the severest resistances to accepting the obligations of our situation. Such resistances, however, conflict with equally strong patriotic motives. In such a situation, when one's own resistance to loyal acceptance of unpalatable obligations, such as paying high taxes, are particularly strong, it is easy to impute disloyal intentions to others.

Our present emotional preoccupation with the problem of loyalty indicates above all that the crisis is not, as some tend to think, primarily concerned with fundamental values, but rather with their implementation. It is true that certain features of the pattern of reaction, such as tendencies to aggressive nationalism and to abdication of responsibilities, would, if carried through, lead to severe conflict with our values. But the main problem is not concerned with doubts about whether the stable political order of a free world is a goal worth sacrificing for, but rather with the question of how our population is rising or failing to rise to the challenge.

The primary symbol that connects the objective external problem and its dangers with the internal strain and its structure is "Communism." "World Communism" and its spread constitute the features of the world situation on which the difficulty of our international problem clearly centers. Internally it is felt that Communists and their "sympathizers" constitute the primary focus of actual or potential disloyalty.

With respect to the external situation, the focus of the difficulty in the current role of Soviet Russia is of course reasonable enough. Problems then arise mainly in connection with certain elements of "obsessiveness" in the way in which the situation is approached, manifested for instance in a tendency to subordinate all other approaches to the situation exclusively to the military, and in the extreme violence of reaction in some circles to the Chinese situation, in contrast to the relative tolerance with which Yugoslavia is regarded.

Internally, the realistic difficulty resides mainly in the fact that there has indeed been a considerable amount of Communist infiltration in the United States, particularly in the 1930's. It is true that the Communist Party itself has never achieved great electoral success, but for a time Communist influence was paramount in a number of important labor unions, and a considerable number of the associations Americans so like to join were revealed to be Communist-front organizations, with effective Communist control behind the public participation of many non-Communists. Perhaps most important was the fact that considerable numbers of the intellectuals became fellow-travelers. In the days of the rise of Nazism and of the popular front, many of them felt that only Soviet Russia was sincere in its commitment to collective security; that there was a Franco-British "plot" to get Germany and Russia embroiled with each other, etc. The shock of the Nazi-Soviet pact woke up many fellow-travelers, but by no means all; and the cause was considerably retrieved by Hitler's attack on Russia.

Two other features of the Communist movement which make it an ideal negative symbol in the context of the present loyalty problem are the combination of conspiratorial methods and foreign control with the progressive component of its ideological system. On the one hand the party has drastically repudiated the procedures of constitutional democracy, and on this issue has broken with all the democratic socialist parties of Europe; it claims the protection of democratic procedures and civil liberties, but does not hesitate to abuse them when this seems to be advantageous. There has further never been any question of the American party determining its own policies by democratic procedures. Perhaps in fact the knowledge of the extent to which the "front" organizations have been manipulated from behind the scenes has been the most disillusioning aspect for liberal Americans of their experience with Communism at home.

At the same time the movement had a large content of professed idealism, which may be taken to account for the appeal of Communism before the Cold War era for such large elements of liberal opinion in the United States, as in other Western countries. Marx was, after all, himself a child of the Enlightenment, and the Communist movement has incorporated in its ideology many of the doctrines of human rights that have formed a part of our general inheritance. However grossly the symbols of democracy, of the rights of men, of peace and brotherhood, have been abused by the Communists, they are powerful symbols in our own tradition, and their appeal is understandable.

Hence the symbol "Communism" is one to which a special order of ambivalence readily attaches. It has powerful sources of appeal to the liberal tradition, but those who are out of sympathy with the main tradition of American liberalism can find a powerful target for their objections in the totalitarian tactics of Communism and can readily stigmatize it as "un-American." Then, by extending their objections to the liberal component of

Communist ideology, they can attack liberalism in general, on the grounds that association with Communist totalitarianism makes anything liberal suspect.

These considerations account for the anti-Communist's readiness to carry over a stereotype from those who have really been party members or advanced fellow-travelers to large elements of the intellectuals, the labor movement, etc., who have been essentially democratic liberals of various shades of opinion. Since by and large the Democratic Party has more of this liberalism than has the Republican, it is not surprising that a tendency to label it as "sympathizing" with or "soft toward" Communism has appeared. Such a label has also been extended, though not very seriously, to the Protestant clergy.

But there is one further extension of the association that is not accounted for in these terms, nor is the failure to include certain plausible targets so accountable. The extension I have in mind is that which leads to the inclusion as "pro-Communist" of certain men or institutions that have been associated with political responsibility in the international field. Two symbols stand out here. The first is Dean Acheson. Mr. Acheson has for years served the Democratic Party. But he has belonged to the conservative, not the New Deal wing of the party. Furthermore, the coupling of General Marshall with him, though only in connection with China, and only by extremists, clearly precludes political radicalism as the primary objection, since Marshall has never in any way been identified with New Deal views. The other case is that of Harvard University as an alleged "hot-bed" of Communism and fellow-traveling. The relevant point is that Mr. Acheson typifies the "aristocrat" in public service; he came of a wealthy family, he went to a select private school (Groton) and to Yale and Harvard Law School. He represents symbolically those Eastern vested interests, against whom antagonism has existed among the new men of the Middle West and the populist movement, including the descendants of recent immigrants. Similarly, among American universities Harvard has been particularly identified as educating a social elite, the members of which are thought of as "just the type," in their striped trousers and morning coats, to sell out the country to the social snobs of European capitals. It is the combination of aristocratic associations—through the Boston Brahmins—and a kind of urban-bohemian sophistication along with its devotion to intellectual and cultural values, including precisely its high intellectual standards, which makes Harvard a vulnerable symbol in this context.

The symbol "Communism," then, from its area of legitimate application, tends to be generalized to include groups in the population who have been associated with political liberalism of many shades and with intellectual values in general and to include the Eastern upper-class groups who have tended to be relatively internationalist in their outlook.

A second underlying ambivalent attitude-structure is discernible in addition to that concerning the relation between the totalitarian and the progressive aspects of Communism. On the one hand, Communism very obviously symbolizes what is anathema to the individualistic tradition of a business economy—the feared attempt to destroy private enterprise and with it the great tradition of individual freedom. But on the other hand, in order to rise to the challenge of the current political situation, it is necessary for the older balance between a free economy and the power of government to be considerably shifted in favor of the latter. We must have a stronger government than we have traditionally been accustomed to, and we must come to trust it more fully. It has had in recent times to assume very substantial regulatory functions in relation to the economy, and now vastly enhanced responsibilities in relation to international affairs.

But, on the basis of a philosophy which, in a very different way from our individualistic tradition, gives primacy to "economic interests," namely the Marxist philosophy, the Communist movement asserts the unqualified, the totalitarian supremacy of government over the economy. It is precisely an actual change in our own system in what in one sense is clearly this direction that emerges as the primary focus of the frustrations to which the older American system has been subjected. The leaders of the economy, the businessmen, have been forced to accept far more "interference" from government with what they have considered "their affairs" than they have liked. And now they must, like everyone else, pay unprecedentedly high taxes to support an enormous military establishment, and give the government in other respects unprecedentedly great powers over the population. The result of this situation is an ambivalence of attitude that on the one hand demands a stringent display of loyalty going to lengths far beyond our tradition of individual liberty, and on the other hand is ready to blame elements which by ordinary logic have little or nothing to do with Communism, for working in league with the Communist movement to create this horrible situation.

Generally speaking, the indefensible aspect of this tendency in a realistic assessment appears in a readiness to question the loyalty of all those who have assumed responsibility for leadership in meeting the exigencies of the new situation. These include many who have helped to solve the internal problems of the control of the economy, those who in the uneasy later 'thirties and the first phase of the war tried to get American policy and public opinion to face the dangers of the international situation, and those who since the war have tried to take responsibility in relation to the difficult postwar situation. Roughly, these are the presumptively disloyal elements who are also presumptively tainted with Communism. Here again, admittedly, certain features of our historical record and attitudes provide some realistic basis for this tendency. In fact many elements in both parties have failed lamentably to assess correctly the dangers of the situation, both internally and externally. New Dealers have stigmatized even the most responsible elements of the business world as economic royalists and the like, while many elements in business have clung long past a reasonable time to an outmoded belief in the possibility of a society with only a "night watchman" government. In foreign affairs, some members of the Democratic Party have been slow to learn how formidable a danger was presented by totalitarian Communism, but this is matched by the utopianism of many Republicans about the consequences of American withdrawal from international responsibilities, through high tariffs as well as political isolationism. The necessity to learn the hard realities of a complex world and the difficulty of the process is not a task to be imposed on only part of the body politic. No party or group can claim a monopoly either of patriotic motive or of competent understanding of affairs.

In a double sense, then, Communism symbolizes "the intruder." Externally the world Communist movement is the obvious source of the most serious difficulties we have to face. On the other hand, although Communism has constituted to some degree a realistic internal danger, it has above all come to symbolize those factors that have disturbed the beneficent natural state of an American society which allegedly and in phantasy existed before the urgent problems of control of the economy and greatly enhanced responsibility in international affairs had to be tackled.

Against this background it can perhaps be made clear why the description of McCarthyism as simply a political reactionary movement is inadequate. In the first place, it is clearly not simply a cloak for the "vested interests" but rather a movement that profoundly splits the previously dominant groups. This is evident in the split, particularly conspicuous since about 1952, within the Republican Party. An important part of the business elite, especially in the Middle West and in Texas, the "newest" area of all, have tended in varying degrees to be attracted by the McCarthy appeal. But other important groups, notably in the East, have shied away from it and apparently have come to be more and more consolidated against it. Very broadly, these can be identified with the business element among the Eisenhower Republicans.

But at the same time the McCarthy following is by no means confined to the vested-interest groups. There has been an important popular following of very miscellaneous composition. It has comprised an important part of those who aspire to full status in the American system but have, realistically or not, felt discriminated against in various ways, especially the Mid-Western lower and lower middle classes and much of the population of recent immigrant origin. The elements of continuity between Western agrarian populism and McCarthyism are not by any means purely fortuitous. At the levels of both leadership and popular following, the division of American political opinion over this issue *cuts clean across the traditional lines of distinction between "conservatives" and "progressives,"* especially where that tends to be defined, as it so often is, in terms of the capitalistic or moneyed interests as against those who seek to bring them under more stringent control. McCarthyism is *both* a movement supported by certain vested-interest elements *and* a popular revolt against the upper classes.

Another striking characteristic of McCarthyism is that it is highly selective in the liberal causes it attacks. Apart from the issue of Communism in the labor unions, now largely solved, there has been no concerted attack on the

general position of the labor movement. Further, the
social program aimed toward the reduction of racial
discrimination has continued to be pressed, to which fact
the decision of the Supreme Court outlawing segregation
in public education and its calm reception provide dramatic evidence. Nevertheless, so far as I am aware there has
been no outcry from McCarthyite quarters to the effect
that this decision is further evidence of Communist influence in high circles—in spite of the fact that eight out of
nine members of the present court were appointed by
Roosevelt and Truman.

Perhaps even more notable is the fact that, unlike the
1930's, when Father Coughlin and others were preaching
a vicious anti-Semitism, anti-Semitism as a public issue
has since the war been very nearly absent from the
American scene. This is of course associated with full
employment. But particularly in view of the rather large
and conspicuous participation of Jewish intellectuals in
the fellow-traveling of the 1930's, it is notable that Jewish-
ness has not been singled out as a symbolic focus for the
questioning of loyalty. A critical difference from German
Nazism is evident here. To the Nazis the Jew was the
primary negative symbol, the Communist the most prominent secondary one. But it must also be remembered that
capitalism was symbolically involved. One of the functions
of the Jew was to *link* Communism and capitalism together. This trio were the "intruders" to the Nazis. They
symbolized different aspects of the disturbance created
by the rapid development of industrialism to the older
pre-industrial *Gemeinschaft* of German political roman-
ticism. It was the obverse of the American case—a new
economy destroying an old political system, not new
political responsibilities interfering with the accustomed
ways of economic life.

Negatively, then, the use of the symbol "Communism"
as the focus of anxiety and aggression is associated with

a high order of selectivity among possibly vulnerable targets. This selectivity is, I submit, consistent with the hypothesis that the focus of the strain expressed by McCarthyism lies in the area of political responsibility—not, as Marxists would hold, in the structure of the economy as such, nor in the class structure in any simple, Marxian-tinged sense.

The same interpretation is confirmed by the evidence on the positive side. The broadest formula for what the McCarthyites positively "want"—besides the elimination of all Communist influence, real or alleged—is perhaps "isolationism." The dominant note is, I think, the regressive one. It is the wishful preservation of an old order, which allegedly need never have been disturbed but for the wilful interference of malevolent elements, Communists and their sympathizers. The nationalistic overtones center on a phantasy of a happy "American way" where everything used to be all right. Naturally it is tinged with the ideology of traditional laissez-faire, but not perhaps unduly so. Also it tends to spill over into a kind of irritated activism. On the one hand we want to keep out of trouble; but on the other hand, having identified an enemy, we want to smash him forthwith. The connection between the two can be seen, for example, in relation to China, where the phantasy seems to be that by drastic action it would be possible to "clean up" the Chinese situation quickly and then our troubles would be over.

The main contention of these pages has been that McCarthyism is best understood as a symptom of the strains attendant on a deep-seated process of change in our society, rather than as a "movement" presenting a policy or set of values for the American people to act on. Its content is overwhelmingly negative, not positive. It advocates "getting rid" of undesirable influences, and has amazingly little to say about what should be done.

This negativism is primarily the expression of fear, secondarily of anger, the aggression which is a product of frustration. The solution, which is both realistically feasible and within the great American tradition, is to regain our national self-confidence and to take active steps to cope with the situation with which we are faced.

On the popular level the crisis is primarily a crisis of confidence. We are baffled and anxious, and tend to seek relief in hunting scapegoats. We must improve our understanding and come to realize our strength and trust in it. But this cannot be done simply by wishing it to be done. I have consistently argued that the changed situation in which we are placed demands a far-reaching change in the structure of our society. It demands policies, and confidence, but it demands more than these. It demands above all three things. The first is a revision of our conception of citizenship to encourage the ordinary man to accept greater responsibility. The second is the development of the necessary implementing machinery. Third is national political leadership, not only in the sense of individual candidates for office or appointment, but in the sense of social strata where a traditional political responsibility is ingrained.

The most important of these requirements is the third. Under American conditions, a politically leading stratum must be made up of a combination of business and non-business elements. The role of the economy in American society and of the business element in it is such that political leadership without prominent business participation is doomed to ineffectiveness and to the perpetuation of dangerous internal conflict. It is not possible to lead the American people *against* the leaders of the business world. But at the same time, so varied now are the national elements which make a legitimate claim to be represented, the business element cannot monopolize or dominate political leadership and responsibility. Broadly, I think, a political elite in the two main aspects of "politicians" whose specialties consist in the management of public opinion, and of "administrators" in both civil and military services, must be greatly strengthened. It is here that the practical consequences of McCarthyism run most directly counter to the realistic needs of the time. But along with such a specifically political elite there must also be close alliance with other, predominantly "cultural" elements, notably perhaps in the universities, but also in the churches.

In the final sense, then, the solution of the problem of McCarthyism lies in the successful accomplishment of the social changes to which we are called by our position in the world and by our own domestic requirements. We have already made notable progress toward this objective; the current flare-up of stress in the form of McCarthyism can be taken simply as evidence that the process is not complete.

6

The Polls on Communism

and Conformity[1]

NATHAN GLAZER AND
SEYMOUR MARTIN LIPSET

TEN OR twenty years ago, no one could have predicted that the defense of civil liberties would become the complicated matter it became in the Fifties. A generation raised on campaigns for the defense of the civil liberties of socialists, pacifists, anarchists, and an outspoken or queer teacher here or there, found the problem simple. It could even extend its protection to the odd teacher or crackpot who supported the Nazis and the Fascists; there were too few of them to matter. But now the matter is more complicated. The Communist Party, however few actual party members there may have been at any given time, did have a far greater influence over American intellectual and cultural life, and in American government too, than anything that can be legitimately called Nazism or Fascism. And there is no question, too, that the American people—however defined —feel more intensely about Communists than they felt about Nazism and Fascism. This attitude was stiffened by the disclosures of past Communist influence, particularly the espionage roles of some hidden units in government, by the rising chill of the cold war, and by the aggression of the Communists in Korea. Security became a natural issue—almost a national *idée fixe*—at least on the official levels of opinion and government. So, the last ten years have seen the creation of a whole system of law, administrative regulations, regulative bodies, and private agencies devoted, at one extreme, to putting Communists in jail, and at the other, to simply making life miserable for people who might have been or might be Communists.

In the resulting hullaballoo and confusion, many people have been properly concerned over the erosion or abrogation of civil liberties—of Communists and non-Communists; other people have been properly concerned over the extent of the threat of Communism, and whether these measures form a really effective defense against the Communist movement. But how concerned were the American people about Communism? And who among them manifested these concerns, and to what extent? How far would Americans go in supporting restrictions on Communists and who among the people would go farthest? How much support could Senator McCarthy mobilize for his charges? The book which was published under the sponsorship of the Fund for the Republic—*Communism, Conformity, and Civil Liberties* by Samuel A. Stouffer of Harvard—is intended as an answer to some of these questions. It is, we should understand, a limited contribution and deals with only one part of the problem. It is a survey of opinions. From any survey of opinions we find out what people *think*. In this book we find out what the

American people think about allowing advocates of public ownership of industry, opponents of religion, suspected Communists, and admitted Communists, to speak, publish, teach, hold government jobs, and so on. To a much smaller and less adequate extent, we find out how serious they consider the danger posed by domestic Communists to be.

But this means (and perhaps this labors the obvious), that we will not find out whether, *in fact,* the civil liberties of advocates of public ownership, atheists and Communists have been infringed, whether they should be limited, how the present situation in this respect compares with the past, and whether it is likely to deteriorate or improve in the future.

Nor does this, as a study of opinions, concern itself with other realities—that socialists and atheists and even Communists regularly publish newspapers, and make speeches, and that, despite the "will of the American people" as reflected in opinion polls, persons in the first two categories teach and work for the government and for colleges and even school boards without major disturbances; in short, that liberty is not to be measured, or not solely, by the opinions of a random sample, the vast majority of whom have never thought about or considered the questions with which they are confronted; and that legislatures and courts and constitutions and the customary practices of our institutions are surer defenses of liberty than the off-the-cuff feelings of the man on the street. It seems, indeed, that it is almost in an absent-minded or abstracted way that the average American will propose very drastic measures for Communists. Most people just don't seem to be terribly concerned with domestic Communism—or any political issue. Almost half the population, 44 per cent, report that they hardly ever follow news about Communists. When asked, "Do you happen to know the names of any Senators and Congressmen who have been taking

a leading part in these investigations of Communism?"
30 per cent of the national cross-section "could not come
up with a single correct name—not even the name of
Senator McCarthy!" It is clear from other data in the
study, that this non-interested group overlaps considerably
with those Americans who do not vote and are uninter-
ested in politics in general. This group with presumably
little or no weight in the body politic is actually much
more anti-civil libertarian than those persons who are
interested in the Communist problem, or in politics generally. Yet, whether people think about Communism,
which people think about it, and, of that group, what
they think ought to be done about it, is itself one of the
most important facts in the situation. If public opinion
is indifferent or enlightened, then government leaders
may safely take whatever measures they think the extent
of the Communist threat requires. If public opinion is
violently anti-Communist and badly informed, then legis-
lators and officials may have to take measures which they
feel are unwise, or the braver ones may have to undertake
the difficult job of educating public opinion. So, despite
the necessary limitations of the techniques used, much of
value can be uncovered by a survey of what people think.

Let us turn now to the study. Two organizations—Gallup's American Institute of Public Opinion and the National Opinion Research Center—conducted independent
interviewing, using the same questionnaire, and drawing
samples of roughly the same size—2,400 persons in each
sample—so that they could check their results against each
other. In most cases, the differences were minor, so we
can accept these results as reliable. In addition to this
national sample of 4,800 cases, a second sample of community leaders was interviewed by the two organizations.
In a random sample of over 100 cities of more than
10,000 and fewer than 150,000 people, fourteen leaders—
political leaders, business and civic leaders, labor leaders,

and heads of major voluntary organizations—were interviewed, being given the same questionnaire that was administered to the national sample. Thus, some 1,500 community leaders were interviewed and it became possible to compare people of position and substance in the middle-sized cities of the country with the rest of the people of those towns, and with the country as a whole.

Generally speaking, we find that a large proportion of the American people are intolerant on a variety of issues. Only 37 per cent of the general sample answered affirmatively the question: "If a person wanted to make a speech in your community against churches and religion, should he be allowed to speak or not?" Even more startling, only 12 per cent of the population would allow "such a person . . . to teach," while three-fifths would favor removing a book attacking churches and religion from public libraries.[2]

While critics of religion are in an especially vulnerable position, many Americans would also deny traditional rights to those who, while *not* Communists, favored the nationalization of industry. Fewer than three-fifths of Americans answered yes to the question: "If a person wanted to make a speech in your community favoring government ownership of all the railroads and big industries, should he be allowed to speak or not?" Only a slim majority, 52 per cent, would retain a book favoring government ownership in the public library. Only one-third would permit an advocate of government ownership "to teach in a college or university."

As might be expected, the freedoms of Communist advocates find short shrift with the American public. Only 27 per cent would allow an admitted Communist to make a speech. Nine-tenths of the population would not allow him to teach in a high school or university. Two-thirds would remove a book by a Communist from the public library. Approximately two-thirds would not allow a Communist to work as a clerk in a store or be a radio singer. Over 75 per cent would take away his citizenship. Slightly over half, 51 per cent, would put an admitted Communist in jail. So concerned are Americans with suppressing Communism, that almost three-fifths of the people thought it more important "to find out all the Communists even if some innocent people should be hurt," while less than a third chose the alternate statement that it was more important "to protect the rights of innocent people even if some Communists are not found out." (If it is any consolation, the "level of tolerance"—if we measure it by what people say—has never been assuringly high. ". . . even in 1943, after the battle of Stalingrad, two out of five Americans would have prohibited any Communist party member from speaking on the radio. By 1948 this proportion was up to 57 per cent; by 1952 it had risen to 77 per cent; and in . . . January, 1954 the figure was 81 per cent. . . . An NORC survey before the war found 25 per cent who would deny socialists the right to publish newspapers; by 1953 [this figure had risen to] 45 per cent.")

The finding that the majority of Americans tend to be politically intolerant is checked by the converse report of a larger proportion who felt that many civil liberties were being denied. Only 56 per cent agreed with the statement that "all people in this country feel as free to say what they think as they used to"; 31 per cent believed that some people do not feel as free as before, and 10 per cent stated that "hardly anyone feels as free to say what he thinks as he used to."

When asked about themselves personally, 13 per cent of the sample replied that they felt *less* free to speak their mind than in years before. One can interpret these findings in two ways: *only* 13 per cent felt less free than before, or *as many as* 13 per cent of the American people now feel less free. Our inclination is to choose the latter interpretation, for in any society few people ever want to speak their mind on a political subject and, if 13 per cent of the adult population, presumably 13,000,000 Americans, feel inhibited to speak out politically, this is a serious situation. (Unfortunately, Professor Stouffer does not tell us who this 13 per cent may be.)

Rather than deal with these very many questions on many specific issues, however, Dr. Stouffer combines fifteen questions to form a "scale of tolerance," and then examines the distribution of tolerance in the population.[3] In effect he maps out those elements in the population which are strongest in their feeling for liberty, and those which are most indifferent, or most actively opposed to it for certain groups.

If we arbitrarily take a cut-off point in the scale of tolerance, and call those achieving this score the "more tolerant" we find that:

31 per cent of the national sample are "more tolerant."

39 per cent of the people who live in metropolitan areas are "more tolerant."

46 per cent of the people who live in the West are "more tolerant."

47 per cent of those aged 21-29 are "more tolerant."

66 per cent of college graduates are "more tolerant."

The concentrations of the "less tolerant" are to be found among the old, the poorly educated, Southerners, small-town dwellers and workers and farmers. Of course, all these factors—and some others of lesser weight in determining tolerance—may be interrelated. The young tend to be better educated than the old, the people who live in big cities tend to be better educated than those in small towns, a higher proportion of Westerners than of Southerners live in big cities, etc.

What is it then that makes a man more tolerant, when two or more of these factors come together, as they often do? One wishes that the author had done more to determine which of these factors was more important, but, even without this help, it seems that education is by far the most important. Two indications of its importance extracted from the data are these: if one takes all those between the ages of 21 and 60 and who are high-school graduates or of lesser education—and this forms a huge block of the population—one finds that age seems to have *no* effect on tolerance while *amount of education is decisive*. Thus, in this group, roughly 20 per cent of those with only grade school education, about 30 per cent of those with some high school education and close to 45 per cent of high school graduates are "more tolerant"— regardless of the ages in these educational categories.

Another case: the South is far less tolerant than the other regions of the country; thus, only 16 per cent of the South is rated "more tolerant" as against 31 per cent of the Midwest, 39 per cent of the East, and 46 per cent of the West. But these very large differences are reduced to very small ones if one compares *educated* Southerners with educated people from other regions. Of college graduates in metropolitan areas, 62 per cent of Southerners are among the "more tolerant," compared (for the same category) with 64 per cent of the Middle West, 78 per cent of the East, and 73 per cent of the West. Pretty much the same story is told when we compare those with "some college." It is only when we get to those with a high school education or less that we find the great gap between the South and the rest of the country.

Education is perhaps most closely related to what is generally called "socio-economic status" or class, and which in many public opinion studies appears in the form of occupation. There is, however, considerable evidence to suggest that among men at the same educational level, occupational variation does make for a difference in their political attitudes.[4] Unfortunately, and most surprisingly, there is little data reported directly on this point, with the exception of one table and chart which indicate that farmers are the least tolerant group, followed in order of increasing tolerance by manual workers, clerical and sales people, proprietors, managers and officials, and as the most tolerant group, professionals and semi-professionals.

These findings on education and occupation prepare us for a major conclusion of the study, namely that, by contrast with the opinions of the American people as a whole, the community leaders stand forth as bulwarks of civil liberties. Almost 85 per cent of the community leaders, as against only 58 per cent of the population as a whole, would allow an individual who favored nationalization of industries to speak. (Seventy-six per cent of American Legion post commanders and 75 per cent of D.A.R. regents would also allow him to speak.) A heavy majority of the national cross-section (60 per cent) would not allow a man to make a speech against church and religion, while only a third of the community leaders would take the same position. Slightly over half (51 per cent) of the national cross-section said an admitted Communist should be jailed, while only 27 per cent of the community leaders held the same position. (The fact that commanders of American Legion posts and regents of the Daughters of the American Revolution are far more liberal than the American people in general is a surprise. But this may be a reflection less of a concern for civil liberties by the Legion and D.A.R. than the fact that the American people in general are indifferent to the ordinary requirements of democracy.)

These community leaders are drawn from the well-educated, professional and upper-level business classes.[5] The majority of the following categories of community leaders, according to Stouffer, are in the more tolerant group: mayors (60 per cent), presidents of school boards (62 per cent), presidents of library boards (79 per cent), chairmen of Republican county central committees (70

per cent), chairmen of the equivalent Democratic committees (64 per cent), presidents of chambers of commerce (65 per cent), presidents of labor unions (62 per
cent), chairmen of Community Chests (82 per cent),
presidents of bar associations (77 per cent), newspaper
publishers (84 per cent), presidents of Parent-Teacher
Associations (68 per cent).

In only three groups of community leaders did the proportion in the "more tolerant" group fall below 50 per
cent: Commanders of the American Legion, regents of
the Daughters of the American Revolution, and presidents
of women's clubs. These leaders, however, who fell in
the range of 46 to 49 per cent, were about as tolerant as
the lower strata of the non-manual sector of the population, or high school graduates. Since one would guess
that the bulk of the leaders in these three categories have
higher educational and status backgrounds than these,
this finding would suggest that these three groups tend
to recruit the less tolerant individuals among people in
their class position.

There can be little doubt that in the United States the
rights of dissidents and of Communists are protected primarily by the powerful classes who accept the traditional
norms under which a democratic system operates. This
seems to be true in other countries as well, that is, the
upper and better educated strata are more likely to be
tolerant of dissent, and to recognize the need for civil
liberties than the workers, the farmers, and the less educated. The question may be raised as to why, if similar
forces are operating here as elsewhere, the United States
is more extreme in its reactions than other democratic
countries. This problem was outside the focus of Professor
Stouffer's study. Some reasons are suggested in the chapter that follows.

Having mapped out the areas of tolerance and intolerance, we come to the really difficult questions that must

precede any sort of deeper understanding. What does it mean to say, for example, that the less educated, the people in rural areas, the Southerners, and the old people are less tolerant? If we were to educate the uneducated, and encourage migration from rural areas to cities, and from the South to the North, does it mean that the level of tolerance in this country would be raised and our problems solved? At times Dr. Stouffer writes almost as if they would be, but this would be to take an extremely limited view. Clearly there are two problems. The first might legitimately be called that of intolerance—the meanness and narrowness that are the natural consequences, at least in America, of isolation, poverty, "lack of advantages," and old age. The intolerant are as likely to keep a socialist from opening his mouth as to throw a Communist into jail. Communism as a peculiar problem does not affect this kind of person—his intolerance predates it and will outlive it. This is, in effect, a social problem. The Communists and their actions are occasions for the expression of this intolerance rather than its own true cause. Dr. Stouffer is right in linking this kind of intolerance to Communism with intolerance of unorthodoxy in the fields of economics and religion. About this aspect of the problem, Dr. Stouffer tells a fairly complete story.

But second, there is the fact that the level of political tolerance and intolerance changes from one period to another. For example, data reported in the Stouffer study indicate that the proportion of the population who would have denied various freedoms to Communists, socialists, or other deviants from conventional national values, was somewhat lower during the 1930s and World War II. Obviously the increase in intolerance is not a result of the fact that there now are more poorly educated people, or that the farm population has increased. The reverse is, of course, true. The important factor which has affected the degree of tolerance is the political problem of Communism and how to deal with it, which is intimately related to the state of civil liberties. But this question is more dependent on changes in international affairs and domestic American politics than on the raising of the educational level.

Basically, there is a failure to distinguish between what we may call the *intolerant*—those who will say "Kill the Communists" as easily as they will say "Jail the sex deviants" and "Fire a teacher who is a freethinker"—and the *concerned*—those who are sincerely worried about Communism, and think strong measures are necessary to deal with it. These two very different forms of what might be called intolerance are never distinguished in the analysis. The majority rules in public opinion research as in voting; and if the majority of the intolerant are poorly educated, come from backward areas, are old—why, then, that characterizes all the "intolerant."

These are admittedly subtle distinctions for a public opinion poll—not that they could not be made if one were aware of their importance. We think that they are crucial for an understanding of the whole problem of Communism, conformism, and civil liberties which Dr. Stouffer has taken up. If one does not make these distinctions, one can easily, by a process of damnation by association, dismiss important political problems which deserve to be discussed on their own merits, and not dismissed on the basis of who holds them. One cannot dispose of the question of what measures are necessary to deal with Communism by demonstrating that the poor and ignorant predominate among those who want to get tough with Communists, and that the well educated, the middle classes, and the community leaders tend to favor unlimited civil liberties.

This confusion between important categories becomes apparent in the construction of the scale of tolerance itself. The scale studies a single variable—tolerance. It assumes that the attitudes and motivation affecting a person who would deny certain civil liberties to Communists, but grant them to atheists and socialists, are of the same order—only different in degree—from the attitudes and motivations that would lead a person to deny civil liberties to all three categories. Mathematically, it appears that Dr. Stouffer is justified in his procedure— the theory of scales asserts that when there is a certain pattern in the answers to a series of questions, then all the questions are measuring a single variable. But one must then say that while the scale is mathematically rational it is not politically rational. Regardless of what mathematics tells us, we *know* from our experience of politics that a person's attitude toward the question of rights for Communists may involve completely different considerations from those affecting his attitude toward rights for atheists and socialists.

The difficulties inherent in operating with a simple dichotomy of the tolerant and intolerant emerge most strikingly when Dr. Stouffer directly takes up the problem of considering just what is the relationship between concern with Communism and tolerance. As the reader will recall, a measure of tolerance was derived from a series of questions about advocates of government ownership of industry, opponents of religion, and accused and actual Communists. A new factor is now introduced—that of "perception of the internal Communist threat." This is measured by a scale which includes such questions as "Do you think there are any Communists teaching in American public schools (or working in American defense plants, etc.?") followed by the question, "How much danger is there that these Communists can hurt the country. . . ." The author considers the relationships between the perception of the internal Communist threat and tolerance of great importance, on the ground that, if there is a positive relationship we might expect an increase in tolerance if the internal Communist threat is perceived as falling; while a negative relationship—that is, the fact that people could be intolerant even though they perceived the internal Communist threat was unimportant—would suggest the need for "a long-sustained program of public education" to increase tolerance. It turns out that there is a positive relationship. And on this basis, the author concludes, "The relationship is high enough and consistent enough to suggest that *if* the internal Communist threat is now exaggerated, and *if* the American people were told this and believed it, tolerance of non-conformists would increase."

Now something important has gone wrong in this demonstration. Dr. Stouffer has so set up his problem that any lover of tolerance should logically desire the perception of the Communist danger to be low—for low perception, his figures show us, is related to high tolerance. This means, consequently, that if we desire tolerance, we should want people to believe what may be a falsehood (that is, the non-existence of a Communist threat in America); for this would make them more tolerant.

Now this is not the first time that the values of tolerance and truth have been in apparent opposition. If we want people to be more tolerant to Negroes, it is possibly best that they should not believe that there are more Negro than white criminals, dope addicts, paupers, and so on— even though the facts are that there are more Negro criminals, paupers, and dope addicts. However, as Paul Kecskemeti argued in *Commentary* (March 1951) in his review of *The Authoritarian Personality*, there is something mechanical and ultimately false about this procedure of saying that everything associated with a good is itself a good. Dr. Kecskemeti pointed out that if anti-Semitism is associated with hostility to Soviet Russia, and lack of anti-Semitism with friendliness to Soviet Russia, it does not follow that we have to encourage

friendliness toward the Soviet Union to encourage friend-
ship for the Jews. These relations are, if not fortuitous,
then certainly historical, products of given moments,
given combinations of events. These relations may change.
It then becomes incumbent on us to decide, from the
point of view of our own values and our own conception
of the world, what is good and what is true, and try to
achieve that directly, rather than to mechanically follow
the pattern of accepting whatever cluster of attitudes fall
together at any given moment as organically and necessarily related.

In the present situation, it would follow that if we
believe it is true that native Communists exist and have
played a considerable role in American government,
society, and culture, and still play some role, then we
need not resign ourselves to having these truths forgotten
or actively denied, simply because that denial is related
to tolerance.

As a matter of fact, of course, there are many people,
even in Dr. Stouffer's sample, who take the sensible attitude of being aware of the extent of Communist activity
in this country, without being intolerant (just as there are
others who rate low in perception of the internal Communist threat and are intolerant). Perhaps it is just those leadership groups—the educated, and those in professional
occupations—who in general turn out to be the main
supporters of tolerance who both perceive the Communist danger and yet are tolerant. Dr. Stouffer, however, is so interested in following the majority, that large
group which has a high perception of the Communist
danger and are intolerant, that he gives little consideration to these perhaps crucial minority groups. We find
out little about them—who they are, where they live,
and how their numbers might be increased. Dr. Stouffer
operates with one major value—tolerance. Everything else
is secondary. And what is associated with intolerance

(statistically speaking) should wither away and die, if we are to have a good society. Recall his conclusion: "If the internal Communist threat is now exaggerated, and if the American people were told this and believed it, tolerance of non-conformists would increase."

It would seem crucial to determine whether the internal Communist threat is exaggerated or not: if it is, there is no conflict between the values of truth and tolerance. If it is not, then there is a conflict, for Dr. Stouffer seems to take it for granted that the sensible position of being aware of the threat and yet upholding tolerance cannot be expected to grow. But on this crucial *if,* Dr. Stouffer does not commit himself. Dr. Stouffer, it seems, would like to take the position that the threat is exaggerated but, hampered by a crippling notion of scientific objectivity, never quite decides to take the leap. He seems to have fallen a victim of that canon of contemporary scientific research which defines the universe of any study by the methods used in that study. Because there is no way of deciding the extent of the Communist threat with the methods of public opinion research, Dr. Stouffer finds it impossible to take a stand on this question. And yet, if social science is to make a contribution to a problem it must try to encompass it in all its reality—and not limit itself to that part of it which falls within the purview of a given method.

To return then to our distinction between the intolerant and the concerned—between those who want to throw the Communists into jail just as they want to throw anyone with whom they disagree into jail, and those who are aware of the existence of a Communist problem, and diverge in their views as to what measures are necessary to deal with it. Dr. Stouffer has told us the story about the first group, which must indeed always concern us, and in doing so he has made a contribution to sociology. The second group, however, is for the most part lost in his sample, and its crucial characteristics cannot be easily discerned. It is this group which is most important politically. Their tolerance (or intolerance) is different from that of the less educated majority; their perception of the internal Communist threat (or lack of it) is also different. It is possible to be tolerant out of complete indifference to political developments and abysmal ignorance. It is also possible to be tolerant out of a commitment to democracy. It is possible to be intolerant out of a sadistic and brutal attitude to other people. It is also possible to be intolerant out of love of one's country and a rational and strong belief that it is so seriously threatened that certain measures, unnecessary in other times and in the face of other enemies, may be necessary. Without an awareness of these distinctions—and these distinctions play no role in Dr. Stouffer's study—one can make no contribution to the *political* problems of Communism and civil liberties.

The failure to be interested in the political problem of civil liberties led Dr. Stouffer to make little use of one of the unique aspects of this study, the interviews with 1,500 community leaders. We learn little or nothing about the factors which affect the differences in attitude toward Communism and civil liberties within this group, or among the privileged and educated classes from whom they are largely selected. In a *political* context, it is the views of these groups which matter most because they write to the newspapers, fill the legislatures, and control the local communities. If this upper stratum was more unified in its support of civil liberties, as are seemingly comparable groups in Great Britain and English-speaking Canada, then the fact that the large majority was intolerant would be of little significance politically.[6]

If we look at this elite group, we find many individuals who are convinced that Communists represent a "very great" or a "great" danger to the country, but nevertheless

are high in tolerance. There is comparatively little difference between the proportion of community leaders, 37
per cent, who believe that Communists are a "great" or
"very great" danger and the 43 per cent of the general
population who have the same sentiments. However, 57
per cent of the community leaders who believe Communists present a serious threat are high on the scale of
tolerance, while only 27 per cent of the general population who are similarly fearful of Communists hold a comparable position on the tolerance scale. Or if we compare
the reactions of the college educated and those who did
not go beyond grammar school to perception of the
Communist danger, we find very little difference. Twenty-
nine per cent of the college group score high on the scale
of perception of the internal Communist threat, as contrasted with 27 per cent of the least educated group.
The differences are striking, however, with regard to
tolerance. Half of the college group who score high on
perception of the threat also score high on tolerance,
while only 11 per cent of the grammar school group
who see a serious Communist menace are high in tolerance.

The ability of many individuals to differentiate between
sensitive areas, and the diffuse attacks on civil rights of
Communists and dissidents, is brought out sharply by the
responses to the specific items which make up the tolerance scale. Although community leaders are much more
tolerant than the bulk of the population, they do not
differ from the lower classes and the uneducated on the
question whether Communists should work in defense
plants, or teach. Close to 90 per cent of both groups would
deny these forms of employment to Communists—i.e. for
them, a sensitive area. On the other hand, the majority
of the population favor putting an admitted Communist
in jail, but only 27 per cent of the community leaders
have the same opinion.

These variations in the responses of different groups

suggest the need for a more elaborate politically oriented classification of groups, rather than simply high and low on tolerance. It is possible to differentiate among four groups: those who perceive the Communist danger as great, and are intolerant; those who perceive the danger as great, but are tolerant; those who see little danger and are tolerant; and a group who see little danger and are still intolerant. The great debate in America as to how to treat Communists has been carried out among the first three groups. And we would suggest that the strongest supporters of civil liberties in the country are those who recognize the Communist threat as great, but who would still maintain all the guarantees of political freedom for obnoxious and even dangerous minorities. When we argue with people who think that Communists are a danger, and who favor harsh measures against them, it is the latter attitude, not the perception of danger which should be changed. Dr. Stouffer could have added greatly to the debt that we already owe him for this informative study, if he had told us more about the factors which are related to such a pattern of tolerance.

One other major problem arises in using the survey technique. While the polls can tell us in considerable detail the nuances of attitude difference among a wide variety of stratified groups, these results are often misleading if interpreted without reference to the specific organizational commitments which in action may modify or even contradict the abstract attitude. To take a sharp example: In Australia, in 1951, a national referendum was held on the proposal, advanced by the Liberal government, to outlaw the Communist Party. Just prior to the announcement of the referendum, a Gallup poll showed that 80 per cent of those questioned favored such a move. Yet, the vote in the referendum held three months later was 50.6 per cent *against* outlawing the Communist Party. What had happened? As a general fact, most of the Australian people, especially the Catholics, were in favor of the action. But because it was proposed by the government, it became a party issue, with the Labor Party and the trade unions coming out in strong opposition. In the end, the Catholics were *less* in favor of outlawing the Communist Party than any Protestant group. The reason is that three-fourths of the Catholics, as workers, vote Labor. Their political and trade-union loyalties turned the trick.[7]

From Stouffer's data we see that Democrats, being in greater proportion workers, and less educated, are, in consequence, less tolerant than Republicans. Yet, on the questions reported in the final chapter dealing with Congressional investigations, Democrats are more hostile to the anti-Communist investigations than Republicans. Here again context modified attitude, for party position became the chief determinant.

The question of what determines the party's attitude is quite a complex one. Generally speaking, the weight of party strategy is still determined by economic class issues, and these traditionally carry with them ideological commitments. Sometimes these are along liberal-and-conservative lines, defined historically. Sometimes these are shaped by other traditional attitudes. This is confirmed, strikingly, in the picture of the South, as seen on Stouffer's scales. On the questions of civil liberties, the South is the least tolerant section of the country. However, the South was the most anti-McCarthy section of the country. There are many reasons: the traditional attachment to the Democratic Party and the fact that McCarthy is a Republican; McCarthy is a Catholic and the South is the most anti-Catholic section in the country; McCarthy attacked the Army, and the South has traditionally been the most pro-military section of the country; the South is politically the least informed and people follow local leaders and local opinion which may be more unrelated to national issues at large. Whatever the source of the contradictions, knowing that the South, in general, is intolerant, does not tell us how it will react to a specific instance of intolerance.

The problem of attitude and context can be examined, too, against the background of European history. A study by the UNESCO institute in Cologne showed that upper-class Germans were more in favor of a democratic political structure (a multi-party as compared to a one party or no party system) than lower-class groups. (Similar findings were reported, too, for Japan with regard to concern for civil liberties.) Education here too, tended to make the upper-class groups more pro-democratic than the lower-class groups. But the political parties supported by the upper- and middle-class groups have tended to be anti-democratic, while those of the working-class have fought harder for democratic rights. Clearly the relationship between "authoritarian" attitudes and party and political structure is quite complex. Clearly too, political events, in the large, are the results mainly of what organized groups do, and this may have little relevance to the sentiments of their members or supporters considered in the mass.

The relationship between attitude and context is discussed by Dr. Stouffer towards the end of his book (pages 210-215) and we have no quarrel with him on this score. If we were to make a criticism it is that in writing a book concerned with the dynamic factors affecting civil liberties, he stresses static structural variables such as education, sex, and religion, and for the most part ignores the way in which the interplay of different institutional and political factors may affect any actual problem of civil liberties. Thus the possible effect of an increase in the educational level of the American population seems more important in this book than a change in the policy of the Republican leadership. But as we have seen, a change in Republican policy toward

Senator McCarthy has sharply changed the climate of opinion within a short space of time. Thus the optimistic thought that as the young grow older and more people become better educated there will be an increase in "tolerance," may not be warranted. This depends on the political situation.

The most significant problem of civil liberties in America is not why did a minority launch an attack on the rights of others, but rather why was the defense to that attack so weak at first, and so late in coming. Some partial reasons may be suggested. The conservative upper class individuals who believe in civil liberties did not respond to the attack by leftists and liberals with whom they disagreed, because it was put as a party issue. The liberals and Democrats, on the other hand, were initially unable to distinguish between legitimate exposés of Communist subversion and espionage, and the indiscriminate red-baiting and attacks on liberals; as a result the Democrats fought *every* charge of Communism or espionage as a political smear. Since some of the charges were true, the liberals and Democrats either buried their heads in the sand, or later sought to outdo the Republican anti-Communists. Thus the Democratic members of Congress for a long time shied away from fighting Senator McCarthy because they felt they were vulnerable to the charge of having accepted Communist support, or because public opinion polls, which did not differentiate among the politically potent and impotent as Stouffer has done, indicated that large sections of the American population supported McCarthy. And later, to demonstrate their anti-Communism, three of the most liberal members of the Senate pushed through the bill to outlaw the Communist Party.

Actually the right-wing attacks were halted only when the conservative defenders of civil liberties stood up to the issue. McCarthy was stopped in the Senate by Eisenhower and the southern Democrats. In the local communities, vigilante attacks against schools, colleges and libraries have been stopped most effectively when leaders of the conservative upper class stepped in, and defended civil liberties. In this instance, at least, the instincts of the American conservative group finally responded to the tradition of civil liberties and democratic procedure, rather than to political advantage. Whether these conservative groups would respond in similar fashion to the defense of democratic rights on a direct economic class issue is a moot point—to the extent that American business accepts its own ideology of fighting state intervention, and to the extent it remembers how fascist states throttled business, too, it will respect democratic rights in these matters as well.

Unfortunately, no effort has been made to combine the techniques of survey research, so admirably employed in the Stouffer study, with an intensive study of those aspects of American society which encourage or challenge efforts to reduce civil liberties. One cannot criticize Professor Stouffer for not dealing with such problems, yet it would cast much light on American politics if we had some answers. For example, who are the minority of community leaders who are intolerant? Some clues are provided by the different roles of such leaders, i.e. those who are tied to patriotic functions tend to be more intolerant; but who among the possible adherents of the American Legion or the D.A.R. participate in such groups? (One answer might be that people who psychologically tend to be authoritarian, within the family and society, are intolerant of deviation in general, and tend to be more patriotic and nationalistic. The Stouffer data show a relationship between such indicators of an "authoritarian personality," and intolerance.)

From sociological hypotheses, we would expect that support of right-wing extremism in American life is to be found disproportionately among the upward-mobile, the *nouveaux riches,* and among the downward mobile as well. This is perhaps particularly true of minority ethnic groups, which in becoming upward mobile, have tended to take over the norms of 100 per cent Americanism in order to become accepted. (Unfortunately, Stouffer reports no data relating ethnic groups or social mobility and intolerance.) And, one may point to the fact that two centers of right-extremist and intolerant activity, Texas and southern California, are also areas in which, on an elite level, there are a disproportionate number of *nouveaux riches.* It is to these sociological hypotheses— and an attempt to locate such groups in the social structure—that the next chapter is addressed.

[1] The authors wish to acknowledge the kind cooperation and advice of Mr. David Riesman. The suggestion for the chapter grew out of discussions with him. They have been guided by some of the ideas expressed by Mr. Riesman in his critique of the Stouffer book presented before the American Association for Public Opinion Research in Madison, Wisconsin, April, 1955.

[2] Professor Stouffer in interpreting these findings describes them as reactions to atheists. The questions, however, dealt with attacks on churches and religion, not advocacy of atheism. The two are not necessarily the same.

[3] In this chapter, we shall follow Dr. Stouffer's use of the term "tolerant" to describe people who would allow Communists, and religious and political dissidents basic civil liberties. While we do not want to argue the question in detail here, we are somewhat troubled by the use of the term tolerance to describe the right of minority free expression. When Republicans support the right of Democrats to speak or run candidates, they are not being "tolerant"; presumably they believe that the welfare of the country requires the existence of opposition. The original meaning of the word "tolerance" involved an assumption that one "tolerated" the existence or rights of someone who was in error. The American Creed is not a creed of tolerance, but rather the belief that the greater good for society comes out of opposition and free discussion.

[4] Data on businessmen, from the Stouffer study, which the book omits, is reported in the May, 1955 *Fortune.* These data reveal a wide variation in the attitudes of businessmen between the poorly educated and the well educated. One would want to know whether this difference corresponds to the variation between small and large businessmen, or independent businessmen and the executives of large corporations.

[5] Unfortunately, Professor Stouffer did not compare community leaders with other individuals in the same socio-economic strata; whether com-

munity participation draws the more tolerant individuals, or whether the responsibility of community leadership makes one more tolerant would have been an interesting question to pursue.

[6] It is interesting to note that a survey of Canadian opinion on civil liberties indicates that the bulk of the population in that country are as opposed to civil liberties for Communists as are Americans. For example, in a poll taken in Canada in 1950, 58 per cent favored a law to "make it a criminal offense to be a member of any Commmunist organization." Stouffer's 1954 study reports that 51 per cent of the Americans favor putting "an admitted Communist in jail." The same Canadian survey reports that 83 per cent would bar a Communist from government employment, and 57 per cent supported a law to "prevent a Communist from voting in any election." Stouffer does not have any comparable questions to these, but the 83 per cent figure for Canadians who would bar Communists from public employment, compares with the 86 per cent of Americans who would not allow Communists to teach in colleges.

The difference between Canadian *political* reactions to the problem of internal Communism as compared with those which occurred in the United States appears to rest more on the nature of its elite and political structure than on differences in basic sentiments of the population. See Chapter 7 for a discussion of this problem.

[7] See Leicester Webb, *Communism and Democracy in Australia* (New York: Frederick A. Praeger, 1955).

7

The Sources of the
"Radical Right"[1]

SEYMOUR MARTIN LIPSET

IN THE last five years we have seen the emergence of an important American political phenomenon, the radical right. This group is characterized as radical because it desires to make far-reaching changes in American institutions, and because it seeks to eliminate from American political life those persons and institutions which threaten either its values, or its economic interests. Needless to say, this movement is opposed to the social and economic reforms of the last twenty years, and to the internationalist foreign policy pursued by the successive Administrations in that period.

The activities of the radical right would be of less interest if it sought its ends through the traditional democratic procedures of pressure-group tactics, lobbying, and the ballot box. But, while most individuals and organizations which we shall consider as part of the radical right do use these means, many use undemocratic methods as well. The singular fact is that radical right agitation has facilitated the growth of practices which threaten to undermine the social fabric of democratic politics. The threats to democratic procedure which are, in part, an outgrowth of radical right agitation involve attempts to destroy the right of assembly, the right of petition, the freedom of association, the freedom to travel, and the freedom to teach or conduct scholarly research without conforming to political tests.[2] This movement, therefore, must be seriously considered by all those who would preserve democratic constitutional procedures in this country.

In evaluating the activities of the radical right, this chapter is divided into three sections: Part 1 deals with continuing sources of extremist politics in America as they have their sources in American history; Part 2 analyzes the social groups which are more prone than others to support the radical right today; and Part 3 deals with the specific character of McCarthyism as the principal expression of radical right ideology on the current scene.

1

STATUS AND CLASS POLITICS

Any analysis of the role of political extremism in the United States must recognize two fundamental political forces operating under the varying historical conditions of American society. These forces may be distinguished by the terms *status politics* and *class politics*. Class politics refers to political division based on the discord between the traditional left and the right, i.e., between those who favor redistribution of income, and those favoring the preservation of the *status quo*. Status politics, as used here, refers to political movements whose appeal is to the not uncommon resentments of individuals or groups who desire to maintain or improve their social status.[3]

In the United States, political movements or parties which stress the need for economic reform have usually gained strength during times of unemployment and depression. On the other hand, status politics becomes ascendant in periods of prosperity, especially when full employment is accompanied by inflation, and when many individuals are able to improve their economic position. The groups which are receptive to status-oriented appeals are not only those which have risen in the economic structure and who may be frustrated in their desire to be accepted socially by those who already hold status, but also those groups already possessing status who feel that the rapid social change threatens their own claims to high social position, or enables previously lower status groups to claim equal status with their own.

The political consequences of status frustrations are very different from those resulting from economic deprivation, for while in economic conflict the goals are clear— a redistribution of income—in status conflict there are no clear-cut solutions. Where there are status anxieties, there is little or nothing which a government can do. It is not surprising, therefore, that the political movements which have successfully appealed to status resentments have been irrational in character, and have sought scapegoats which conveniently serve to symbolize the status threat. Historically, the most common scapegoats in the United States have been the minority ethnic or religious groups. Such groups have repeatedly been the victims of political aggression in periods of prosperity, for it is precisely in these times that status anxieties are most pressing.[4]

American political history from this perspective emerges in a fairly consistent pattern. Before the Civil War, there was considerable anti-Catholic and anti-immigrant activity. Such agitation often took the form of organized political parties, the most important of which was the Know-Nothing or American Party. And it was during a prosperous decade that these parties and movements were at their height. The Know-Nothings who polled one fourth of the total popular vote for President in 1856 reached their greatest power in a period of widespread prosperity and inflation and practically vanished in the depression year 1857.[5] The American Protective Association (A.P.A.), which emerged in the late 1880's, was the next major organized anti-Catholic movement and it too arose in a period of renewed prosperity. A contemporary analyst of this movement has pointed to the status concerns which motivated many of the members of the A.P.A.

Latter day Know-Nothingism (A.P.A.ism) in the west, was perhaps due as well to envy of the growing social and industrial strength of Catholic Americans.

In the second generation American Catholics began to attain higher industrial positions and better occupations. All through the west, they were taking their place in the professional and business world. They were among the doctors and the lawyers, the editors and the teachers of the community. Sometimes they were the leading merchants as well as the leading politicians of their locality.[6]

Interestingly enough, the publisher of many anti-Catholic A.P.A. works was also the publisher of the Social Register, which was first copyrighted in 1887, the year in which the A.P.A. was organized,[7] a fact which suggests a possible link between this mass organization and the desire of high-status, old family Americans to resist the upward mobility of the second generation Catholics. A large number of individuals listed in the Social Register

were among the important financial supporters of the
A.P.A., as well as of other anti-immigration organizations.

The Progressive movement, which flourished from
1900-1912, is yet another protest movement which attracted the interest and participation of large numbers
of Americans during a period of high prosperity. This
movement, while differing considerably from the others,
since it was concerned with liberal social reforms, may,
nevertheless, be a reflection of status politics. Richard
Hofstadter has suggested that it was based in large measure on the reaction of the Protestant middle class against
threats to its values and status.[8] The Progressive movement had two scapegoats—the "plutocrat" millionaires,
and the immigrants.[9] The rise of the "robber barons," the
great millionaires and plutocrats of the late nineteenth
and early twentieth centuries, served to challenge the
status of many old, upper-middle-class American families
which had previously considered themselves the most
important group in society; these new millionaires were
able to outdo them in philanthropy and in setting new
styles of life. The Progressive movement, like previous
expressions of status politics, was also opposed to immigration. It viewed the immigrant and the urban city
machines based on immigrant support as a basic threat
to American middle-class Protestant values.

And finally the Ku Klux Klan, which vigorously attacked
the rights of minority groups, also emerged in prosperous
times, the 1920's. It is important to note, however, that
while the Klan was against Jews, Catholics and Negroes,
it also represented the antagonism of the small town and
provincial city Protestant lower-middle class and working
class against the "cosmopolitanism" of the upper classes.
The upper-class, largely metropolitan-centered, Protestant
churches were a frequent target of Klan attack. The
English minister of a high Protestant church, divorced
women who were accused of "playing around," physicians

who had allegedly engaged in sexual irregularities with patients, were among those subjected to Klan violence.[10]

At its height, the Klan had the support of millions of individuals, and dominated political life in Indiana, Maine, Colorado, Oklahoma, Texas, Oregon, Arkansas, Ohio, and California. It would be rash to give any simplified interpretation of the factors underlying such an important social movement. If, however, one asks what had occurred on the American scene to encourage such a mass expression of provincial resentment, one important factor is the growing predominance of the large metropolitan centers, which were centers of Catholics, Jews, and high-status Protestants. In the changing world of post-World War I America, the fundamentalist provincial was faced with the fact that he and his communities had lost much of their independence and status. The war boom, and later, the prosperity of the twenties, made it possible for many individuals to rise economically, including members of previously lower-class minority groups, such as the Jews and Catholics. The Catholics were also beginning to get national political power. These changes were paralleled by a seeming decline in basic morality, and a growth in religious cynicism. The Klan, with its attack on metropolitan "cosmopolitanism" and the more traditional minority ethnic scapegoats, seems to have provided an outlet to the frustrated residents of provincial America, who felt their values, power, and status slipping away.

The hypothesis that the Klan represented the reaction of a large section of provincial America to the frustrations of boom-time social change may, of course, be questioned in view of the fact that it declined considerably as an organization after 1926, before prosperity ended. This decline, however, seems in large measure to be related to the fact that the overwhelming majority of Klan leaders were publicly exposed as obvious charlatans, who were using the organization to feather their own nest, and to the social pressure directed against the Klan by the upper class and every section of the press. The loss of respectability led to a rapid withdrawal from the organization by its middle-class adherents, and the jailing for fraud of some of its leaders soon disillusioned the large section of working-class supporters.

The 1928 Presidential election campaign, however, witnessed a new outburst of bigotry directed against the Catholic Democratic candidate, Al Smith (which showed that the sentiments which gave rise to the Klan had not vanished). In this election, the Democratic Party increased its vote in the large metropolitan centers, while reaching its lowest point in decades in the smaller communities.

These four movements, Know-Nothings, A.P.A., Progressives, and Ku Klux Klan, all illustrate the way in which American society has thrown up major protest movements in periods of prosperity, thus confounding the general assumption that protest politics are primarily products of depressions. The prosperity movements differ from those groups who are products of economic crises in that they find "scapegoats" who threaten their value system, while other protest groups have direct economic targets. The Progressives, a group one does not normally see this way, were concerned with the manner in which the *nouveaux riches* and the immigrants were corrupting American institutions, while the Klan, a status-resentment group par-excellence, attacked the "cosmopolitanism" of Catholics, Jews, and the metropolitan elite, which undermined the middle-class Protestant virtues. Perhaps the most significant single fact concerning the strength of the Klan and the role of organized bigotry in America is that every effort to build a mass social movement based on bigotry during the great depression of the 1930's had little success. It is the common concern with the protection of "traditional" American values that characterizes "status politics" as contrasted with the regard for jobs, cheap credit, or high farm prices, which have been the main emphases of depression-born "class politics."

If we assume that this is a pattern in American politics, it is not surprising that the continuing prosperity of the late nineteen forties and early fifties should also have developed a political movement resembling the four discussed above. McCarthyism, like its predecessors, is characterized by an attack on a convenient scapegoat, which is defined as a threat to American institutions, and also involves an attempt to link "cosmopolitan" changes in the society to a foreign plot.[11]

THE STATE OF TOLERANCE IN AMERICA

A second important factor to consider in evaluating present trends in American politics is the traditional attitude toward tolerance in American society. The historical evidence, some of which has been cited above, indicates that, as compared to the citizens of a number of other countries, especially Great Britain and Scandinavia, Americans are not a tolerant people. In addition to discrimination against ethnic and religious minorities, each war and most pre-war situations have been characterized by the denial of civil liberties to minorities, often even of minorities which were not opposed to the war. Abolitionists, for example, faced great difficulties in many areas, North as well as South, before the Civil War. Many were fired from schools and universities. During World War I, German-Americans and Socialists often experienced personal physical attacks, as well as economic discrimination. In the last war, the entire Japanese-American population on the west coast was denied the most elementary form of personal freedom.[12]

Political intolerance has not been monopolized by political extremists or wartime vigilantes. The Populists,

for example, discharged many university professors in
state universities in states where they came into power in
the 1890's. Their Republican opponents were not loath
to dismiss teachers who believed in Populist economics.
Public opinion polls, ever since they first began measuring
mass attitudes in the early thirties, have repeatedly shown
that sizable numbers, often a majority, of Americans oppose the rights of unpopular political minorities.[13] In both
1938 and 1942, a majority of the American public opposed
the right of "radicals" to hold meetings.

The state of current attitudes toward civil liberties has
been reported on in detail in a study by Samuel Stouffer,
based on interviews with a random sample of Americans in the spring of 1954. Large sections of the
American population opposed the rights of atheists,[14]
Socialists,[15] and Communists[16] to free speech and free
publication.

One important factor affecting this lack of tolerance
in American life is the basic strain of Protestant puritanical morality which has always existed in this country.
Americans believe that there is a fundamental difference
between right and wrong, that right must be supported,
and that wrong must be suppressed, that error and evil
have no rights against the truth. This propensity to see
life in terms of all black and all white is most evident,
perhaps most disastrous, in the area of foreign policy,
where allies and enemies cannot be gray, but must be
black or white.[17]

The differences in fundamental economic philosophy
and way of life between the Democrats and Republicans
in this country are far less than those which exist between
Conservatives and Socialists in Great Britain. Yet political
rhetoric in this country is comparable in Europe only for
those campaigns between totalitarians and their opponents. While McCarthy has indeed sunk American politi-

cal rhetoric to new depths, one should not forget that his type of invective has been used quite frequently in American politics. For example, Roosevelt called some of his isolationist opponents, "Copperheads," a term equivalent to traitor.[18] If various impressionistic accounts are to be believed, many Republicans, especially Republican businessmen, have a far deeper sense of hatred against Roosevelt and the New Deal, than their British or Scandinavian counterparts have against their socialist opponents.

Although Puritanism is probably one of the main sources of American intolerance, there are certainly many other elements which have contributed to its continuance in American life. The lack of an aristocratic tradition in American politics helped to prevent the emergence of a moderate rhetoric in political life. Almost from the start of democratic politics in America with the early adoption of universal male suffrage, the political machines were led by professional politicians, many of whom were of lower-middle-class or even poorer origins, who had to appeal to a relatively uneducated electorate. This led to the development of a campaign style in which any tactic that would win votes was viewed as legitimate. Thus, Jefferson was charged with "treason," and with being a French agent before 1800, while Republicans waved the "bloody shirt" against the Democrats for decades following the Civil War. In order to involve the masses in politics, politicians have sought to make every election appear as if it involved life or death for the country or for their party.

Another factor which has operated to diminish tolerance in this country has been mass immigration. The prevalence of different cultural and religious ways of life has always constituted a threat to American stability and cultural unity. In order to build a nation, it was perhaps

necessary that men should be intolerant of the practices
of newcomers, and should force them to assimilate. All
through world history, the intermingling of people from
different cultural backgrounds has resulted in strife. Such
conflict is obviously not conducive to the emergence of a
tradition of civic discipline, in which everyone has the
right to live out his life as he sees fit, and in which
minorities are protected.

The minority immigrant groups themselves have contributed to the support for conformity. One of the principal reactions of members of such groups to discrimination—to being defined as socially inferior by the majority
culture—is to attempt to assimilate completely American
values, to reject their past, and to overidentify with
Americanism. They tend to interpret indiscrimination
against their ethnic group as a consequence of the fact
that they are foreign and they behave differently, that in
short they are insufficiently American. Many of those who
adopt the assimilationist solution attempt to enforce conformity within their own group, and are intolerant of
those who would perpetuate foreign ways and thus earn
the enmity of those of Anglo-Saxon origin.[19]

At least one other element may be suggested as having
operated against the development of tolerance: those
situations which have encouraged or required men to take
the law into their own hands in order to enforce the moral
values of the dominant groups in society. Such events
occurred in the South after the Civil War, and in the
West continuously with the expansion of the frontier. In
the South, as Myrdal has pointed out, the conservative
groups have resisted legal procedures in order to maintain
white supremacy. On the western frontier, many men
considered it necessary to engage in vigilante activities
to eliminate lawlessness. Both of these traditions, especially the continuing Southern one, have helped to destroy
civic discipline.

AMERICANISM AS AN IDEOLOGY:
UN-AMERICANISM

A third element in American life related to present political events is the extent to which the concept of Americanism has become a compulsive ideology rather than simply a nationalist term. Americanism is a creed in a way that "Britishism" is not.

The notion of Americanism as a creed to which men are converted rather than born stems from two factors: first, our revolutionary tradition which has led us to continually reiterate the superiority of the American creed of equalitarianism, of democracy, against the old reactionary, monarchical and more rigidly status-bound systems of European society; and second, the immigrant character of American society, the fact that people may become Americans—that they are not simply born to the status.

But if foreigners may become Americans, Americans may become "un-American." This concept of "un-American activities," as far as I know, does not have its counterpart in other countries. American patriotism is allegiance to values, to a creed, not solely to a nation. An American political leader could not say, as Winston Churchill did in 1940, that the English Communist Party was composed of Englishmen, and he did not fear an Englishman.[20]

Unless one recognizes that Americanism is a political creed, much like Socialism, Communism or Fascism, much of what is currently happening in this country must remain unintelligible.[21] Our national rituals are largely identified with reiterating the accepted values of a political value system, not solely or even primarily of national patriotism. For example, Washington's Birthday, Lincoln's Birthday, and the Fourth of July are ideological celebrations comparable to May Day or Lenin's Birthday in the Communist world. Only Memorial Day and Veteran's Day may be placed in the category of purely patriotic, as distinct from ideological, celebrations. Consequently, more than any other democratic country, the United States makes ideological conformity one of the conditions for good citizenship. And it is this emphasis on ideological conformity to presumably common political values that legitimatizes the hunt for "un-Americans" in our midst.

THE MULTIPLE ELITES

While factors persistent in the culture have exerted great pressure towards conformity to the creed of Americanism, yet the rapid growth, and size, of the United States has prevented American society from developing an integrated cultural or power structure similar to those in smaller and older tradition-oriented European nations. One cannot, for example, speak of *an* American elite, be it economic, political or cultural. The elites that exist are fractioned regionally, ethnically, and culturally, so that friction and competition constantly arise among these segmented groups: West against East, North against South, new rich versus old rich, Anglo-Saxons against minority ethnics, the graduates of Ivy League schools against others, etc.

This segmentation has facilitated the emergence of new social movements, religions, and cultural fads. But it also has prevented any one of them from engulfing the country. Each new movement is opposed by some segment of a rival elite, as well as that part of the general population which follows it. Thus Populism, the Ku Klux Klan, the abortive labor and socialist parties, the Progressive movement, and the Know-Nothings, have all had important successes within specific regions, communities, or ethnic groups; but each died away without coming to national power. In the United States, seemingly, with the exception of prohibition, it has been impossible to build a durable national movement on a single issue, or on an appeal to a single interest group.

While the heterogeneity and sheer size of the United States apparently bar any extremist ideological group from coming to national power, it also promotes the emergence of such groups on a more parochial base since any can almost always find enough supporters, leaders, and financial backers to make an impression on the body politic. Any appeal, be it anti-Catholicism, anti-Semitism, Huey Long's "Share the Wealth movement," Townsend's Old Age pension crusade, monetary reform, Technocracy, or others such as those mentioned earlier, will have some appeal. It is almost an axiom of American politics that any movement can find some millionaire backing, and it does not take many millionaires to set up an impressive looking propaganda apparatus. Each of the various radical groups, the Socialist Labor Party, the Socialist Party, and the Communist Party, has had its millionaires. In recent decades, the Communists were more successful than others on the left in this regard.

The fact that it is relatively easy to build a new political or economic reform movement in America has often been overlooked by many observers because of the failure of every effort to construct a third major political party—a difference, obviously, between the ease of a *movement* and the difficulty of a *party*. The failure of third-party efforts has been a consequence, however, of the American electoral system with its requirement that only one party can control the executive branch of the government at one time. Actually, the two major American parties are coalitions, and the underlying base of American politics is much closer to the French multi-party system than it is to the British two-party political structure. American

parties are coalitions of distinct and often conflicting
factions, and no one interest group is able to dominate
the government. As in France, however, it is relatively
simple for a new ideological or interest group to gain
representation, but it is almost impossible for it to secure
majority control of the government.[22] For example, in the
1920's many Klan-backed individuals were elected to
Congress, state legislatures, and some governor's office.
At about the same time, the quasi-socialist Non-Partisan
League won control of the Republican Party and the
state government in North Dakota, and had considerable
influence in a number of other midwest states, while an
offshoot of it captured the Democratic Party and the
governor's chair in Oklahoma. In the 1930's the Democratic Party of California, Oregon and Washington, was
captured temporarily by Socialist factions—i.e., Upton
Sinclair's EPIC movement in California, and the Cooperative Commonwealth Federation in the other two coast
states. At the same time, three Northern midwestern
states were actually governed by left-wing offshoots of
the Republican Party—the Non-Partisan League in North
Dakota, the Progressive Party in Wisconsin, and the
Farmer-Labor Party in Minnesota. Townsend, Huey
Long, Father Coughlin, and the Communists were also
able to send some men to Congress through the mechanism of winning primary contests in one of the major
parties. Today, as in the past, various ideological or
interest factions strive to increase their representation in
government through rather than against the traditional
parties.

The fact that the leaders of American political parties
have much less influence over the men whom they elect
than do the heads of parties in the British Commonwealth
also facilitates the emergence of dissident political tendencies. A Labor or Tory member of the British parlia-
ment could never engage in a one-man crusade with a

power comparable to control of a Senate committee such as Senators Langer, La Follette, and McCarthy, have done at different times.

The tendency of American society to throw up new movements or organizations is, of course, not limited to the political field. Tocqueville, more than a century ago, called attention to the American propensity, as compared with the greater lassitude of Europeans, to form organizations for various purposes. The reason for this distinctive pattern lay in the fact that America did not have a distinct aristocratic elite which could fulfill the functions of organization and leadership performed by the elite in Europe. And, Tocqueville argued, the very multitude of existing voluntary associations facilitated the emergence of new ones, since the older associations, because they train men in the skills of organization, provide a resource when some new need or new social objective is perceived.[23] What little comparative data exist, suggest that this empirical generalization is still valid.[24]

It is hardly surprising, therefore, that Americans who regard Communism as a great evil should form associations to combat it. These groups are but one more manifestation of American political and moral activity, much like the popular attempts to ban liquor, gambling, or immorality in comic strips. One may point to similar developments in the sphere of religion. Perhaps no other country, including Israel, has thrown up so many new religious sects. Spiritualism, the Mormon Church, Jehovah's Witnesses, Seventh Day Adventists, Christian Science, and the Churches of God, are but some of the sects with over 100,000 church members which were born in the United States.

The various dissident social and religious movements have reflected the openness of the American social order. Conventional morality is not supported by a cohesive system of social control since there are, in effect, a variety of moralities. This generalization does not contradict the previous discussion of intolerance in American life, for intolerance to be effective on a national scale must represent the will of a majority or all-powerful group. Fortunately, with the exception of groups which are defined as agents of a foreign actual or potential military enemy, it has been impossible for any group to convince the country to actively support restrictions against others who do not conform to the beliefs of one or another segment of American society. A Canadian sociologist, S. D. Clark, has commented on this aspect of American society. He suggests that the much tighter political and social control structure of Canada frustrates efforts at dissident movements before they can develop, while the United States permits them to emerge, but frustrates their dreams of power:

> Critics outside the country [the United States] might well pause to consider not the intolerance which finds expression in McCarthyism but the tolerance which makes it possible for McCarthyism to develop. In Canada it would be hard to conceive of a state of political freedom great enough to permit the kind of attacks upon responsible political leaders of the government which have been carried out in the United States. More careful examination of the American community in general, and perhaps of the academic community in particular, would probably reveal that, in spite of the witch hunts in that country, the people of the United States enjoy in fact a much greater degree of freedom than do the people of Canada.[25]

THE SHIFT TO THE RIGHT

Four aspects of American society have been suggested as contributing to an understanding of extremist political developments in the United States: the role of the status-driven during periods of prosperity, their fear of other groups which threaten their status; the absence of a firm tradition of civic discipline or tolerance; the definition of Americanism in ideological terms; and the lack of an integrated cultural and political social control structure.

In order to understand the recent manifestations of political intolerance, however, it is necessary to discuss a fifth factor, the consequences of a liberal or conservative climate of opinion on the power of extremist groups. The period from 1930 to 1945 saw the predominance of liberal sentiment in American politics. This was largely the result of two factors, the depression and the threat of Fascism. The depression emphasized the need for socio-economic reforms and helped to undermine the legitimacy of conservative and business institutions. It was followed immediately by a war which was defined as a struggle against Fascism. Since Fascism was a rightist movement, this fact tended to reinforce the political predominance of leftist liberal sentiments.

During this period the political dynamic in most democratic countries was in the hands of the left, and it used this strength to undermine the prestige of conservatism. In the United States, for example, several Congressional Committees conducted exposés of "undemocratic" activities of big business. In the thirties, the Nye Committee "exposed" the way in which Wall Street bankers had helped plunge the United States into World War I in order to maintain their investments, while the La Follette Committee revealed that large corporations employed labor spies and gangsters to prevent their employees from forming trade unions. The famous Truman Committee often exposed big business profiteering during World War II. All three committees helped to foster an anti-business and anti-conservative climate of opinion. It is quite true that the House Un-American Activities Committee operated at the same time as the liberal committees, but though it secured considerable publicity, it was relatively unimportant compared with the role of anti-subversive committees in the post-war years.

The period of liberal supremacy was also marked by a great growth in the influence of the Communist Party. In the United States, the Communists were concerned with penetrating and manipulating liberal and moderate left groups, rather than with building an electoral party. The Communists, by concealing their real objectives, by acting positively for liberal causes, by being the best organizers of the left, were able to penetrate deeply into various liberal organizations and into the labor movement. An index of their success may be seen in the fact that close to a dozen Congressmen, one state governor, many members of the staffs of liberal Congressmen and Congressional Committees, and a number of high-ranking civil servants, showed by their subsequent political behavior that they were close followers of the Communist Party.

The post-war period, on the other hand, has seen a resurgence of conservative and rightist forces. This has resulted from two factors, a prolonged period of prosperity and full employment, and second, the change in foreign policy. Where once we warred against Fascism, which is identified with the "right," we now war against Communism, which identifies with the "left." And while Fascism and Communism are much closer to each other in moral consequences and actual practice than either is to the democratic right or left, by the general populace, the one is considered right and the other left.[26] And just as the Communists were able to secure considerable influence during the period of liberal ascendency, right-wing extremists have been able to make considerable headway during the conservative revival. Thus, the period from 1947-8 to 1954 presents a very different picture from the previous decade and a half. The conservatives and the extreme right are now on the offensive. The "free enterprise" system which provides full employment is once more legitimate. Liberal groups feel in a weak position politically, and now wage a defensive battle, seeking to preserve their conquests of the thirties, rather than to extend them.

It is striking to observe the similarities in the rhetoric of the liberals and conservatives when on the offensive. In the thirties, conservatives, isolationists, business leaders, Republican Senators and Congressmen were criticized by some liberals as being semi-Fascist, or with being outright Fascists. Similarly in the last half-decade, many conservatives have waged an attack on liberals, Democrats and opponents of a vigorous anti-Russian foreign policy for being pro-Communist, or "creeping Socialists." The sources of the violent attack on conservatism in the earlier period came in large measure from the Communists and their fellow travelers, although it was voiced by many liberals who had no connection with the Communist Party and were unaware of the extent to which they had absorbed a Communist ideological position. More recently, the extreme right wing, the radical right of the American political spectrum, has been successful in setting the ideological tone of conservatism.

It is important to note the parallelism in the rhetoric employed by liberals when criticizing the State Department's policy toward the Loyalists in the Spanish Civil War of 1936-1939, and that used by many extreme rightists toward the policy of the same department a few years later in the Chinese Civil War. The liberal left magazines portrayed an American foreign office staffed by men who were sympathetic to extreme conservatism if not outright Fascism, and who tricked Roosevelt and Hull into pursuing policies which helped Franco. Various individuals, some of whom are still in the State Department, such as

Robert Murphy, were labeled as pro-Franco. The recent right-wing accusations that our Chinese policies were a result of Communist influence in government sound like a rewritten version of the Fascist conspiracy of the thirties. The same allegations about the social background of State Department members, that many of them come from Groton, Harvard, and the Brahmin upper class, were used by the Communists in the thirties to prove that the State Department was ultra-rightist in its sympathies, and are used today by McCarthy and other radical rightists to account for presumed sympathies with Communism.[27] The State Department's refusal to aid Loyalist Spain was presented as convincing proof of the presence of Fascist sympathizers within it. In the same way, the radical right now refuses to acknowledge that men may have made honest errors of judgment in their dealing with the Russians or the Chinese Communists.

So similar are the political approaches of the radical right and the Communists that one may fittingly describe the radical right doctrine as embodying a theory of "Social Communism" in the same sense as the Communists used the term "Social Fascism" in the early thirties. The Communists, before 1934, argued that all non-Communist parties including the Socialists were "Social Fascists," that is, they objectively were paving the way for Fascism. The principal organ of the radical right today, the *Freeman,* contends that all welfare state and planning measures are "objectively" steps toward the development of a totalitarian Communist state. The New Deal, Americans for Democratic Action, the C.I.O. Political Action Committee, all are charged with "objective" totalitarianism. Both the Communists and writers for the *Freeman* have argued that the "social" variety of Fascism or Communism is more dangerous than the real thing, for the public is more easily deceived by a sugar-coated totalitarian program. The Communists in pre-Hitler Germany concentrated their fire not on the Nazis, but on the "Social Fascists," the socialists and liberals, and the *Freeman* and other sections of the radical right let loose their worst venom on the American liberals.

An example of the violent character of this ideology may be seen in a 1950 *Freeman* article which contended that, "This new political machine, which . . . rules the old Democratic Party is an outgrowth of the CIO's Political Action Committee (PAC)." It further claimed that "every single element in the Browder [Communist Party] program was incorporated in the PAC program. It has been the policy of the Administration ever since." The labor movement organized around Truman because of the Taft-Hartley Act. Why, asked this *Freeman* writer, did labor unite against this act, which though it "injured the Communists . . . certainly did not injure the workers." . . . Because the Communists executed another strategic retreat. They let go of their prominent offices in the CIO but they still had control of the press, and the policy-making and opinion-forming organs. Then they got their ideas into the opinion-forming agences of the AFL, especially its League for Political Education.

"How could the AFL be captured by the Communist policy-makers? It had a great tradition, but in face of CIO 'gains,' its leaders thought they had to 'do something.' And the Communists were ready and waiting to tell them what to do—policies nicely hidden behind the cloak of higher wages, more benefits, but still fitting perfectly the symbols laid down to guide policy-makers by Earl Browder in 1944."

The article went on to ask, "What proof have we that the Politburo in Moscow wanted the election of Wallace? Wallace certainly did not poll the total Communist vote. For eight years they had worked on getting control of a major party. Why give up the Truman party? . . .

"Practically every word of Truman's campaign came,

again, from Browder's pattern of 1944, which is the policy
of the PAC. Practically every word of his attack on the
80th Congress can be found earlier in the pages of the
Daily Worker and the *People's Daily World*.

"What then was the role of Wallace and the third
party? It was the old Communist dialectic. By setting up
Wallace as the 'left,' the Communists could make Truman's platforms and speeches look like the 'center.' "[28]

Here is a picture of the real world that should be
placed side by side with that of the Communists. As they
see a country controlled by a self-conscious plot of Wall
Street magnates, of two "capitalist" parties competing
just to fool the people, this radical rightist sees a night-
marish world in which the Communists also have two
political parties in order to fool the people, in which
Wallace's million votes only represented a presumably
small part of total Communist strength.

In both periods, the thirties and the fifties, the extremists have been able to capitalize on sympathetic
predispositions. These ideological predispositions have
not reflected sympathy with extremism by the average
liberal or conservative, but rather led men to view with
sympathy any attack directed against their principal
political opponents. The lack of any normative restrictions against violent political rhetoric in American politics,
to which attention was called earlier, facilitated the
adoption by basically unideological politicians of termi-
nology which in large part resembles that used by rival
totalitarians in Europe. In effect, the extreme left and
right have been able to influence the ideological setting
of American politics since the early thirties. The radical
right today, like the Communists before them, have been
able to win influence far outweighing their numerical
support in the general population, because they have
seemingly been the most effective fighters against those
policies and groups which are repugnant to all conservatives.

2

THE TWO CONSERVATIVES

The conservative elements in American society can be divided into two groups, the moderate conservatives and the radical right. These two may be differentiated by their attitude toward the New Deal era. The moderates are generally willing to accept the past within limits, that is, they do not want "to turn the clock back." They accept various Roosevelt reforms; they tolerate the labor movement; they tend to be internationalist in ideology and to accept the policies of Roosevelt in the last war. Moderate conservatives also believe in constitutional processes, civil liberties, and due process.

The radical right, on the other hand, refuses to accept the recent past, or is radical in the quixotic sense that it rejects the status quo. Most, though not all of the radical right are opposed to: (1) the welfare state; (2) the labor movement; (3) the income tax; (4) World War II—the radical right sees the war as an avoidable mistake, and prefers in retrospect a policy of Russia and Germany fighting it out alone.[29]

In a larger sense, the radical right views our entire foreign policy from the recognition of Russia to Potsdam as appeasement, treason and treachery. It is opposed to membership in the United Nations, and to entangling foreign commitments. It is Asia-oriented, rather than Europe-oriented. It is suspicious of Great Britain as a Machiavellian power which has manipulated us into two wars, and now refuses to back us in our time of need.

Since the radical right believes that both our domestic and foreign policies over the last twenty years have represented tremendous setbacks for the country, it seeks an explanation of these calamitous errors, and finds it in the penetration of the government and the agencies of opinion formation by the Communist movement. The radical right is far from having a unified ideology. Some groups are more concerned with our past and present foreign policy, others with domestic affairs. But the common denominator which unites the radical right is the identification of the policies which it opposes, either in the economic or foreign sphere, with the "softness" of Franklin Roosevelt and the Democratic Party to the Soviet Union and the American Communist Party.

To some extent the two principal sources of bitter opposition to Roosevelt and the Democrats, the extreme economic conservatives and the isolationists, have tended to come together and adopt each other's ideologies. For example, right-wing Texans were ardent advocates of American entry into World War II. The Texas legislature by an almost unanimous vote passed a resolution telling Charles Lindbergh that he was not welcome in Texas during his leadership of America First. Today, however, many of the same Texans regard our participation in World War II as a blunder. On the other hand, a number of isolationists, such as Burton K. Wheeler, William Henry Chamberlain, and others, who were liberal or radical in economic matters, have become domestic conservatives. John T. Flynn is perhaps the outstanding example. He wrote regularly for the *New Republic* during the thirties and criticized Roosevelt's domestic and international policies from a left-wing point of view. With the onset of World War II, Flynn joined the America First movement. This action subjected him to vicious smears from liberal interventionists, who charged that he cooperated with Fascists.[30] He found increasingly that his audiences and the magazines that would accept his articles were right-wing conservatives, and gradually in joining with the right in foreign policy, he accepted their position on economic issues as well.

It is difficult to demonstrate that similar changes in political ideology have occurred among sections of the general population. A cursory inspection of election results in Wisconsin and other midwest states, however, indicates that many voters who once supported liberal isolationists are now backing right-wing nationalists. It would be interesting to know, for example, what proportion of those who supported the isolationist but progressive Bob La Follette in Wisconsin now backs McCarthy. Conversely, some of the economic radical rightists such as the new millionaires of Texas, or men who were involved in the Liberty League in the thirties, have accepted the isolationist interpretation of the past, even thought they were not isolationists before World War II.

Increasingly, a coherent radical right ideology has emerged which attacks past Democratic foreign policy as pro-Soviet, and criticizes New Deal economic policy as Socialist or Communist inspired. What are the sources of the support of the radical right in this country? It is difficult to answer this question since the groups who back the efforts to suppress the civil rights of men with whom they disagree, do not themselves agree on all or even most issues. The common denominator on which all the supporters of extremist action in the political arena agree is vigorous anti-Communism. This issue, today, has replaced anti-Catholicism or anti-immigrant sentiment as the unifying core for mass right-wing extremist action. One can identify some of the groups which play important roles in the anti-Communist crusade. These include groups reacting to the need for status policies, both the upward mobile ethnic population, and some of the downward mobile old American groups; groups responding to economic as well as status appeals; the *nouveaux riches,* and the insecure small businessmen; the traditionalist and authoritarian elements within the working-class groups whose values or ties to groups in other countries make

them especially vulnerable to anti-Communist appeals
(such as the Catholics or people coming from countries
occupied by the Communists); and the traditional isolationists, especially those of German ancestry.

STATUS POLITICS AND THE RADICAL RIGHT

One traditional source of extreme conservatism in the
United States is the derivation of status from a claim to
the American past—the people who belong to such filio-
pietistic organizations as the Daughters of the American
Revolution, the Colonial Dames, veterans' organizations,
historical commemoration societies, patriotic groups, etc.
The point one must always recognize in considering such
organizations is that few of them are actually what their
name implies. That is, most of these organizations which
supposedly contain all those who have a right to membership in the groups by virtue of their own actions or those
of their ancestors only are supported by a minority of
those who are eligible. The Daughters of the American
Revolution, for example, do not contain all the female
descendants of Revolutionary soldiers, but only a small
segment, those who choose to identify themselves in that
fashion.[31] The same point may be made about the membership of groups commemorating the War of 1812, the
Civil War, the Confederacy, and other comparable
groups. Further, in practice, the members who are active
in these groups, who set policy, constitute an infinitesimal
minority of the total membership.

What is the minority deriving status and other gratifica-
tions from such membership? Various sociological insights
may be of some help here although unfortunately there
is little or no research on their membership. It has been
suggested that individuals who participate in such societies tend disproportionately to be people who have little

other claim to status. They may be members of families which once were important, but whose present position is such that on the basis of personal achievement alone they would have little right to social prestige. Many such individuals tend to magnify this one claim to status, a claim to history, a claim to lineage, an identification with a heroic American past, which other people cannot have. It is their defense against the newcomers, against the rising minority ethnic groups. And consequently, such individuals and their organizations make a fetish out of tradition and past styles of life, and tend to be arch-conservative. Thus the groups which have the greatest sense of status insecurity will oppose both economic reform and internationalism, both of which are viewed as challenges to tradition.

While on one hand, the status-threatened old-family American tends to over-emphasize his identification with American conservative traditions, and thus be potentially or actually a supporter of the radical right, the new American, the minority ethnic, also is in strong need of asserting his status claims. For while the old American desires to maintain his status, the new American wishes to obtain it, to become accepted. This is particularly true for those members of the minority groups who have risen to middle or upper class position in the economic structure. These groups, having entered at the bottom, tend to view the status hierarchy as paralleling the economic ladder; they believe that one need only move up the economic scale to obtain the good things of the society. But, as they move up economically, they encounter social resistance. There is discrimination by the old-family Americans, by the Anglo-Saxon against the minority ethnics. The Boston Brahmins, for example, do not accept the wealthy Irish.[32] As Joseph Kennedy, father of the present Senator and former Ambassador to Great Britain, once put it in reaction to the fact that the Boston press continually made reference to him as Irish: "I was born here, my children were born here. What the hell do I have to do to be an American?" All through the country, one can find ethnic groups, often composed of third and fourth generation Americans, who have developed their own middle and upper classes, but who are still refused admittance into the social circles of Anglo-Saxon Protestants. One of the major reactions to such discrimination, as indicated earlier, is to become overconformist to an assumed American tradition. Since many members of these ethnic groups do not want to be defined as European, they also tend to become isolationist, ultra-patriotic, and even anti-European. For them, as for the old American traditionalist, the positive orientation towards Europe of liberals, of moderate conservative internationalists, creates a challenge to their basic values and to their rejection of Europe. Thus the status-insecure old-family American middle-class, and the status-striving minority ethnics, both arrive at similar political positions.

But to return at this point to the theme developed in the earlier discussion of status politics, status insecurities and status aspirations are most likely to appear as sources of frustration, independent of economic problems, in periods of prolonged prosperity. For such times make it possible for individuals and groups who have moved up to constitute a visible threat to the established status groups; while at the same time the successfully mobile begin to search for means of improving their status. It is obvious that there are always many who do not prosper in periods of prosperity. And it is precisely members of the older prestigeful groups who are disproportionately to be found among the rentier class economically, with many living on fixed incomes, old businesses and the like —sources of income which are prone to decline in their relative position.[33]

Thus, clearly, prosperity magnifies the status problem

by challenging the economic base of the older groups, and accentuating the claim to status of the emerging ones. As a general hypothesis I would suggest that the supporters of the radical right in the 1950's come disproportionately from both the rising ethnic groups, and those old-family Americans who are oriented toward a strong identification with the past.[34]

THE ECONOMIC EXTREMISTS

A second source of support for extreme right-wing activities, here as in other countries, is the important group of newly wealthy individuals thrown up by great prosperity. New wealth most often tends to have extremist ideologies, to believe in extreme conservative doctrines in economic matters.[35] The man who makes money himself feels more insecure about keeping it than do people who possess inherited wealth. He feels more aggrieved about social reform measures which involve redistribution of the wealth, as compared with individuals, still wealthy, who have grown up in an old traditionalist background, which inculcates the values of tolerance traditionally associated with upper-class aristocratic conservatism. It is not without reason that the new millionaires, such as those in Texas, have given extensive financial support to radical right movements, politicians, and to such propaganda organizations as Facts Forum.

While the most important significance of the newly wealthy lies in the power which their money can bring, rather than in their numbers, there is a mass counterpart for them in the general population, the small independent businessmen. Statistical data on social mobility in the United States indicates a great turnover in the ranks of these groups.[36] A large proportion, if not a majority of them, come from other social strata: the small storekeepers and businessmen often are of working-class origin; the small manufacturer often comes out of the ranks of executives, white collar or government workers.

These small businessmen, perhaps more than any other group, have felt constrained by progressive social legislation and the rise of labor unions. They are squeezed harder than large business, since their competitive position does not allow them to pay increases in wages as readily as can big firms. Governmental measures such as social security, business taxes, or various regulations which require filling out forms, all tend to complicate the operation of small business. In general, these people are oriented upwards, wish to become larger businessmen, and take on the values of those who are more successful, or perhaps more accurately, they tend to take over their *image* of the values of more powerful groups, values which are often those of the radical right. Thus, as an hypothesis, it may be suggested that in terms of economic interest motivation, the principal financial support of the radical right comes from those who have newly acquired wealth, and from small business.[37]

Extreme conservatism on economic matters is, of course, not new. During the thirties it was represented by the Liberty League, and by various measures of organized business groups to block the development of trade unions. In general, one could probably safely say that most big business was willing to use undemocratic restrictive measures, such as labor spies and thugs, to prevent the emergence of trade unions in the twenties and thirties. The basic difference between the radical right and the moderate right, at present, however, is that the moderate right, which seemingly includes the majority of big business, has come to accept the changes which have occurred in the last twenty years, including trade unions and various social reforms, whereas the radical right still looks upon these as basic threats to its position. In practice

economic rightists' efforts to turn the clock back have
been successful in many states which are characterized
by the lack of metropolitan areas, by rural and small-town
predominance in the legislatures. In such states, laws
have been passed outlawing the closed union shop, the
amendment to repeal the income tax amendment to the
Constitution has been endorsed by the legislature, and
other legislation designed to destroy the reforms of the
thirties and forties has been enacted. The fact remains,
however, that the bulk of the reforms and institutions the
liberal left created in the thirties and forties remain intact,
and the business conservatives and the radical right cannot feel secure or victorious.

THE "TORY" WORKER

The previous sections have dealt with factors differentiating middle and upper-class supporters of right-wing
extremism from those who back more moderate policies.
The stress on the radical right backers in these strata does
not mean that the principal support of this type of politics
lies here. In fact, survey as well as impressionistic data
suggest that the large majority of these classes adhere to
moderate politics, principally those of the moderate conservative, and that the overwhelming majority of the
middle and upper groups have been consistently opposed
to McCarthy and the whole radical right movement. The
various studies of attitudes toward civil liberties and
McCarthy suggest that the lower a person is in socio-
economic status or educational attainment, the more likely
he is to support McCarthy, favor restrictions on civil
liberties, and back a "get tough" policy with the Communist states.[38]
    The lack of tolerance exhibited by large sections of the
lower classes as compared with the middle classes is, of

course, quite understandable. Support of civil liberties or tolerance for persons with whom one strongly disagrees requires, one would guess, both a high degree of material and psychic security, and considerable sophistication. As compared with the bulk of the middle and upper classes, the working class lacks these attributes. The consequences of these differences are manifest not only in the political arena, but in religion as well, for chiliastic evangelical religions have tended to draw their support from the lower classes, while liberal "tolerant" denominations have almost invariably been middle and upper class groups.

When one attempts, however, to go beyond the variables of economic status and education, in distinguishing between support or opposition to McCarthy or greater or less tolerance in civil liberties among the lower classes, the principal differentiating factors seem to be party allegiance, and religious beliefs. In the United States and Great Britain, the conservative workers, those who back the Tory or Republican parties, tend to have the most intolerant attitudes. Comparative impressionistic data suggests that these differences are not inherent in varying social strata, but rather are a consequence of partisan identifications and values. That is, the Democratic and Labour parties are more concerned with propagating a civil libertarian value system than are the conservative parties. Within the Democratic and Labour parties, however, the working class is more intolerant than the middle class.[39]

The support which a large section of the American working class gives to right-wing extremism today may also be related to the greater sense of status deprivation felt by "failures" in periods of prosperity discussed earlier. Workers who fail to get ahead while some friends, classmates, and fellow war veterans do, are also likely to feel embittered. This prosperity-born bitterness should result in more varied forms of protest in America than in

Europe, since American workers, unlike European ones, do not have a Socialist ideology which places the blame for individual failure on the operation of the social system.[40] While the lower strata constitute the largest section of the mass base of the radical right, especially of McCarthy, who, as we shall see later, makes a particular appeal to them, in power terms they are the least significant. Up to now, there are no organized working-class groups, other than some of the fundamentalist churches, which support radical right activities.[41] And unlike the middle and upper-class supporters of rightist opinions in the area of civil liberties, and foreign policy, who are also economic conservatives, many of the lower-class followers of radical right leaders are in favor of liberal economic policies. Those workers who tend to back extreme right policies in economic as well as civil liberties and foreign policy areas tend to be the most traditionalistic and apolitical in their outlook. The principal significance of lower-class attitudes, therefore, lies in the votes and responses to public polls which they contribute to the radical right rather than in their potential utilization as part of a mass base for an organized movement.[42]

THE ISOLATIONISTS

A fourth basis of strength of the radical right has developed out of the old isolationist-interventionist controversy. The traditional isolationists have become, in large measure, a base of the radical right. If one looks over the background of isolationism in this country, it seems largely rooted in ethnic prejudices or reactions, ties to the homeland, and populist xenophobia. Samuel Lubell, for example, suggests, "The hard core of isolationism in the United States has been ethnic and emotional, not geographic. By far the strongest common characteristic of the isolationist-voting counties is the residence there of ethnic groups with a pro-German or anti-British bias. Far from being indifferent to Europe's wars, the evidence argues that the *isolationists* are over-sensitive to them."[43]

During two wars, the pro-German ethnic groups have been isolationists. In addition to the Germans, and some midwestern Scandinavian groups tied to them by religious and ecological ties, many Irish also have opposed support of Britain in two wars. Because German influence was concentrated in the Midwest, and in part because isola-tionist ideologies were part of the value system of agrarian radicalism, isolationism has been centered in the Midwest, especially among once-radical agrarians. The agrarian radicals of the Midwest tended to be xenophobic, suspi-cious of eastern and international finance capitalism. The various agrarian movements regarded efforts to involve the United States in European conflicts as motivated by the desire of eastern bankers to make money. The radical agrarian character of isolationism, however, gradually began to change for at least two reasons: (1) numerically its mass Midwest base became less and less rural as the farm population declined, and more and more small-town middle class in character; and (2) interventionism was identified with the New Deal and social reform.[44] Thus the small-town midwestern middle class was anti-New Deal, conservative and isolationist; this all added up to a fervent opposition to Roosevelt and his domestic and foreign policy.

This former isolationist group, especially its German base, was under a need to justify its past, and to a certain extent, to gain revenge.[45] The Germans, in particular, were considered disloyal by the Yankees and other native American stock in two wars. Consequently, campaigns which seem to demonstrate that they were right and not disloyal would obviously win their support. The way in which one can understand the resentment against the UN and other international agencies is that these organizations are symbolic of American foreign policy and especially of the foreign policy of World War II, of collective security, of internationalism, of interventionism; and thus the attack on UNESCO, the attack on the UN is an attack on the past, an attack on Roosevelt, an attack on our whole foreign policy from '33 on.

The common tie which binds the former isolationist with the economic radical conservative is on the one hand the common enemy, Roosevelt and the New Deal, and secondly, the common scapegoat with which they can justify their past position. Both can now suggest that they were right, right in opposing the foreign policy or correct in opposing certain economic policies because these past policies were motivated or sustained by Communism or the Communist Party. Thus, both have an interest in magnifying the Communist plot, in identifying liberal and internationalist forces in American society with Communism.

THE CATHOLICS

A fifth source of mass support for the radical right in the recent period are many Catholics. As a rapidly rising group which was largely low status until recently, Catholics might be expected to be vulnerable to status-linked political appeals. In addition and probably more significant, however, Catholics as a religious group are more prone to support anti-Communist movements than any other sect with the possible exception of the fundamentalist Protestant churches.[46] This predisposition derives from the long history of Catholic opposition to Socialism and Communism, an organized opposition which has been perhaps more formalized in theological church terms than

in almost any other group. This opposition has, in recent
years, been magnified by the fact that a number of countries taken over by the Communists in eastern Europe are
Catholic, and it is notable that in Europe those countries
which are most in danger of Communist penetration are,
in fact, Catholic.

In the past, however, Catholics in the United States
and other English-speaking countries, have been traditionally allied with more left-wing parties. For example,
in Great Britain, Australia and New Zealand, the Catholics tend to support the Labor Party. In the United States,
they have backed the Democratic Party, while in Canada
they support the Liberal Party.[47]

The identification of Catholicism with the left in the
English-speaking countries, as compared with its identification with the right in Western Europe, is related to the
fact that the Catholic Church is a minority church in the
English-speaking countries, and has been the church of
the minority ethnic immigrants who have been largely
lower class. As a lower status group, Catholics have been
successfully appealed to by the out-party, by the party
of the lower class.

The rise of the Communist threat, however, and the
identification of Communism with the left has created a
conflict for many Catholics. Historically, this ideological
conflict has developed just as the Catholic population in
most of these countries has produced a sizable upper and
middle class of its own, which in economic terms is under
pressure to abandon its traditional identification with the
lower class party. The Republican Party in the United
States and the (conservative) Liberal Party in Australia
as well, it is interesting to note, are now given an opportunity to break the Catholics from their traditional political mores. The conservatives face the problem in the era
of the welfare state, that welfare politics obviously appeal

to lower-class people. Consequently, for the conservatives to gain a majority (and here I speak not only of the radical right but of the moderate conservatives as well), they must have some issues which cut across class lines, and which can appeal to the lower classes against the party of that class. Traditionally, nationalism and foreign policy issues have been among the most successful means for the conservatives to break through class lines. In this specific case, if the conservatives can identify the left with Communism they may gain the support of many Catholics, both lower and middle class. This combination of the party desire to win elections plus the general desire of conservatives to dominate the society has led them to adopt tactics which normally they would abhor.

It may be appropriate to recall that the use of bigotry as a tactic by the conservatives to gain a political majority is not unknown in American history. The Whig Party before the Civil War, faced with the fact that increased immigration, largely Catholic, was constantly adding to the votes of the Democratic Party, realized that they might never obtain a majority. (They were in much the same position as the Republican Party from 1932 to 1952.) The Whigs, led largely by the so-called aristocratic elements in American society, upper-class Protestants both north and south, supported mass movements which were anti-Catholic and anti-immigrant, because of the belief that this would be the only way to win elections against the party of the "Demagogues," as they described the Democratic Party.

The upper-class Whigs hoped to break lower-class white Protestants from their support of the Democratic Party by identifying that party with the immigrants and with the Catholics. Today, of course, the position is reversed. The attempt is not so much to break Protestants from the Democrats, but to win the Catholics from the

Democrats. The Republicans wish to break the Democratic allegiance of the Catholics, rather than use them as a scapegoat to secure lower-class Protestant voters.[48]

It is also interesting to note that, since liberal groups draw so much support from the Catholics, it is an exceedingly delicate matter for them to defend themselves against the charge that they once made common cause with the Communists. American liberals are under pressure to deny their past, rather than defend it. To admit that liberals ever had sympathy for the Soviet Union, or that they ever in any way collaborated with Communists would be akin to confession, at least so far as their Catholic supporters are concerned, of collaboration with the Devil. In order to defend itself and to retain its Catholic base, the liberal left must either outdo the right in Communist charges, or at least tacitly agree with it. It fears that a large part of its mass base agrees with the radical right on the Communist question.[49]

The introduction of a bill to outlaw the Communist Party by the most liberal members of the United States Senate is an example of this phenomenon. Many of them are vulnerable to the charge of Communist collaboration. Paul Douglas, as a Socialist, visited the Soviet Union, and was addressed as Comrade by Stalin. This interview was published by the Communist Party. Wayne Morse was strongly backed by Harry Bridges in his election to the United States Senate. Hubert Humphrey was elected to the Senate by the Democratic-Farmer-Labor Party, shortly after the Communists captured the old Minnesota Farmer-Labor Party, and merged it with the Democratic Party of the state. None of these men ever supported the Communist Party, or even has any record of fellow-traveling for a brief period. Nevertheless, facts such as these would be difficult to explain without these men giving repeated evidence of their being strongly anti-Communist.

The situation in the Catholic community, today, is similar to conditions in the Jewish community during the thirties. The Jews, concerned with the growth of Nazism, felt the need to do something about it. Nazism became an important political issue for them. This situation played into the hands of the Communists who used the fight against Nazism as their principal appeal. And it is a fact that the Communists had considerable success among the Jews in this period.[50] Perhaps even more important was the fact that this influence often affected the political ideology and tactics of Jewish organizations which were in no way Communist.

Today the Catholics face the Communist issue as the Jews did Nazism. Even unscrupulous anti-Communism, the sort which is linked to motives and policies unrelated to the problem of fighting Communists, can win support within the Catholic community. And just as the Communists were able to press forward various other aspects of their ideology among the Jews in the 1930's, so the radical right, stressing the anti-Communist issue, is able to advance other parts of its program. The radical right uses the anti-Communist issue to create or sustain hostility among the Catholics against the New Deal, against social reform, at the same time identifying liberalism with Communism.

It is, therefore, impossible to analyze the impact of the radical right on American life without considering the vulnerability of the Catholics to the Communist issue, and the effect of this Catholic sensitivity on the political strategy of both Republican and Democratic politicians in their reactions to the radical right. For politic reasons many existing analyses of the radical right have found it convenient to ignore the Catholics, and attempts have been made to interpret the problem in terms of other variables or concepts, some of which, like the minority ethnic's reaction to status deprivation, have been suggested in this chapter as well. While such processes are important, it should not be forgotten that the majority of Catholics is still proletarian, and not yet in a position to make claim to high status. The role of the Catholic vulnerability to the radical right today, like the similar reaction of the Jews to the Communists a decade ago, must be considered independently of the fact that both groups have also reacted to the situation of being an ethnic minority.[51]

THE CATALYTIC ELEMENTS

No analysis of the social strata and political tendencies which make up the radical right can be complete without a discussion of the catalytic elements, members of near Fascist and so-called borderline organizations, or individuals who though never members of such groups have maintained right-wing authoritarian sentiments. These groups and individuals have advocated extremist right-wing ideologies for a long time. Although their number may vary and their strength may fluctuate, they remain as a chronic source of potential extremist sentiments and organization. During the thirties, there were many avowedly authoritarian Fascist and racist organizations. Racism, at least in the form of anti-Semitism, lost much of its appeal during and following World War II. But while racism became even less useful politically than it ever had been, exposés of Communist plots, a traditional activity of most right-wing authoritarians, fitted in with the popular mood. It is probable that the neo-Fascist groups and individual authoritarians today use the Communist issue instead of anti-Semitism.[52] For many of them hunting Communists with the seeming approval of society is much more palatable than attacking Jews. Engaging in attacks on alleged Communists or subversives may now serve to enhance their status, while attacks on minority groups meant accepting the role of a political and social deviant.

Here again, the analogy may be made with the role of the Communists in the late thirties and early forties. Being pro-New Deal and anti-Fascist, political values which were held by a large part of the population, made it psychologically much easier for Communists to operate than when they were primarily engaged in an avowed struggle for Communism. A number of former Communists have reported that many of the party members and leaders seemed much happier in this role in the late thirties and early forties than in their earlier phase as avowed revolutionaries. In this latter period, the Communist movement was much more effective in initiating campaigns which appealed to large sections of the population.

While there is no right-wing conspiracy equivalent to that of the Communist Party (the various organizations and groups are disunited and often conflict with each other), nevertheless, there is an amorphous radical right extremist movement which receives the support of many who are not open members of extremist organizations. These may be termed the fellow-travelers of the radical right. In sociological terms, these groups should come disproportionately from the categories discussed earlier, that is, from the status-threatened or the status-aspiring, from the *nouveaux riches,* from the small businessman, from the ardent Catholics. However, it may be suggested that some of the research findings of studies such as the *Authoritarian Personality*[53] are relevant in this context. The *Authoritarian Personality* and similar studies suggest that for a certain undefined minority of the population various personality frustrations and repressions result in the adoption of scapegoat sentiments. Such individuals are probably to be found disproportionately among the

members of various patriotic and anti-Communist societies, in the crackpot extremist groups, and significantly in
the committees of various Communist-hunt groups, for
example, in the un-American activities committees of
local Legion posts, and other groups. No one can object to
people fighting Communists. If a minority in an organization denounces individual X or Y as a Communist, one
may expect a general tendency for other members of the
group to accept the charge in terms of their identification
with the organization. Thus, with the climate of opinion
shifted to the right, and with the Communist issue important to many people, that minority of individuals who for
one reason or another feel the need to hunt out local
subversive conspirators will be supported by many individuals and groups, who left alone would rarely engage
in such activities.[54]

One other group is important in the development of the
radical right since World War II: the ex-Communists.
Some of them, along with some other former non-Communist radicals, have given a coherent tone and ideology
to the radical right. Basically, the radical right is unintel-
lectual. Its leaders know very little about Communism or
international affairs, and as a matter of fact, have little
interest in international affairs. The former radicals and
Communists can pinpoint for the ideologists and spokesmen of the radical right those areas in American life
where Communists have been important, those aspects
of American foreign policy which are most vulnerable
to attack. Perhaps the best example of this phenomenon
is to be found in *The Freeman.* Many of the writers for
this magazine have been former leftists, such as James
Burnham, William Schlamm, John Chamberlain, Ralph De
Toledano, J. B. Matthews, Freda Utley, Eugene Lyons,
John T. Flynn, George Schuyler, and Charlotte Haldane.

Before concluding this review of general tendencies,
one interesting and important contradiction between radi-

cal right ideology in the United States and the consequences of its promulgation should be stressed. Most of
the intellectual and political spokesmen of the radical
right proclaim a belief in complete liberty for all. *The
Freeman* reads like a philosophical anarchist magazine.
Its present editor, Frank Chodorov, has proclaimed the
libertarian gospel in two recent books, *One is a Crowd,*
and *The Income Tax: Root of All Evil.* The New Deal is
often denounced for having endangered civil liberties and
individual freedom by increasing the power of the state
and trade unions. Many of the speakers at the November
29, 1954 Madison Square Garden rally to protest the
Senate censure of Senator McCarthy demanded the preservation of a "government of limited powers." Writers
for *The Freeman* often criticize the tariff. Basically, the
ideology of extreme conservatism in this country is *laissez-
faire.* McCarthy's young intellectual spokesman, William
Buckley, strongly supported the doctrines of Adam Smith
in the same book in which he demanded a purge of
American university faculties of left-wingers.[55] In a real
sense, the radical right is led by the Frondists of American
society, those who want to turn the clock back to a
golden age of little government.

3

McCARTHYISM: THE UNIFYING IDEOLOGY[56]

Extreme conservatism cannot ever hope to create a
successful mass movement on the basis of its socio-
economic program alone. Except during significant economic crisis, the majority of the traditional middle and
upper class conservative elements are not likely to support
extremist movements and ideologies, even when presented
in the guise of conservatism, and the lower classes do not

support movements in defense of privilege. The problem of the radical right is to develop a political philosophy which will have appeal to its traditional rightist support, but will also enable it to win a mass base. Nazism was able to do this in Germany by combining a strong nationalist appeal to the status-threatened German middle and upper class, together with an "attack on Jewish international capitalism" designed to win over those most concerned with economic reform. As a number of European political commentators have suggested, anti-Semitism has often been the extreme rightist equivalent for the Socialist attack on capitalism. The Jewish banker replaces the exploiting capitalist as the scapegoat.

In the United States, the radical right had to find some comparable method of appealing to the groups which have a sense of being underprivileged, and McCarthy's principal contribution to the crystallization of the radical right in the 1950's has been to locate the key symbols with which to unite all its potential supporters.[57] McCarthy's crusade is not just against the liberal elements of the country, cast in the guise of "creeping Socialists;" he is also campaigning against the same groups midwest Populism always opposed, the Eastern conservative financial aristocracy. In his famous Wheeling, West Virginia speech of February 9, 1950, McCarthy began his crusade against internal Communism by presenting for the first time an image of the internal enemy:

> The reason why we find ourselves in a position of impotency is not because our only potential enemy has sent men to invade our shores, but rather because of the traitorous actions of those who have been treated so well by this nation. It is not the less fortunate, or members of minority groups who have been selling this nation out, but rather those who have had all the benefits the wealthiest nation on earth has had to offer—the *finest homes*, the *finest college educations*, and the *finest jobs* in the govern-

ment that we can give. This is glaringly true in the
State Department. There the *bright young men who
are born with silver spoons in their mouth are the
ones who have been worse.*[58]

This defense of the minority groups and the underprivileged, and the attack on the upper class has characterized the speeches and writings of McCarthy and his
followers. McCarthy differs considerably from earlier
extreme right-wing anti-Communists. He is rarely interested in investigating or publicizing the activities of
men who belong to minority ethnic groups. The image
of the Communist which recurs time and again in his
speeches is one of an easterner, usually of Anglo-Saxon
Episcopalian origins, who has been educated in schools
such as Groton and Harvard.

The attack on the elite recurs frequently in the current
writings of the radical right. *The Freeman* magazine
writes that "Asian coolies and Harvard professors are
the people . . . most susceptible to Red propaganda."[59]
Facts Forum describes intellectuals as the group most vulnerable to Communism, and defines intellectuals as,
"lawyers, doctors, bankers, teachers, professors, preachers,
writers, publishers."[60] In discussing the Hiss case, Facts
Forum argued that the forces defending Hiss which were
most significant were not the Communists, themselves,
but "the American respectables, *the socially pedigreed,*
the culturally acceptable, the certified gentlemen and
scholars of the day, dripping with college degrees. . . . In
general, it was the 'best people' who were for Alger
Hiss."[61] In discussing McCarthy's enemies, the *Freeman*
stated: "He possesses, it seems a sort of animal, negative-
pole magnetism which repels alumni of Harvard, Princeton, and Yale. And we think we know what it is: *This
young man is constitutionally incapable of deference to
social status.*"[62]

Over and over again runs the theme, the common men
in America have been victimized by members of the upper

classes, by the prosperous, by the wealthy, by the well educated. When specific names are given, these are almost invariably individuals whose names and backgrounds permit them to be identified with symbols of high status. As McCarthy could attack other individuals and groups, this concentration on the Anglo-Saxon elite is no accident. What are the purposes it serves?

Since McCarthy comes from Wisconsin, where for forty years isolationism and attacks on eastern business and Wall Street were staple political fare, he may have been searching for an equivalent to the La Follette appeal. Much of the electorate of Wisconsin, and other sections of the Midwest, the German-Americans and those who were sympathetic to their isolationist viewpoint, have been smarting under the charge of disloyalty. McCarthy has argued that it was not the isolationists, but rather those who favored our entry into war with Germany who were the real traitors, since by backing Great Britain they had played into the hands of the Soviet Union. The linkage between the attacks on Anglo-Saxon Americans and Great Britain may be seen in McCarthy's infrequent speeches on foreign policy; these invariably wind up with an attack on Great Britain, sometimes with a demand for action (such as economic sanctions, or pressure to prevent her from trading with Red China).[63] Thus McCarthy is in fact attacking the same groups in the United States and on the world scene, as his liberal predecessors.

On the national scene, McCarthy's attacks are probably much more important in terms of their appeal to status frustrations than to resentful isolationism. In the identification of traditional symbols of status with pro-Communism the McCarthy followers, of non-Anglo-Saxon extraction, can gain a feeling of superiority over the traditionally privileged groups. Here is a prosperity-born equivalent for the economic radicalism of depressions. For the resentment created by prosperity is basically not against the economic power of Wall Street bankers, or Yankees, but against their status power. An attack on their loyalty, on their Americanism, is clearly also an attack on their status. And this group not only rejects the status claims of the minority ethnics, but also snubs the *nouveaux riches* millionaires.

The celebrated Army-McCarthy hearings vividly presented to a national television audience the differences between the McCarthyites and their moderate Republican opponents. Every member of McCarthy's staff who appeared on television, with but one exception, was either Catholic, Jewish or Greek Orthodox in religion, and Italian, Greek, Irish, or Jewish in national origin. The non-military spokesmen of the Eisenhower administration on the other hand were largely wealthy Anglo-Saxon Protestants. In a real sense, this televised battle was between successfully mobile minority ethnics and, in the main, upper-class Anglo-Saxon Protestants.

It is also interesting to note that McCarthy is probably the first extreme rightist politician in America to rely heavily on a number of Jewish advisors. These include George Sokolsky, the Hearst columnist, Arthur Kohlberg, a Far-Eastern exporter, and of course, his former counsel, Roy Cohn. (These Jewish McCarthyites are, however, unrepresentative of the Jewish population generally, even of its upper strata, since all survey data as well as impressionistic evidence indicate that the large majority of American Jews are liberal on both economic and civil liberties issues.)

An attack on the status system could conceivably antagonize groups within the radical right: such as the patriotic societies, the Daughters of the American Revolution, and members of old upper-status families like Archibald Roosevelt, who chaired a testimonial dinner for Roy Cohn. Yet, attacks on the Anglo-Saxon Yankee scapegoat do not have this effect because they are directed against majority elements in the society. Criticism of Jews or the Irish, or Italians or Negroes, would have resulted in an immediate response from members of the attacked group. Anglo-Saxon white Protestants, as a majority group, however, are not sensitive to criticism, they are not vulnerable to being attacked, nor do they expect attack. McCarthy, on the one hand, can throw out symbols and images which appeal to the minority ethnics, to the Germans, to the Irish, and the Italians, without at the same time securing the hostility of radical rightists who also are members of the D.A.R., the Sons of the American Revolution, the Patriotic Dames or any other comparable group.[64] And in spite of his populist-type symbols, he can retain the support of these groups and the cooperation of some big businessmen. This is his peculiar power. To the status-deprived he is a critic of the upper class; to the privileged, he is a foe of social change and Communism.

ANTI-COMMUNISM: THE WEAKNESS OF A SINGLE ISSUE

In spite of its early successes in intimidating opponents, and gaining widespread support behind some of its leaders, the radical right has not succeeded in building even one organization of any political significance. And without organizing its backing, it cannot hope to secure any lasting power. This failure is not accidental, or a result of inept leadership, but stems from the fact rather that the only *political* issue which unites the various supporters of radical right politicians is anti-Communism.[65] It is only at the leadership level that agreement exists on a program for domestic and foreign policy. The mass base, however, is far from united on various issues. For example, as McCarthy well knows, the dairy farmers of

Wisconsin want the government to guarantee 100 per cent parity prices. But this policy is an example of government regimentation to some of the extremist elements on his side.

The Catholic working class remains committed to the economic objectives of the New Deal, and still belongs to trade unions. While McCarthy and other radical rightists may gain Catholic support for measures which are presented under the guise of fighting Communism, they will lose it on economic issues. And should economic issues become important again as during a recession, much of the popular support for McCarthyism will fall away. As a result any attempt to build a radical right movement which has a complete political program is risky, and probably will not occur.

The radical right also faces the problem that it unites bigots of different varieties. In the South and other parts of the country, fundamentalist Protestant groups which are anti-Semitic and anti-Catholic back the radical right in spite of the fact that McCarthy is a Catholic.

One illustration of the way in which these contradictions among his supporters can cause difficulty is a statement which appeared in the New York *Journal-American*: "I think Joe owes the Army an apology but I doubt if our soldiers will get it. The Senator has sure lost his touch since he took up with those oil rich, anti-Catholic Texas millionaires. They are the very same gang which threw the shiv at Al Smith back in 1928."[66]

Perhaps the greatest threat to the political fortunes of the radical right has been the victory of Eisenhower in 1952. As long as the Republican Party was in opposition the radical right could depend upon covert support, or at worst, neutrality from most of the moderate conservative sections of the Republican Party. Even when they viewed the methods of the radical right with distaste, the party leadership saw the group as potential vote gainers.

The frustration of twenty years in opposition reduced the scruples of many Republicans, especially those who were involved in party politics.

The differences between the radical right and the moderate right are evident indeed and open factionalism existed in the party long before the election of Eisenhower. Nevertheless, the evidence is quite clear that a large proportion, if not the majority of the moderate Republicans, did not view McCarthy or the radical right as a menace to the party, until he began his attack upon them. Walter Lippmann once persuasively argued that when the Republicans were in office they would be able to control the radical right, or that the radical right would conform for the sake of party welfare. Most Republicans probably at the time agreed. However, the program of Eisenhower Republicanism has not been one of turning the clock back, nor has it fed the psychic needs of the radical right in domestic or foreign policy. Eisenhower's policies in the White House have certainly not reduced the needs of radical right groups for political action, for scapegoatism. They have not reduced McCarthy's desires to capitalize upon popular issues to maintain power and prestige in the general body politic. As a result, the radical right is now forced to struggle openly with the moderate conservatives, essentially the Eisenhower Republicans, who in large measure represent established big business.[67] This is a fight it cannot hope to win, but the danger exists that the moderates in their efforts to resist charges of softness to Communism, or simply to defeat the Democrats, will take over some of the issues of the radical right, in order to hold its followers, while destroying the political influence of its leaders.

The development of open warfare between the moderate Republican, high status, and big business groups on one hand, and McCarthy and the radical rightists on the other, has probably represented the turning point in the power of the latter. Thirty years earlier, the Ku Klux Klan was severely crippled by the emerging antagonism of the traditional power groups. As was pointed out earlier, many of its middle-class members dropped out of the organization when they discovered that such membership would adversely affect their status and economic interests. Today as in 1923-24, the moderate conservative upper-class community has finally been aroused to the threat to its position and values represented by the radical right.[68]

It is extremely doubtful that the radical right will grow beyond the peak of 1953-54. It has reached its optimum strength in a period of prosperity, and a recession will probably cripple its political power. It cannot build an organized movement. Its principal current significance, and perhaps permanent impact on the American scene, lies in its success in overstimulating popular reaction to the problem of internal subversion, in supplying the impetus for changes which may have lasting effects on American life, e.g., the heightened security program, political controls on passports, political tests for schoolteachers, and increasing lack of respect for an understanding of the Constitutional guarantees of civil and juridical rights for unpopular minorities and scoundrels.

It is important, however, not to exaggerate the causal influence of the radical right on the development of restrictions on civil liberties in American life. More significant than the activities of any group of active extremists are the factors in the total political situation which made Americans fearful of Communism. Perhaps most important of all these is the fact that for the first time since the War of 1812, the United States has been faced with a major foreign enemy before whom it has had to retreat. The loss of eastern Europe, of China, the impasse in Korea, Indo-China and Formosa, the seeming fiasco of our post-war foreign policy, have required an explanation. The theory that these events occurred because we were "stabbed in the back" by a "hidden force" is much more palatable than admitting the possibility that the Communists have stronger political assets than we do. The fear and impotence forced on us by the impossibility of a nuclear war requires some outlet. And a hunt for the internal conspirators may appear as one positive action. Political extremists are capitalizing on our doubts and fears, but it is the situation which creates these doubts and fears, rather than the extremists, that is mainly responsible for the lack of resistance by the political moderates.

Every major war in American history has brought with it important restrictions on civil liberties. Recognition of this fact has often led Americans who were primarily concerned with the preservation of civil liberties to oppose our entry into war. Before World War II, such ardent anti-Fascists as Robert Hutchins and Norman Thomas opposed an interventionist policy, on the grounds that entry into a prolonged major war might result in the destruction of American democracy. History fortunately records the fact that they were mistaken. The current situation, however, is obviously more threatening than any previous one, for one can see no immediate way for the United States to win the fight against Communism. And we now face the serious danger that a prolonged cold war may result in the institutionalization of many of the current restrictions on personal freedom which have either been written into law, or have become normal government administration procedure. Those who regard extremist anti-civil libertarian phases of American history as temporary and unimportant in long-range terms should be cautioned that one of the consequences of the Ku Klux Klan and the post World War I wave of anti-radical and anti-foreigner hysteria was the restrictive immigration laws based on racist assumptions. The Klan died and the anti-radical hysteria subsided, but the quota restrictions based on the assumption of Nordic supremacy remained. Clearly the recent defeat of Senator McCarthy and the seeming decline of radical right support have not resulted in an end or even modification of many of the measures and administrative procedures which were initiated in response to radical right activity. Consequently if the cold war continues, the radical right, although organizationally weak, may play an important role in changing the character of American democracy.[69]

[1] The intellectual sources of this paper are far more numerous than the footnote references acknowledge. In particular, I am indebted to Richard Hofstadter, whose "The Pseudo-Conservative Revolt" forms chapter 2 of this volume, and Immanuel Wallerstein's "McCarthyism and the Conservative" (M.A. thesis in the Department of Sociology, Columbia University, 1954). This paper is Publication No. A169 of the Bureau of Applied Social Research, Columbia University, one of a series prepared for the Fund for the Republic.

[2] I do not assert that every or even most individuals or groups I classify in the radical right are involved in, or sympathetic to efforts to reduce personal freedom. In fact, as is made clear later in this paper, the ideology of the radical right is a belief in as much *laissez-faire* as possible. Most supporters of radical right politics believe that they are helping to increase democratic rights for everyone. The point is, however, that the nature of their attacks on political opponents, the definition they make of liberal or left politics as illegitimate, un-American, creeping socialism, fellow-traveling or worse, does have the consequence of encouraging the denial of civil liberties to their political opponents.

[3] For a discussion of class and status politics in another context see, S. M. Lipset and R. Bendix, "Social Status and Social Structure," *British Journal of Sociology*, II (1951), especially pp. 230–33. Similar concepts are used by Richard Hofstadter in Chapter 2.

[4] It is important to note that scapegoat and ethnic prejudice politics have not been exclusively the tactic of prosperity-based movements. Anti-Semitic movements, in particular, have also emerged during depressions. The Populist movement and Father Coughlin's National Union for Social Justice are perhaps two of the most significant ones. It should be noted, however, that both of these movements focused primarily on proposed solutions to economic problems rather than racism. Initially, these groups were concerned with solving economic problems by taking away control of the credit system from the private bankers. Anti-Semitism emerged in both as a means of symbolizing their attack on eastern or international financiers. It is interesting to note that many movements which center their explanation of the cause for depressions on the credit system often wind up attacking the Jews. The Social Credit movement is the most recent example of this pattern. Apparently the underlying

cultural identification of the international financier with the international Jew is too strong for these groups to resist. In each case, however, Populism, Coughlinism, and Social Credit, the economic program preceded anti-Semitism.

5 Historians have traditionally explained the decline of the Know-Nothings as a result of their inability to take a firm position on the slavery issue. Recent research, however, suggests that the depression may have been even more important than the slavery agitation. Detailed study of pre-Civil War electoral behavior indicates that the slavery issue played a minor role in determining shifts from one party to another. Evidence for these statements will be found in a forthcoming monograph by Lee Benson of the Bureau of Applied Social Research, Columbia University.

6 Humphrey J. Desmond, *The A.P.A. Movement* (Washington: The New Century Press, 1912), pp. 9–10.

7 While the A.P.A. arose and won strength in a prosperous era, it continued to grow during the depression of 1893. Gustavus Myers, however, suggests that one of the major reasons for its rapid decline in the following two or three years was the fact that many of its leaders and members became actively involved in the class politics which grew out of this depression. That is, many A.P.A.ers either joined the Bryan movement or actively supported McKinley, depending on their socio-economic position. Thus, the decline of the A.P.A., also, may be laid in large part to the fact that a depression accentuates economic issues and makes status concerns less important.

See Gustavus Myers, *History of Bigotry in the United States* (New York: Random House, 1943), pp. 244–245.

8 R. Hofstadter, *The Age of Reform* (New York: Alfred A. Knopf, 1955).

9 Quantitative evidence which fits in with this interpretation of the Progressive movement may be found in an unpublished paper, "The Genteel Revolt Against Politics—A study of the New York State Progressive Party in 1912," by Richard Ravitch. He summed up his statistical analysis as follows:

"It would be wrong to assume that the Progressives were anti-Catholic, but it was unusual for a political party in New York to have only one Catholic in its midst. Several Bull Mooses [Progressives] had belonged to the Guardians of Liberty, an organization which attacked the Church; but they withdrew to avoid the political repercussions. Certainly it can be said that the overwhelming religious affiliation was that of the Conservative [high status] Protestant sects.

"They were men conspicuous for their lack of association with the two groups which were slowly becoming the dominant forces in American life—the industrialist and the union leader. They were part of an older group which was losing the high status and prestige once held in American society. The Progressives represented the middle-class of the nineteenth century with all its emphasis on individualism and a set of values that was basically provincial. Resenting the encroachment on 'his' America by the corporations and urban masses, the formation of the Progressive Party may be considered his way of protesting what was now his defensive position in the bewildering 'drift' which characterized 20th century society."

Evidence that anti-Catholic sentiment was strong during the pre-World War I prosperity may also be adduced from the fact that a leading anti-Catholic paper, *The Menace*, had a circulation of 1,400,000 in 1914.

Emerson H. Loucks, *The Ku Klux Klan in Pennsylvania* (Harrisburg, Pennsylvania: The Telegraph Press, 1936), p. 16.

[10] This discussion is based largely on an unpublished paper by Nathan Glazer. For documentation of the various points made here see John Moffat Mecklin, *The Ku Klux Klan: A Study of the American Mind* (New York: Harcourt Brace and Co., 1924); E. H. Loucks, *op. cit.*; Henry Fry Peck, *The Modern Ku Klux Klan* (Boston: Small, Maynard and Co., 1922); Frank Bohn, "The Ku Klux Klan Interpreted," *American Journal of Sociology*, January 1925, pp. 385–407.

[11] It is interesting to note in this connection that much of the earlier extremist agitation also dealt with supposed plots of foreign agents. For example, the agitation leading to the Alien and Sedition Acts before 1800, the anti-Catholic movements, all involved claims that agents of a foreign power or of the Pope sought to subvert American life and institutions. The leaders of these movements all argued that men with loyalties to foreign institutions had no claim to civil liberties in America. "Can a Romanist be a good citizen of America . . . ? Romanism is a political system—as a political power it must be met. . . . *No ballot for the man who takes his politics from the Vatican.*" Reverend James B. Dunn, leader of the A.P.A. quoted in Myers, *op. cit.*, p. 227. (Emphasis in Myers.)

The present situation, of course, differs from these past ones in that there *is* a foreign directed conspiracy, the Communist Party. But today, as in the past, the new right seeks to link native, non-Communist expression of dissent to foreign powers as well.

[12] Morton Grodzins, *Americans Betrayed, Politics and the Japanese Evacuation* (Chicago: University of Chicago Press, 1949).

[13] See Herbert Hyman and Paul Sheatsley, "Trends in Public Opinion on Civil Liberties," *Journal of Social Issues*, IX (1953), No. 3, pp. 6–17.

[14] Samuel A. Stouffer, *Communism, Conformity, and Civil Liberties* (New York: Doubleday and Co., 1955), p. 32–33; see the summary and discussion of his findings in Chapter 6.

[15] *Ibid.*, pp. 28–31.

[16] *Ibid.*, pp. 39–46.

[17] David Riesman has suggested that the factors sustaining extreme moralism in American life are declining as more and more Americans are becoming "other-oriented," more concerned with being liked than being right. While Riesman's distinction between inner-oriented and other-oriented people is useful for analytical purposes, I still believe that viewed cross-culturally, Americans are more likely to view politics in moralistic terms than most Europeans. No American politician would say of an ally, as did Churchill of Russia, that I will ally with the "devil, himself," for the sake of victory. The American alliance with Russia had to be an alliance with a "democrat" even if the ally did not know he was democratic. Both the liberal reaction to the possibility of alliance with Chiang Kai-shek and Franco, and the conservative reaction to recognition of Communist China are but the latest examples of the difficulty which morality creates for our international diplomacy. See

David Riesman, *The Lonely Crowd* (New Haven: Yale University Press, 1950), for a discussion of the decline of such morality; and George Kennan, *American Diplomacy, 1900–1950* (New York: New American Library, 1952). Gabriel A. Almond, *The American People and Foreign Policy* (New York: Harcourt, Brace & Company, 1950), Chap. III, "American Character and Foreign Policy"; Raymond Aron, *The Century of Total War* (London: Derek Verschoyle, 1954), pp. 103–104, for analysis of the way in which morality in politics hampers our foreign policy.

[18] See Will Herberg, "Government by Rabble-Rousing," *The New Leader*, Jan. 18, 1954.

[19] It is true, of course, that there has been an alternative nationalist reaction, such as Zionism among the Jews, the Garvey movement among the Negroes, and identification with national societies among other groups. In large measure, however, these patterns have been the reaction of lower-status, usually foreign-born members of immigrant groups. Once assimilated, and accepted, immigrant groups often adopt the so-called "third generation" pattern in which they attempt to re-identify with their past national traditions. While this pattern would seem to conflict with assumption that conformity is the norm, I would suggest that it fits into the needs of individuals in a mass urban culture to find symbols of belongingness which are smaller than the total society.

[20] Churchill made this statement in the House, in defending his refusal to declare the Communist Party, then opposed to the war, illegal.

[21] See Leon Samson, *Toward A United Front* (New York: Farrar and Rinehart, 1933).

[22] For further comments on this theme see S. M. Lipset, "Democracy in Alberta," *The Canadian Forum*, November and December 1954, pp. 175–177, 196–198.

[23] Alexis de Tocqueville, *Democracy in America* (London: Oxford University Press, 1946), pp. 376–381.

[24] Arnold Rose, "Voluntary Associations in France," in *Theory and Method in the Social Sciences* (Minneapolis: University of Minnesota Press, 1954), pp. 72–115. Mass Observation, *Puzzled People* (London: Victor Gollancz, 1947), pp. 119–122.

[25] S. D. Clark, "The Frontier and Democratic Theory," *Transactions of the Royal Society of Canada*, Volume XLVII, Series III, June 1954, p. 72.

[26] That this is somewhat legitimate may be seen by analyzing the social bases of support of these totalitarian movements. In general, Communists, where strong, receive support from the same social strata which vote for democratic socialist or liberal groups in countries with weak Communist movements. Conversely, Fascist and right authoritarians, such as De Gaulle, have received their backing from previous supporters of conservative parties. There is little evidence of an authoritarian appeal *per se*. Rather, it would seem that under certain conditions part of the conservative group will become Fascists, while under others, part of the support of the democratic left will support the Communists. See S. M. Lipset, et al., "Psychology of Voting," in Gardner Lindzey, ed., *Handbook of Social Psychology* (Cambridge: Addison Wesley, 1954), pp. 1135–1136.

[27] For a discussion of the way in which the radical right systematically attacks the Brahmin upper class in the State Department, see pp. 210–11 of this essay. Even as late as 1952, the left-wing journalist I. F. Stone attempted to bolster his attack on American policy in Korea by calling attention to the fact "that Acheson on making his Washington debut at the Treasury before the war, had been denounced by New Dealers as a 'Morgan man,' a Wall Street Trojan Horse, a borer-from-within on behalf of the big bankers." I. F. Stone, *The Hidden History of the Korean War* (New York: Monthly Review Press, 1952), p. 204.

It should be noted that, in so far as education at Harvard, Yale or Princeton is an indicator of upper-class background, the extremist critics of the State Department are correct in their claim that persons with a high-status background are disproportionately represented in the State Department. A study of 820 Foreign Office Officers indicated that 27 per cent of them graduated from these institutions, while only 14 per cent of high-ranking civil servants in other departments had similar collegiate backgrounds. (R. Bendix, *Higher Civil Servants in American Society* [Boulder: University of Colorado Press, 1949] pp. 92–93.)

Some evidence that elite background is even of greater significance in the higher echelons of the State Department may be found in a recent article published in the *Harvard Alumni Bulletin*:

"The new United States Ambassador to the Federal Republic of Germany (James B. Conant, Harvard '14, and former president of the University) will find, if he looks about him, fellow alumni in comparable positions. Across the border to the south and west, the Belgian ambassador is Frederick M. Alger, Jr. '30, and the French ambassador is C. Douglas Dillon, '31. Down the Iberian Peninsula the ambassadors to Spain and Portugal are John D. Lodge '25, and James C. H. Bonbright '25. A bit to the north, Ambassador Conant will find Ambassador Robert D. Coe '23 in Denmark and John M. Cabot '23 in Sweden. In the forbidden land to the east of him is Charles E. Bohlen '27, Ambassador to the U.S.S.R. Near at hand, across the Channel, is the senior member of Harvard's ambassadorial galaxy, Winthrop W. Aldrich '07, LL.D. '53, Ambassador to Great Britain. . . . There seem to be enough Harvard ambassadors for a baseball team in Europe. . . ." ("Ambassadors" in *Harvard Alumni Bulletin*, vol. 57, May 21, 1955, p. 617.)

[28] Edna Lonergan, "Anatomy of the PAC," *The Freeman*, November 27, 1950, pp. 137–139.

[29] A good example of extreme right ideology is contained in the newspaper report of a speech delivered at a meeting of Alliance, Inc., a right-wing group sponsored by Archibald Roosevelt:

"Gov. J. Bracken Lee of Utah declared last night that 'We have in Washington what to my mind amounts to a dictatorship.'

"Asserting that high spending was heading the country toward poverty, he . . . [said] that the end result of all dictatorships was the same. 'They end up with a ruling class and all the rest of us are peons.' . . .

"There was no difference, he continued, between the Government in Russia and an all powerful central government in Washington. . . .

". . . all the trouble in Washington began when a constitutional amendment authorized the income tax. He assailed the United Nations, foreign aid and Federal grants to the states.

"He appealed to those who felt the way he did 'to speak up now.' When a voice in the audience asked, 'How,' he replied: 'If you feel that McCarthy's on our side say so.' This reference to Senator Joseph R. McCarthy of Wisconsin evoked applause, cheers and whistles."

See "Governor of Utah Sees Dictatorship," *New York Times,* February 18, 1955, p. 19.

For a description of the ideology of the radical right, or as he calls them, the ultra-conservatives, see Clinton Rossiter, *Conservatism in America* (New York: Alfred A. Knopf, 1955) pp. 183–186.

[30] One hypothesis which may explain the subsequent bitterness of some of the former liberals and leftists who broke with Roosevelt over his foreign policies is contained in a defense of the Moscow trials of the 1930's written by John T. Flynn in his more leftist days.

"Americans found it difficult to believe that the old Bolsheviks recently executed in Russia, after all their years of warfare against capitalism, could have been really guilty of intriguing with Italy and Germany to destroy Stalin. That seemed unbelievable. *This incredulity struck me as possible only by ignoring the strange distance which the human mind and heart can lead a man of strong feeling when they begin to generate hatreds.* Now we have a weird case of it in our own far more composed country. Would anyone have believed, four years ago for instance, that in 1937 we would behold John Frey, of the A.F.L.—as fine a person as one would care to meet—actually consorting with a company union in steel to defeat and destroy a singularly successful industrial union movement led by John L. Lewis? Yet this fantastic thing has occurred. It is no stranger than a Russian editor full of hatred of Stalin seeking to circumvent that gentleman's plans by teaming up for the moment with Hitler." *New Republic,* March 24, 1937, pp. 209–210 (my emphasis).

[31] It is worth noting that existing evidence suggests that there is a substantial difference in the reactions of men and women to the radical right. Women are much more likely to support repressive measures against Communists and other deviant groups than are men as measured by poll responses, and many of the organizations which are active in local struggles to intimidate school and library boards are women's groups. In part this difference may be related to the fact that women are more explicitly concerned with family status in the community than are men in the American culture, and hence, may react more than the men do to status anxieties or frustrations. The organizations of old family Americans which are concerned with claiming status from the past are predominantly female. Hence, if the thesis that status concerns are related to rightist extremism and bigotry is valid, one would expect to find more women than men affected by it.

Secondly, however, evidence from election and opinion studies in a number of countries indicates that women are more prone to be concerned with morality in politics. They are much more likely to support prohibition of liquor or gambling, or to vote against corrupt politicians than men. This concern with morality seems to be related to the greater participation in religious activities by the female sex. Since Communism has come to be identified as a moral crusade against evil by every section of American public opinion, one should expect that women will be more likely to favor suppression of evil, much as they favor suppression of liquor and gambling. The propensity to support efforts to repress "corrupt ideas" is probably intensified by the fact that much of the concern with the activities of Communists is related to their potential effect on the young. See H. Tingsten, *Political Behavior: Studies in Election Statistics* (London: P. S. King, 1937), pp. 36–75 for a report of comparative data on women's attitudes and political behavior. In the 1952 Presidential election in the United States, more women voted Republican than Democratic for the first time in many years. It has been suggested that this was a product of the raising of strong moral issues by the Republicans. See L. Harris, *Is There A Republican Majority?* (New York: Harper's and Sons, 1954), Chapter VI.

The recent Stouffer study of attitudes toward civil liberties further tends to validate these inferences. The data indicate clearly that in 1954 women were much more intolerant of Communists, critics of religion, and advocates of nationalized industry than men. Similarly, presidents of women's clubs were less tolerant than any other group of community leaders interviewed with the exception of officers of the D.A.R. and the American Legion. (See S. A. Stouffer, *op. cit.*, pp. 131–55, 52.) Part of the difference in attitudes between men and women reported in this study is accounted for by the fact that women are more religious than men, and religious people are more likely to be intolerant than the non-religious. However, even when religious participation is held constant, women are more likely to be intolerant than are men. I would suggest that part of this difference is related to the fact that women are more likely than men to reflect the political concerns derived from status. Unfortunately, the Stouffer study does not attempt to measure the effect of status concerns on political beliefs. For an excellent study which does attempt to do this in the context of analyzing the electoral support of British political parties see Mark Benney and Phyllis Geiss, "Social Class and Politics in Greenwich," *British Journal of Sociology*, 1950, Vol. I, pp. 310–324. The authors of this study found that women were more likely to report themselves in a higher social class than men at the same occupational level, and those who reported themselves to be higher status were more conservative.

[32] For an excellent description of the reactions of the Boston Brahmins to the Irish, see Cleveland Amory, *The Proper Bostonians* (New York: E. P. Dutton and Company, 1947), p. 346.

[33] In an article written shortly before his death, Franz Neumann suggested that one of the social sources of political anxiety which led to individuals and groups accepting a conspiracy theory of politics is social mobility:

"In every society that is composed of antagonistic groups there is an ascent and descent of groups. It is my contention that persecutory anxiety—but one that has a real basis—is produced when a group is threatened in its prestige, income, or its existence. . . .

"The fear of social degradation thus creates for itself 'a target for the discharge of the resentments arising from damaged self-esteem.' . . .

"Hatred, resentment, dread, created by great upheavals, are concentrated on certain persons, who are denounced as devilish conspirators. Nothing would be more incorrect than to characterize the enemies as scapegoats, for they appear as genuine enemies whom one must extirpate and not as substitutes whom one only needs to send into the wilderness. The danger consists in the fact that this view of history is never completely false, but always contains a kernel of truth and, indeed, must contain it, if it is to have a convincing effect."

Franz L. Neumann, "Anxiety in Politics," *Dissent,* Spring 1955, pp. 141, 139, 135.

³⁴ One study of McCarthy's appeal indicates that, among Protestants, he gets much more support from persons of non-Anglo-Saxon ancestry than from those whose forefathers came from Britain. The polls are not refined enough to locate old Americans who support patriotic organizations, but the activities of groups which belong to the Coalition of Patriotic Societies are what would be expected in terms of the logic of this analysis. See Wallerstein, *op. cit.*

³⁵ These observations about the *nouveaux riches* are, of course, not new or limited to current American politics. William Cobbett commented in 1827:

". . . this hatred to the cause of public liberty is, I am sorry to say it, but too common amongst merchants, great manufacturers, and great farmers; especially those who have risen suddenly from the dunghill to chariot."

G. D. H. Cole and Margaret Cole, eds., *The Opinions of William Cobbett* (London: The Cobbett Publishing Co., 1944), pp. 86–87; see also Walter Weyl, *The New Democracy,* (New York: The Macmillan Co., 1912), pp. 242–243 for similar comments on the American *nouveaux riches,* in the late nineteenth and early twentieth centuries.

³⁶ See S. M. Lipset and Reinhard Bendix, "Social Mobility and Occupational Career Patterns II. Social Mobility," *American Journal of Sociology,* Vol. LVII (March 1952), pp. 494-504.

³⁷ Again, poll data fit this hypothesis. Material from a 1952 Roper poll shows that the most pro-McCarthy occupational group in the country is small businessmen. See Wallerstein, *op. cit.* For an excellent discussion of the reactionary politics of upward mobile small business, see R. Michels, "Psychologie der anti-Kapitalistischen Massenbewegungen," *Grundriss der Sozialokonomik,* Vol. IX, No. 1, p. 249. A recent study of post-war elections in Great Britain also suggests that small businessmen react more negatively to welfare state politics than any other occupational group. John Bonham reports that a larger proportion of small businessmen shifted away from the Labor Party between 1945 and 1950 than any other stratum. See the *Middle Class Vote* (London: Faber and Faber, 1954), p. 129.

³⁸ There is a considerable body of evidence which indicates that economic liberalism (support of the labor movement, government planning, and so forth) is correlated inversely wtih socio-economic status, while non-economic "liberalism" (support of civil liberties, and internationalism), is associated positively with socio-economic status. That is, the poor are for redistribution of wealth, while the more well-to-do are liberal in non-economic matters. See G. H. Smith, "Liberalism and Level of Information," *Journal of Educational Psychology,* February 1948, pp. 65-81; Hyman and Sheatsley, *op. cit.,* pp. 6-17; reports of the American Institute of Public Opinion, *passim.*

These findings are paralleled by various reports which suggest that lower status and education are associated with high scores on scales designed to measure degree of authoritarianism. See H. H. Hyman and P. B. Sheatsley, "The Authoritarian Personality—A Methodological

Critique," in M. Jahoda and R. Christie, *Studies in the Scope and Method of 'The Authoritarian Personality'* (Glencoe, Ill.: The Free Press, 1954), p. 94; R. Christie, "Authoritarianism Re-examined," in *ibid.*, pp. 169-175.

Janowitz and Marvick have reported the interesting finding based on a national sample that the two most "authoritarian" groups are the poorly educated lower class, and the poorly educated lower middle class. See M. Janowitz and D. Marvick, "Authoritarianism and Political Behavior," *Public Opinion Quarterly*, Summer 1953, pp. 185-201.

The Stouffer study reports results similar to these earlier ones. In addition it indicates that leaders of community organizations, most of whom are drawn from the upper part of the class structure and are college educated, are much more favorable to civil liberties than the general population. See S. A. Stouffer, *op. cit.*, pp. 28-57, and *passim.*

[39] Zetterberg in an unpublished study of attitudes toward civil liberties in a New Jersey community found that working-class respondents were much more intolerant on civil-liberties questions than middle-class respondents, and that working-class Republicans were somewhat more anti-civil libertarian than working-class Democrats. Similar conclusions may be deduced from various reports of the American Institute of Public Opinion (Gallup Poll) and the Stouffer study. The first indicates that lower-class respondents are more favorably disposed to McCarthy than middle and upper class, but that Democrats are more likely to be anti-McCarthy than are Republicans. Stouffer reports similar findings with regard to attitudes toward civil liberties. Unfortunately, neither the Gallup Poll nor Stouffer have presented their results by strata for the supporters of each party separately. See S. A. Stouffer, *op. cit.*, pp. 210-215. A survey study of the 1952 elections indicates that at every educational level, persons who scored high on an "authoritarian personality" scale were more likely to be Eisenhower voters than were those who gave "equalitarian" responses. Robert E. Lane, "Political Personality and Electoral Choice," *American Political Science Review*, March 1955, p. 180.

In Britain, Eysenck reports that "middle-class Conservatives are more tender-minded [less authoritarian] than working-class Conservatives; middle-class Liberals are more tender-minded than working-class Liberals; middle-class Socialists more tender-minded than working-class Socialists, and even middle-class Communists are more tender-minded than working-class Communists." H. J. Eysenck, *The Psychology of Politics* (London: Routledge and Kegan Paul, 1954), p. 137. Similar findings are indicated also in a Japanese study which reports that the lower classes and the less educated are more authoritarian than the middle and upper strata and the better educated, but the supporters of the socialist parties are less authoritarian than those who vote for the two "bourgeois" parties. See Kotaro Kido and M. Sugi, "A Report on Research on Social Stratification and Social Mobility in Tokyo (III). The Structure of Social Consciousness," *Japanese Sociological Review*, January 1954, pp. 74-100. See also National Public Opinion Research Institute (of Japan) Report No. 26, *A Survey of Public Attitudes Toward Civil Liberty* (Tokyo 195).

An as yet unpublished secondary analysis of German data collected by the UNESCO Institute at Cologne yields similar results for Germany. The working classes are less favorable to a democratic party system than are the middle and upper classes. However, within every occupational stratum men who support the Social-Democrats are more likely to favor democratic practices than those who back the more conservative parties. The most anti-democratic group of all are workers who vote for non-Socialist groups. (This analysis was done by the author.)

It is also true that the working class forms the mass base of authoritarian parties in Argentina, Italy, and France. Ignazio Silone is one of the few important Socialists who have recognized that recent historical events challenge the belief that the working class is inherently a progressive and democratic force.

". . . the myth of the liberating power of the proletariat has dissolved along with that other myth of the inevitability of progress. The recent examples of the Nazi labor unions, those of Salazar and Peron . . . have at last convinced of this even those who were reluctant to admit it on the sole grounds of the totalitarian degeneration of Communism. . . . The worker, as we have seen and as we continue to see, can work for the most conflicting causes; he can be Blackshirt or partisan." Ignazio Silone, "The Choice of Comrades," *Dissent*, Winter 1955, p. 14.

It may in fact be argued that the lower classes are most attracted to chiliastic political movements, which are necessarily intolerant and authoritarian. Far from workers in poorer countries being Communists because they do not realize that the Communists are authoritarian, as many democratic Socialists have argued and hoped, they may be Communists because the evangelical "only truth" aspect of Communism is more attractive to them than the moderate and democratic gradualism of the social democracy.

[40] See R. K. Merton, "Social Structure and Anomie," in his *Social Theory and Social Structure* (Glencoe, Ill.: Free Press, 1949), Chapter IV.

[41] The large Catholic working class, although predominantly Democratic, also contributes heavily to the support of extremist tendencies on the right in questions dealing with civil liberties or foreign policy. This pattern stems in large measure from their situation as Catholics, and is discussed in a later section.

[42] It is interesting to note in this connection that the large group of persons who are inactive politically in American society tend to be the most conservative and authoritarian in their attitudes. These groups, largely concentrated in the lower classes, do, however, contribute to the results of public opinion polls since they are interviewed. Consequently such polls may exaggerate greatly the effective strength of right-wing extremism. Stouffer reports that those less interested in politics are less tolerant of the civil liberties of Communists and other deviants than are those who are interested. See S. A. Stouffer, *op. cit.*, pp. 83-86. Sanford, who found a negative relationship between socio-economic status and authoritarian attitudes, states: "We have data showing that authoritarians are not highly participant in political affairs, do not join many community groups, do not become officers in the groups they become members of." F. H. Sanford, *Authoritarianism and Leadership* (Philadelphia: Stephenson Brothers, 1950), p. 168; see also G. M. Connelly and H. H. Field, "The non-voter—Who he is, what he thinks," *Public Opinion Quarterly*, Vol. 8, 1944, pp. 175-187. Data derived from

a national survey in 1952 indicate that when holding education constant, individuals who score high on an "authoritarianism" scale are more likely to belong to voluntary associations than those who score low. The high "authoritarians," however, are less likely to engage in political activity or have a sense that they personally can affect the political process. Robert E. Lane, *op. cit.*, pp. 178-179. On the other hand Bendix suggests that the apathetic traditionalist group was mobilized by the Nazis in the final Weimar elections; see R. Bendix, "Social Stratification and Political Power," *American Political Science Review*, Vol. 46, 1952, pp. 357-375.

[43] Samuel Lubell, *The Future of American Politics* (New York: Harper and Bros., 1952), p. 132. Lubell's thesis has been challenged by R. H. Schmuckler, "The Region of Isolationism," *American Political Science Review*, June 1953, pp. 388-401. Schmuckler denies that the statistical evidence proves that any one factor is basically correlated with voting behavior of isolationist members of Congress. Lubell, however, uses other indicators of the effect of ethnic attitudes on voting on foreign policy issues, the changes in the election of 1940. Regardless of who is correct, the basic hypothesis that feelings about past American policy which are linked to the position of different ethnic groups, affect the current political behavior of these groups may still be valid.

[44] Among once liberal Midwest isolationist politicians who were first liberals and became extreme rightists were Senators Nye, Wheeler and Shipstead.

[45] "The memory of opposition to the last war seems the real mainspring behind present-day isolationism. What really binds the former isolationists is not a common view on foreign policy for the future, but a shared remembrance of American intervention in the last war. The strength of the Republican appeal for former isolationist voters is essentially one of political revenge." Lubell, *op. cit.*, p. 152.

[46] Various national surveys have indicated that Catholics are more likely to be favorable to Senator McCarthy than adherents of other denominations. (See the reports of the American Institute of Public Opinion.) The recent survey of attitudes toward civil liberties reports that outside of the South, church-going Catholics are more intolerant than church-going Protestants. See S. A. Stouffer, *op. cit.*, pp. 144-145.

[47] See S. M. Lipset, et al., *op. cit.*, p. 1140; Eysenck, *op. cit.*, p. 21.

[48] A similar effort is being made at the current time by the Australian conservatives who are attacking the Labor Party for alleged softness towards Communism, and for allowing itself to be penetrated by the Communists. The presence of a large Catholic population in these countries, traditionally linked to the more liberal party, is probably one of the most important factors affecting the reluctance of the moderate conservative politicians to oppose the tactics of the extremists on their own side.

[49] In Canada, also, the Catholics have provided the main dynamic for threats to civil liberties, which are presented as necessary parts of the struggle against Communism. The government of the Catholic province of Quebec passed legislation in the thirties which gave the government the right to invade private homes in search of Communist activities and to padlock any premises which have been used by the Communists. Civil liberties groups in Canada have charged that these laws have

been used against non-Communist opponents of the government especially in the labor movement.

⁵⁰ There is, of course, no reliable quantitative way of measuring this
influence, although all students of the Communist movement agree that
its success was greatest among Jews. In Canada, where under a parliamentary system, the Communist Party was able to conduct election
campaigns in districts where they had hopes of large support, they
elected members to the Federal House and provincial legislatures from
Jewish districts only. Similarly, in Great Britain, one of the two Communists elected in 1945 came from a London Jewish district.

⁵¹ It is possible to suggest another hypothesis for Catholic support of
political intolerance in this country which ties back to the earlier discussion of the working class. All existing survey data indicate that the
two religious groups which are most anti-civil libertarian are the Catholics and the fundamentalist Protestant sects. Both groups are predominantly low status in membership. In addition, both fall under the
general heading of extreme moralizing or Puritanical religions. In the
past, and to a considerable extent in the present also, the fundamentalists
played a major role in stimulating religious bigotry, especially against
Catholics. It is important, however, to note also that a large part of
the American Catholic church is dominated by priests of Irish birth or
ancestry. French Catholic intellectuals have frequently referred to the
American Catholic church as the Hibernian American church. Irish
Catholics, like French Canadians, are quite different from those in the
European Latin countries. They have been affected by Protestant values,
or perhaps more accurately by the need to preserve the church in a
hostile Protestant environment. One consequence of this need has been
an extreme emphasis on morality, especially in sexual matters. Studies
of the Irish have indicated that they must rank high among the sexually
repressed people of the earth. The church in Ireland has tended to be
extremely intolerant of deviant views and behavior. The pattern of
intolerance among the American Irish Catholics is in large measure a
continuation in somewhat modified form of the social system of Ireland.
Thus the current anti-Communist crusade has united the two most
morally and sexually inhibited groups in America, the fundamentalist
Protestants and the Irish Catholics. I am sure that much could be done
on a psychoanalytical level to analyze the implications of the moral and
political tone of these two groups. For a good report on morality and
sex repression among the Irish in Ireland and America, see John A.
O'Brien, ed., *The Vanishing Irish* (New York: McGraw-Hill, 1953); see
also C. Arensberg and S. Kimball, *Family and Community in Ireland*
(Cambridge: Harvard University Press, 1948).

⁵² Many, however, still make Aesopian references to the Jews. For a
good current report on the anti-Semitic fringe within the radical right
see James Rorty, "The Native Anti-Semite's 'New Look,'" *Commentary*,
Nov., 1954, pp. 413-421.

In reporting on the Madison Square Garden rally called by the Ten
Million Americans Mobilizing for Justice, a group formed to fight the
move to censure McCarthy, James Rorty suggests that many of the par-
ticipants were individuals who had taken part in Fascist rallies in the
thirties.

"Edward S. Fleckenstein, an American agitator and associate of neo-

Nazis whom Chancellor Adenauer had the State Department oust from Germany, had worked overtime to mobilize his Voters Alliance of German Ancestry. So successful were his efforts that Weehawken, Secaucus, and other northern New Jersey communities had sent delegations so large that, according to organizer George Racey Jordan, it had been necessary to limit their allotment of seats, to avoid giving an 'unrepresentative' character to the meeting." James Rorty, "What Price McCarthy Now?", *Commentary*, January 1955, p. 31.

I was present at this rally, and from my limited vantage point, would agree with Rorty. Men who sat near me spoke of having attended "similar" rallies ten and fifteen years ago. Perhaps the best indicator of the temper of this audience was the fact that Roy Cohn, McCarthy's counsel, felt called upon to make a speech for brotherhood, and reiterated the fact that he was a Jew. One had the feeling that Cohn felt that many in his audience were anti-Semitic.

[53] See T. W. Adorno, et al., *The Authoritarian Personality* (New York: Harpers, 1950). See also Richard Christie, *op. cit.*, pp. 123-196, for a summary of more recent work in this field.

[54] Stouffer reports that individuals who support "authoritarian . . . child-rearing practices" and respond positively to the statement: "People can be divided into two classes—the weak and the strong," are prone to also advocate strong measures against Communists, supporters of nationalized industry, and critics of religion. These questions are similar to the ones used on various psychological scales to locate "authoritarian personalities." S. A. Stouffer, *op. cit.*, pp. 94-99.

[55] William Buckley, *God and Man at Yale* (Chicago: Henry Regnery and Co., 1951).

[56] Much of the data in this section are drawn from Wallerstein, *op. cit.*

[57] I am not suggesting that McCarthy or the radical right are Fascists or even precursors of Fascism. For reasons which are discussed below, I do not believe they could build a successful social movement even if they wanted to. Rather, however, I do suggest that the extreme right in all countries, whether Fascist or not, must find a program or issue which can appeal to a section of the lower middle class, if not the working class, if it is to succeed.

[58] *Congressional Record*, February 20, 1950, p. 1954. (My emphasis.)

[59] *The Freeman*, Vol. I, No. 1, p. 13.

[60] *Facts Forum Radio Program*, No. 57.

[61] *Ibid.* (My emphasis.)

[62] *The Freeman*, November 5, 1951, p. 72. (My emphasis.)

[63] "Where have we loyal allies? In Britain? I would not stake a shilling on the reliability of a government which, while enjoying billions in American munificence, rushed to the recognition of the Chinese Red regime, traded exorbitantly with the enemy through Hong Kong and has sought to frustrate American interests in the Far East at every turn." Joseph R. McCarthy, *The Story of General George Marshall, America's Retreat from Victory* (No. publ., 1952), p. 166.

"As of today some money was taken out of your paycheck and sent to Britain. As of today Britain used that money from your paycheck to pay for the shipment of the sinews of war to Red China. . . .

"Now what can we do about it. We can handle this by saying this to our allies: If you continue to ship to Red China, while they are imprisoning and torturing American men, you will not get one cent of American money." Joseph R. McCarthy, quoted in the *New York Times*, November 25, 1953, p. 5: 1-8.

[64] It is, of course, possible that Anglo-Saxon Protestant supporters of McCarthy react similarly to the members of minority ethnic groups to the mention of Groton, Harvard, striped-pants diplomats, and certified gentlemen, that is, that they too, take gratification in charges which reduce the prestige of those above them, even if they are also members of the same ethnic group. In large measure, I would guess that it is the middle-class, rather than the upper-class members of nationalistic and historical societies who are to be found disproportionately among the supporters of the radical right. Consequently, they too, may be in the position of wanting the high and mighty demoted.

[65] In addition much if not most of the support for radical right policies reported by the polls comes from groups which normally show the lowest levels of voting or other forms of political participation, women, members of fundamentalist sects, and conservative workers. These groups are the most difficult to organize politically.

It is unfortunate that most American politicians as well as the general intellectual public do not recognize that the public opinion poll reports on civil liberties, foreign policy, and other issues are usually based on samples of the total adult population, not of the electorate. Consequently, they probably greatly exaggerate the electoral strength of McCarthyism. For a related discussion see David Riesman and Nathan Glazer, "The Meaning of Opinion," in D. Riesman, *Individualism Reconsidered* (Glencoe, Ill.: The Free Press, 1954), pp. 492-507.

[66] Frank Conniff in the *Journal-American*, quoted in *The Progressive*, April 1954, p. 58.

[67] The cleavage in the Republican Party revealed by the vote in the United States Senate to censure McCarthy largely paralleled the lines suggested in this paper. The party divided almost evenly in the vote, with almost all the Republican Senators from eastern states plus Michigan voting against McCarthy, while most of the Republicans from the Midwest and far western states voted for him. The cleavage, in part, reflects the isolationist and China-oriented section of the party on one side, and the internationalist eastern wing on the other. From another perspective, it locates the Senators with the closest ties to big business against McCarthy, and those coming from areas dominated by less powerful business groups on the other. There are, of course, a number of deviations from the pattern.

An indication of the temper of the right wing of the Republican Party may be seen from the speeches and reaction at a right-wing rally held in Chicago on Lincoln's Birthday. Governor J. Bracken Lee of Utah stated, "We have gone farther to the left in the last two years [under Eisenhower] than in any other period in our history. I have the feeling that the leadership in Washington is not loyal to the Republican Party." Brigadier General William Hale Wilbur, U.S. Army, retired, charged that the "great political victory of 1952 is being subverted. . . . American foreign policy is no longer American." McCarthy drew loud cheers while denouncing the evacuation of the Tachens. Senator George W. Malone of Nevada stated that Washington is "the most dangerous town in the United States." *New York Times*, February 13, 1955, p. 54.

⁶⁸ Perhaps the most interesting event in the extremist versus moderate conservative battle occurred in the 1954 senatorial elections in New Jersey. There, a liberal anti-McCarthyite, Clifford Case, former head of the Fund for the Republic, ran on the Republican ticket on a platform of anti-McCarthyism. A small group of right-wingers urged "real Republicans" to repudiate Case and write in the name of Fred Hartley, coauthor of the Taft-Hartley Act on the ballot. This campaign began with considerable publicity, but soon weakened. One reason for its rapid decline was that a number of the largest corporations in America put direct economic pressure on small businessmen, lawyers, and other middle-class people active in Hartley's behalf. These people were told that unless they dropped out of the campaign, they would lose contracts or business privileges with these corporations. It is significant to note that one of the few remaining groups vulnerable to direct old-fashioned pressure from big business is the middle-class backers of right-wing extremism.

⁶⁹ The stress in this paper on the radical right should not lead to ignoring the contribution of the Communist Party to current coercive measures. The presence of a foreign controlled conspiracy which has always operated partially underground, and which engages in espionage has helped undermine the basis of civil liberties. Democratic procedure assumes that all groups will play the game, and any actor who consistently breaks the rules endangers the continuation of the system. In a real sense, extremists of the right and left aid each other, for each helps to destroy the underlying base of a democratic social order.

Index

Acheson, Dean, 50, 53, 57, 92, 111, 113, 132, 223
Adams, Henry, 115
Adams, John, quoted, 8
Adenauer, Konrad, 231
Adorno, Theodore W., 35, 47, 54 f., 231
Aldrich, Winthrop W., 223
Alger, Frederick M., Jr., 223
Almond, Gabriel A., 222
Alsops, 16, 74
Amory, Cleveland, 225
Arensberg, C., 230
Aron, Raymond, 222

Babbitt, Irving, 95, 102, 116
Barr, Stringfellow, 88
Bayard, James Asheton, 7
Beard, Charles A., 30, 100
Beard, Miriam, 31
Bell, Daniel, 31, 75
Bendiz, Reinhard, 219, 223, 226, 229
Benney, Mark, 225
Benson, Lee, 220

Bentham, Jeremy, 25, 31
Berelson, Bernard, 87
Berle, Adolf A., Jr., 57, 114
Bettelheim, Bruno, 55, 70
Biddle, Nicholas, quoted, 7
Boasberg, Leonard, 54
Bohlen, Charles E., 92, 223
Bohn, Frank, 221
Bonbright, James C. H., 223
Bonham, John, 226
Bozell, Brent, 89
Bricker, John W., 13, 102, 104
Bridges, Harry, 204
Brodie, Bernard, 74
Brogan, D. W., 54
Brooks, Van Wyck, 18
Browder, Earl, 187-188
Brownell, Herbert, Jr., 20
Brunswik, Else Frenkel-. *See* Frenkel-Brunswik, Else
Bryan, William Jennings, 19, 89, 92, 220
Buckley, William, 89, 209, 231
Bukharin, Nikolai I., 22
Burke, Edmund, 95, 102, 110

Burnham, James, 20 f., 208
Butler, Richard Austen, 108

Cabot, John M., 223
Calhoun, John C., 28-29
Campbell, Angus, 88
Carnegie, Andrew, 63
Case, Clifford, 233
Chamberlain, John, 208; quoted, 12
Chamberlain, Neville, 102
Chamberlain, William Henry, 190
Chambers, Whittaker, 13
Chiang Kai-shek, 221
Chodorov, Frank, 89, 209
Christie, Richard, 54, 227, 231
Churchill, Sir Winston, 95, 108, 177, 221 f.
Clark, S. D., 182, 222
Clay, Henry, 7
Cobbett, William, quoted, 226
Coe, Robert D., 223
Cohn, Roy, 97 ff., 213, 231
Cole, G. D. H. and M., 226
Coleridge, Samuel Taylor, 102
Commons, John R., 30
Conant, James B., 223
Connally, Tom, 57
Connelly, G. M., 228
Conniff, Frank, 232
Corcoran, Tommy, 74
Coughlin, Rev. Charles E., 6, 94, 98, 103, 137, 180, 219

David, Elmer, 40, 54
de Gaulle, Charles, 222
Desmond, Humphrey J., 220
de Tocqueville, Alexis. See Tocqueville, Alexis de
De Toledano, Ralph, 208
Dewey, Thomas E., 85, 98
Dies, Martin, 57

Dillon, C. Douglas, 223
Dirksen, Everett M., 102, 107, 112
Dodd, Norman, 89
Donnelly, Ignatius, 94
Douglas, Paul H., 204
Dreyfus, Alfred, 97, 99
Dulles, John Foster, 50, 53
Dunn, Rev. James B., quoted, 221

Earle, Edward Mead, 74
Eastman, Max, 20 f.
Eden, Sir Anthony, 108
Eisenhower, Dwight D., 16, 25, 35 f., 41, 53, 57, 68, 73, 98, 107 ff., 113, 134, 162 f., 213, 227, 232
Evans, George Henry, 10
Eysenck, H. J., 227, 229

Fairchild, Henry Pratt, 80
Farley, James A., 55
Fast, Howard, 89
Field, H. H., 228
Flanders, Ralph E., 101, 111
Fleckenstein, Edward S., 230
Flynn, John T., 21, 190, 208; quoted, 224
Forrestal, James V., 73
Fox, Dixon Ryan, 30
Franco, Francisco, 186 f., 221
Frenkel-Brunswik, Else, 87-88; quoted, 55
Frey, John, 224
Frick, Henry Clay, 63

Galbraith, J. K., 114
Gallup, George H., 144, 227
Gaudet, Hazel, 87
Gaulle, Charles de, 222
Geiss, Phyllis, 225
Glazer, Nathan, 16, 30, 221, 232

Godkin, Edwin L., 27
Greenblum, Joseph, 55
Grodzins, Morton, 221
Gurin, Gerald, 88
Guterman, Norbert, quoted, 54

Harriman, Averell, 59, 73
Haldane, Charlotte, 208
Halevy, Eli, 32
Hamilton, Alexander, 7
Handlin, Oscar, quoted, 31
Harrington, James, quoted, 8
Harris, Louis, 30, 225
Harrison, William Henry, 7
Hartley, Fred, 233
Hawthorne, Nathaniel, 115
Hearst, William Randolph, 64
Herberg Will, 108, 222
Hicks, Granville, 21-22, 31, 82
Hiss, Alger, 55, 82, 85, 110, 211
Hitler, Adolf, 55, 94, 130, 186, 224
Hoffman, Paul, 111
Hofstadter, Richard, 15, 88 f., 170, 219 f.
Holcombe, Arthur N., 30; quoted, 10
Hoover, J. Edgar, 57
Hopkins, Harry, 74
Hughes, Howard, 63
Hull, Cordell, 185
Humphrey, George M., 88
Humphrey, Hubert H., 204
Hunt, H. L., 69
Hutchins, Robert, 218
Hyman, Herbert, 221, 226

Jackson, Andrew, 7
Jahoda, Marie, 54, 227
Janeway, Eliot, 75
Janowitz, Morris, 55, 70, 227
Jefferson, Thomas, 9, 104, 175
Jenner, William E., 107

Johnson, Lyndon B., 57
Jordan, George Rainey, 231

Kamenev, Lev B., 22
Kant, Immanuel, 28
Kecszkemeti, Paul, 154
Kennan, George, 222
Kennedy, John F., 193
Kennedy, Joseph P., 193
Kido, Kotaro, 227
Kimball, S., 230
Kirk, Russell, 88
Knowland, William F., 13, 108
Knox, Henry, quoted, 8-9
Kohlberg, Arthur, 213
Kohler, Foy, 14

La Follette, Robert M., Sr., 94, 103, 125, 181, 183, 191, 212
Lane, Robert E., 227, 229
Laski, Harold J., 32
Lazarsfeld, Paul, 87
Lee, Ivy, 63
Lee, J. Bracken, quoted, 223, 232
Lemke, William, 6
Lewis, John L., 224
Lilienthal, David, 114
Lincoln, Abraham, 115
Lindbergh, Charles A., 190
Lindsay, Vachel, 92
Lippmann, Walter, 16, 216; quoted, 27
Lipset, Seymour Martin, 3, 16, 30, 219, 222, 226, 229
Lodge, Henry Cabot, Jr., 92
Lodge, John D., 223
London, Jack, 26
Lonergan, Edna, 223
Long, Huey, 14, 179 f.
Loucks, Emerson H., 221
Lovett, Robert A., 73
Lowenthal, Leo, quoted, 54

Lubell, Samuel, 30, 54, 66, 199, 229
Lyons, Eugene, 21, 208

McAllister, Ward, 63
McCarran, Pat, 94, 112
McCarthy, Joseph R., 3, 13-17 *passim*, 20-24 *passim*, 36, 57 f., 63-67 *passim*, 71, 84, 90, 92 ff., 97-113 *passim*, 136, 142, 144, 160, 162, 174, 181, 186, 191, 197 ff., 209-216 *passim*, 219, 224, 226 f., 229 ff.; quoted, 231
McCloy, John J., 73
McKinley, William, 102, 220
Madison, James, 28, 104, 116; quoted, 8 f.
Malenkov, Georgi M., 111
Malone, George W., 232
Marshall, George C., 132
Marshall, Margaret, 22
Marvick, D., 227
Marx, Karl, 104, 131
Mason, A. T., 30
Matthews, J. B., 208
Maverick, Maury, 56-57
May, Allan Nunn, 13
Mead, Margaret, 46, 55
Mecklin, John Moffat, 221
Melville, Herman, 115
Merton, R. K., 228
Michels, R., 226
Mill, John Stuart, 28, 32, 109
Miller, Warren E., 88
Moody, Dwight, 19
Moos, Malcolm, 68
Morris, Robert, 24
Morse, Wayne, 204
Murphy, Robert, 186
Mussolini, Benito, 53
Myers, Gustavus, 220 f.
Myrdal, Gunnar, 176; quoted, 5

Napoleon, 96
Neumann, Franz L., 32; quoted, 225-226
Niebuhr, H. Richard, 31, quoted, 19
Niebuhr, Reinhold, 23
Nietzsche, Friedrich, 96
Nixon, Richard M., 108, 112
Nye, Gerald P., 94, 183, 229

O'Brien, John A., 230
Owen, Robert, 10
Orwell, George, 21, 100

Paine, Tom, 95 f., 116
Parsons, Talcott, 3, 16, 67
Pearlin, Leonard I., 55
Perón, Juan D., 228
Piatakov, 22

Quill, Mike, 6

Rakovsky, Christian G., 22
Ranulf, Svend, 18, 31
Ravitch, Richard, quoted, 220
Rayburn, Sam, 56
Reece, B. Carroll, 89
Reuther, Walter, 6
Riemer, Neal, 32
Riesman, David, 15, 30, 164, 221, 232
Robespierre, 100
Rockefeller, John D., 62-63
Roosevelt, Archibald, 14, 213; quoted, 223
Roosevelt, Franklin D., 10, 37, 41, 50, 55-57, 59, 72, 74, 83, 89, 93, 102, 104, 124, 137, 175, 185, 189 f., 200 f., 215-216, 224
Roosevelt, Theodore, 14, 27
Roper, Elmo, 226
Rorty, James, quoted, 230-231

Rose, Arnold, 222
Rosenberg, Ethel and Julius, 13, 51, 78
Ross, E. A., 80
Rossiter, Clinton, 224
Rousseau, Jean Jacques, 96
Rovere, Richard, 38, 54

Salazar, Antonio de Oliveira, 228
Samson, Leon, 222
Sanford, F. H., quoted, 228
Schachtman, Max, 104
Schlamm, William, 20 f., 208
Schlesinger, Arthur M., Jr., 23, 88
Schmuckler, R. H., 229
Schultz, Rabbi, 98
Schuyler, George, 208
Sheatsley, Paul, 221, 226
Shils, Edward A., 74
Shipstead, Henrik, 229
Silone, Ignazio, quoted, 228
Sinclair, Upton, 180
Smith, Adam, 25
Smith, Alfred E., 55, 102, 104, 172, 209, 215
Smith, G. H., 226
Sokolnikov, Grigory Y., 22
Sokolsky, George, 213
Stalin, Josef, 204, 224
Stevenson, Adlai, 34, 65, 68, 92, 101, 105-106, 107-113 *passim*
Stimson, Henry L., 73
Stone, I. F., 223
Stouffer, Samuel A., 16, 142-143, 149-165 *passim*, 174, 221, 225, 227 ff., 231
Streit, Clarence, 88
Sugi, M., 227
Sweet, W. W., 31

Taft, Robert A., 36, 89
Tate, Allen, 88
Thomas, Norman, 101, 218
Thoreau, Henry, 115
Tingsten, H., 225
Tocqueville, Alexis de, 31, 102, 181; quoted, 19, 54
Townsend, Francis E., 179 f.
Truman, David, 30
Truman, Harry S., 30, 34, 53, 57, 59, 76, 109, 113, 137, 183, 187-188

Utley, Freda, 21 f., 208

Valtin, Jan, 22
Van Buren, Martin, 7-8
Vaughan, Harry H., 57
Viereck, Peter, 15, 84
Villard, Oswald Garrison, 27
Voltaire, François, 93

Webb, Leicester, 165
Webster, Daniel, 7
Wechsler, James A., 23
Weyl, Walter, 226
Wheeler, Burton K., 94, 190, 229
White, Harry Dexter, 57, 82
Wilbur, William H., 232
Willkie, Wendell, 73
Wilson, Charles E., 88
Wilson, Edmund, 32; quoted, 27
Wilson, Woodrow, 89
Wolfe, Bertram, 14
Wright, Richard, 69

Zetterberg, 227
Zinoviev, Grigori E., 22